HARVARD HISTORICAL STUDIES

PUBLISHED UNDER THE DIRECTION OF
THE DEPARTMENT OF HISTORY

FROM THE INCOME OF

THE HENRY WARREN TORREY FUND

VOLUME XXXV

THE
NATIONAL WORKSHOPS

A Study in the French
Revolution of 1848

BY

DONALD COPE McKAY
Harvard University

HARVARD UNIVERSITY PRESS
CAMBRIDGE, MASSACHUSETTS
1965

To

WILLIAM LEONARD LANGER

FOREWORD

1965

IN 1948, fifteen years after the publication of this book, France like other European countries celebrated the centennial of the great upheavals that shook Europe in the mid-nineteenth century. Commemorative meetings were held everywhere, with the customary addresses, exhibitions, and ceremonies. Above all, a veritable plethora of books and articles gave testimony to the widespread interest in the occasion. Much of what was said and written was merely repetitious of what was already known, but among the scholarly contributions there were some that opened up new vistas or advanced new interpretations.

This new literature tended, on the whole, to emphasize the social aspects of the revolution which, with respect to the French situation, had long been recognized as important. It is probably no exaggeration to say that the crowds of workmen who made the Paris revolution were moved more by economic grievances — low wages, chronic unemployment, inadequate housing, constant shortage of food — than by political aspirations. In any case, the Provisional Government wrestled as best it could with this formidable social problem. It provided relief through the National Workshops, which in the main represented an early form of Works Progress Administration. When, in a matter of months, the situation had gotten out of hand, there ensued the great insurrection in Paris known as the June Days, certainly the greatest uprising of the workingmen in the entire century.

It is this complicated and controversial phase of the revolution that the late Professor Donald McKay undertook to analyze in the present volume. Despite the vast literature that has appeared in the interval since its original publication, this volume still stands as the authoritative account of a crucial and highly dramatic episode of modern history. In fact, I do not hesitate to say that it comes as near to being the "definitive" treatment of the subject as any historical monograph is apt to be.

The author's all-too-early death in 1959 cut short a distinguished career not only in historical teaching and writing but also in government service. During the Second World War Professor McKay served as a member of the Board of Analysts of the Office of Strategic Services, which pioneered modern methods of processing foreign intelligence. It was this close contact with international affairs that led him, in association with the late Sumner Welles, to launch the well-known American Foreign Policy Library series, of which more than a dozen volumes (including his own, *The United States and France*) appeared between 1945 and Professor McKay's death.

The experiences of the war also brought home to Mr. McKay the urgent need for training in the social studies on a regional and interdisciplinary basis. At Harvard he was chiefly instrumental in securing faculty approval for the Regional Studies Programs, from which the Russian Research Center, the Center for Middle Eastern Studies, and the East Asian Research Center, as well as the Center for International Affairs, were later to emerge. His contribution to history and historical study was a notable one and I consider it a privilege as well as a pleasure to introduce this new edition of his *National Workshops*, which is yet another memento of his professional activities and devotion.

William L. Langer
Archibald Cary Coolidge
Professor of History, Emeritus

Harvard University
March 1965

FOREWORD

BERNARD SHAW, who has given us some of the ablest forewords
in the language, has also denounced the practice as indefensible.
Too many bad books have been salvaged by a preface, more
especially in our day when few readers go far beyond that
point. But the habit of taking the reader by the hand is too
well fixed to be easily put aside. Perhaps in the end the best
defence of a preface is its brevity.

The National Workshops — at best an awkward rendering of
an untranslatable term — have logically received the attention
of all those who have written of the Revolution of 1848 in
France. But thus far the question has been studied only incidentally to the general history of the period, and no extended
monographic treatment has appeared.[1] More than many others,
the period has engaged the prejudices of those who have
written its history. For many of its problems are those about
which the heat of political controversy continues to play. As
a foreigner, the writer has perhaps certain advantages. He has
tried in any event to keep before him Ranke's dictum: he has
attempted " to show how it actually happened," and there has
been no effort to imprison the facts within arbitrary formulae.
He has addressed himself primarily to the preponderant political significance of the institution and has given only passing
consideration to the decidedly secondary economic aspects of
the Workshops. The Introduction, which is intended merely
to form a setting for the problem, is based almost entirely on
secondary works.

The writer's attention was first directed to the problem of
the National Workshops by Monsieur Joannès Tramond, of
the *Académie de la Marine*, who has been consistently helpful
in aid, encouragement, and suggestion. Like many Americans

---

[1] The monograph by Picattier (see Bibliography) is negligible. The most satisfactory account is that by Georges Renard in his *République de 1848*.

before him, the writer is deeply indebted to Monsieur Georges Bourgin, *conservateur* of the *Archives nationales,* whose indulgent guidance has made his researches both pleasanter and far more effective. Monsieur Paul Raphaël has been generously helpful in connection with the policy of Falloux, on which he has given the writer numerous suggestions. To his friends, Mr. Merrill T. B. Spalding and Mr. Reginald I. Lovell, he is indebted for substantial aid at a time when both were much occupied: the former read and criticized the manuscript, the latter read the proofs. To Professor William Leonard Langer of Harvard University the writer acknowledges a very special debt. No appeal to his aid or encouragement has been unavailing, while to his sound judgment and wide knowledge of nineteenth century movements the writer has repeatedly recurred. The researches in Paris for the present volume were made possible originally through a fellowship from the Department of History of Harvard University. Certain additions were subsequently made and the volume was prepared for publication while the writer was engaged on another project as fellow of the Social Science Research Council. The researches were carried on primarily in the *Archives nationales,* the *Archives de la Seine,* and the *Bibliothèque nationale*; to the administrations of these institutions the writer wishes to acknowledge his appreciation.

Donald Cope McKay

Paris,
December 28, 1932

CONTENTS

INTRODUCTION

THE Revolution of February in France has almost invariably been described in terms of the Reform Banquets. Its origins have been sought in the political agitation of the parliamentary opposition, and the sudden overturn occasioned by the unexpected successes of the insurgents has been denoted a *surprise accidentelle*. But this leaves insufficiently explained both the tenacious resistance of the Paris workers behind the barricades and their subsequent determined efforts to achieve what they conceived to be the aim of a revolution at once "social and democratic." In short, there existed a proletarian opposition in 1848, whose precise character and whose rôle in the years preceding unfortunately remain obscure. It is obvious that this opposition was poorly regimented. It is true also that its plans for the amelioration of the workers' lot were vague and undeveloped. The existence of such an opposition was of capital importance, however, for the history of the National Workshops. For the establishment of the Workshops was, in the view of the workers, the logical development of the acceptance by the Provisional Government of the "right to work," cornerstone of the proletarian program. And the later campaign for the dissolution of the Workshops the workers viewed as a breach of good faith on the part of those who had earlier promulgated a decree guaranteeing work to all citizens.

Security against unemployment was indeed the principal anxiety of the worker, who had suffered much from *crises de chomage* under the July Monarchy. Paris workers — and it was of course these who had furnished the contingents for the barricades of February — had been hard hit by the economic crisis of the years 1846 to 1848. Their numbers had been considerably increased by the influx of workers who were drawn to the capital between 1840 and 1845 as a result of prosperous conditions then existing and of opportunities for employment on the fortifications of Paris.[1] The total male working-class population of Paris at the beginning of 1848 was about 200,000.[2] The very unsatisfactory unemployment statistics for the week following the Revolution put the figure of those without work at anywhere from 10,000 to 49,000.[3] In any event this number rapidly mounted as businesses were obliged to close following the February Days. Finally, by June 20, there were approximately 120,000 men enrolled in the National Workshops, and it was estimated that there were some 50,000 unemployed to whom admission to the Workshops had been refused.[4] Even if a substantial proportion of those enrolled had come from the provinces and foreign countries, it would still be evident that a large majority of the Paris workers were without formal employment prior to the June Days. It was under these conditions that the Provisional Government had established the National Workshops, in their view a means of remedying an acute condition of unemployment and of immobilizing at the same time possible elements of disturbance.

*   *   *   *   *

Some consideration of the proletariat prior to February, 1848, is essential to an understanding not only of its rôle in the February Days but of the general working-class situation out of which the National Workshops emerged. Attention will be directed to (1) the conditions of the proletariat prior to the economic crisis of 1846-1848; (2) the character of the crisis itself; (3) the economic effects of the depression upon the condition of the proletariat and the concomitant intensification of the revolutionary spirit among the workers.

---

[1] P. Quentin-Bauchart: *La crise sociale de 1848. Les origines de la Révolution de février* (Paris, 1920), p. 196.
[2] G. Renard: *La République de 1848 (1848-1851)* (Paris, 1906?), p. 329, and sources cited in his accompanying *Notes et références* (see p. 365); cf. *Commune de Paris*, March 14.
[3] Quentin-Bauchart: *op. cit.*, p. 241, note 1; *Univers*, July 3, 1848.
[4] See below, p. 130, and Appendix I.

I

The abrupt political transformation from the Napoleonic regime to the Restoration foreshadowed no such rapid change in the economic life of the nation. Despite the progress which characterized the cotton industry and to a lesser extent certain others, French industrial development was slow and conditions similar to those of the *ancien régime* were general. *Petite industrie* everywhere prevailed, and large plants were decidedly the exception.

The July Monarchy witnessed a much more rapid transformation of industry, especially after 1840, characterized by increased production, much wider use of machinery, and the very general appearance of large plants. Beet sugar production, which totalled but 6,000,000 kilograms in the year of the "trois glorieuses," attained a figure of 40,000,000 kilograms in 1836 and 52,000,000 in 1847. Rapid progress was made in textile machinery, and the use of the steam engine was steadily extended. By 1848 *grande industrie* had made great progress, but it was still necessary to make sharp distinctions between different industries and between various regions.[5] It is important to note that Paris was not typical; there *petite industrie* was in the ascendant: 7,000 *patrons* had more than 10 workers each, while 32,000 worked alone or with a single worker; few large factories existed.

With industrial development came its functional concomitant, the growth of the city proletariat and the aggravation of the workers' problems. If these problems were less severe in their total effect than in those countries where the industrial revolution made more rapid progress, they were not less devas-

---

[5] According to the census of 1851, the industrialists *(patrons de grande industrie)* numbered 124,000, and employed 1,306,000 persons (675,000 men and 531,000 women), an average of ten per *patron*. *Petite industrie* included 1,548,000 masters, 1,434,000 men workers, and 1,370,000 women workers, an average of two employees per *patron*. (Figures given by H. Sée: *La vie économique de la France sous la monarchie censitaire (1815-1848)* (Paris, 1927), p. 87.

tating in their effects upon the individual worker. Urbanization proceeded apace. Towns of more than 3,000 population increased by a total of 2,000,000 inhabitants during that period.[6] Lodgings were soon at a premium, rents mounted, and the workers were often obliged either to live in conditions of indescribable squalor or to find quarters in the suburbs and trudge weary miles to and from their work. Infant mortality was high; in the Department of the Haut-Rhin half of those born did not survive the second year.[7] The number of foundlings had increased 30 per cent since 1820.[8] The infanticide rate in the fourteen leading industrial departments, as compared with the rate for the whole of France, was in the ratio of 121 to 41.[9]

Vice, crime, alcoholism, and disease found congenial soil in the squalor of the workers' quarters. Prostitution and drunkenness increased.[10] Crime mounted, and criminal gangs, by no means a monopoly of our own day, were organized for the more systematic exploitation of urban society.[11] Disease, especially tuberculosis and rickets, attacked the workers, whose undernourished systems offered less resistance to its ravages.

Working hours were uniformly long, with considerable variation among regions and among trades. The eleven-hour day was usual in the Paris building trades,[12] while thirteen hours

---

[6] Sée, pp. 87-88.

[7] *Ibid.*, p. 97; E. Levasseur: *Histoire des classes ouvrières et de l'industrie en France de 1789 à 1870* (Second edition, Paris, 1903-1904, 2 vols.), II, p. 267.

[8] L. Blanc: *Organisation du travail* (Fifth edition, Paris, 1848), p. 62. Blanc gives the following figures for *enfants trouvés*: 1820 — 102,103; 1831 — 122,981; 1847 — about 130,000. It will be noted, however, that the increase in the later period, when industrialization was proceeding at an accelerated pace, was much slower than in the period 1820-1831.

[9] Blanc: *Organisation du travail*, p. 61.

[10] Sée, p. 104.

[11] See, e.g., Blanc: *op. cit.*, pp. 46 ff. " . . . en attendant qu'on se décide à organiser l'association des travailleurs, nous voyons s'organiser celle des assassins " (p. 47). Blanc complains bitterly that prevailing ideas of criminal justice took no account of the criminal's environment as influencing his acts (pp. 48-49). It need scarcely be noted that Blanc was far in advance of his times in his ideas on criminal justice.

[12] E. Levasseur: *La Population française* (Paris, 1889-1892, 3 vols.), III, p. 89.

was normal in the factories of the great provincial towns, and much longer hours were by no means exceptional.[13]

Nominal wages were low, but varied greatly by trade and by region. No general statistical picture of a reliable character is possible. The nearest approaches are offered in the two reports, (1) of the government investigation of industrial conditions, conducted between 1840 and 1845, and (2) of the " Investigation of Wages and Working Conditions by Cantons," conducted by the Labor Committee of the National Assembly in 1848. For the sixty-three departments within the purview of the former investigation, the average wage (excluding Paris) was 2.09 francs per day for men, 1.03 for women, and 0.73 for children. The departmental range can be measured by comparing the two extremes, the Departments of the Seine (average 3.50 for men, 1.55 for women) [14] and the Mayenne (1.49 francs for men, 0.68 for women). From the figures of the 1848 investigation only a roughly approximate average can be derived: 1.78 francs per day for men, 0.77 for women, and 0.50 for children. With this general average, the higher level of Paris is to be contrasted: 3.75 to 3.80 for men, and 1.60 for women. The decline in wages indicated by the second report cannot be accurately interpreted; was it due principally to the crisis *preceding* the Revolution of 1848 or to the crisis *precipitated* by the Revolution? Unfortunately the wage statistics of the second report refer in part to conditions prior to February 24, 1848, and in part to those following that date.[15] Despite the unsatisfactory character of our knowledge, it may be stated, says Sée, that nominal wages had approximately doubled

[13] Sée, pp. 97 ff. and sources there cited. The hours were at least fifteen (thirteen and one-half hours of *travail effectif*) in the Department of the Haut-Rhin; thirteen hours was the rule in the Department of the Nord; thirteen at St. Quentin; twelve to twelve and a half at Reims.

[14] Some idea of the differential among trades is given by Levasseur's figures for the building trades of Paris (*Population française*, III, p. 89). The figures for 1840 include: masons, 4.15 francs; stonecutters, 4.20; carpenters, 4.00; roofers (*couvreurs*), 4.50.

[15] For the whole question of the two reports, see Levasseur: *Classes ouvrières,* II, pp. 257-261.

since the end of the *ancien régime*, but still remained very moderate.[16]

The heart of the workers' problem is of course not the *nominal* but the *real* wage. Here one is immediately faced with a paucity of statistics on the cost of living. Three investigators — Charles Dupin, the Baron de Morogues, and Villeneuve-Bargemont — agree that a worker's family with an income of 760 francs a year was in want, while an income of 860 francs would provide *l'aisance*, provided the worker were not living in a large city. In 1845 Sée estimated the minimum expenses of an unmarried worker in Paris at 502 francs, and for a household without children at 750 francs. Even on the basis of the few wage figures given above[17] it will be obvious that many workers did not earn the latter figure.[18]

Adequate statistics on fluctuations in the cost of living are also lacking. The supply of foodstuffs, notably cheese and potatoes, seemed to increase more rapidly than did the population, and there was no rise in the price of bread.[19] Meat prices increased one-fifth in the period 1815-1848, while manufactured products generally showed a substantial decline.[20] But, even if a general improvement in real wages could be demonstrated, it must still be insisted that the worker was subject to recurrent periods of unemployment, occasioned by the inevitable " dead seasons " prevailing in most trades and by the long series of economic crises which marked the Restoration and the reign of Louis-Philippe.[21] If, in normal times, the majority of work-

---

[16] Sée, p. 94.

[17] See p. xv.

[18] Sée, p. 95. Sée cites the usual figures, which appear also in Levasseur: *Classes ouvrières*, II, pp. 271-272.

[19] Sée, p. 96. Sée is obviously referring to the period as a whole, when he considers the price of bread, and not to such exceptional conditions as those prevailing in 1846-1847. The latter year was known as " l'an du pain cher."

[20] Sée, p. 96; cf. F. B. Artz: *France under the Bourbon Restoration* (Cambridge, 1931), p. 271: " . . . the food of the workers was inadequate, consisting chiefly of soup, bread, potatoes, and milk, a diet deficient in meat and vegetables, and in bare quantity often wholly insufficient."

[21] Sée, p. 96. There were no less than ten such crises: 1816, 1818, 1819, 1826, 1827, 1830, 1831, 1836, 1837, 1847. The textile workers suffered the most severely from the resulting unemployment.

ers were able to meet their meagre expenses, their existence was none the less precarious, and a prolonged period of sickness or unemployment almost inevitably led to reliance on public charity, mendicity, or, in the case of women, prostitution.

The appearance of women and children in the factories added another sombre note to the gloomy industrial scene. With the advent of the machine, strength yielded to skill; women adequately filled the places of men, and the diminutive hands of the young were at a premium in the operation and cleaning of machines. Eager industrialists welcomed a new source of cheap labor and applauded the individualistic regime which guaranteed the operation of "natural economic law," permitting wages to be fixed by the forces of supply and demand. Obvious economies could be effected, for women received from a half to a third of the wages of men, and children correspondingly less.

The unhygienic conditions under which the workers only too frequently lived extended also into the factories. The rooms were often narrow, dark, insanitary — sometimes the result of hasty improvisation. Gradually the practical requirements of the machines themselves obliged more spacious construction, and decided progress was made under the July Monarchy in the direction of more healthful working conditions.

Most of the evils of the workers' situation, especially those resulting from economic instability, were exaggerated by the faster tempo of industrial development in the latter half of the reign of Louis-Philippe. The workers were further embittered by their apparent helplessness to remedy their condition. Little could be anticipated in the way of amelioration from employers who declared that they were in business "to become rich men, not philanthropists." The government, too, was saturated in the economic philosophy of *laisser-faire,* so congenial to its bourgeois supporters of the *pays légal.* Its only conspicuous humanitarian measure, the Child Labor Act of 1841, was rendered emasculate by the elimination of a salaried inspectorate, and the substitution therefor of the gratuitous services of inspectors chosen from the manufacturing class.

Despite his enormous handicaps, however, the worker accepted the conditions imposed by the new industrial system in no docile spirit. His reactions gave rise to various phases of an inchoate labor movement in France.

The Great Revolution, which had swept away the ancient gilds, had dealt a serious blow at the right of combination in the *Loi Chapelier* of 1791, which forbade *all* combinations, whether of masters or of men. A natural advantage to the masters, inherent in such a situation, was enhanced by Napoleonic legislation, which provided much heavier penalties for offending workers than for their employers; strikers were to be treated, in the manner of the *ancien régime*, as "rebels" (*séditieux*). Moreover, combinations of masters seem rarely to have been prosecuted, whereas prosecutions of organized or striking workmen appear uninterruptedly in the period from 1815 to 1848. The worker was further subjected to the master's control by the extension of the *livret* to all workers by the law of 1803. In the *livret* were inscribed the signatures of the worker's previous employers, and no man could be hired unless his record with the last employer was satisfactory. The *livret* also contained a list of the loans (*avances*) made to the worker by the master, and thus formed the basis of a very great, sometimes tyrannical, control by the employer.[22]

Yet despite the repressive legislation of the government and the employer's preponderant position, workers' organizations continued to exist and to exert some influence. Principal among these latter was the very old *compagnonnage* (which had always existed in defiance of the law), composed of the *élite* of the unmarried journeymen, for the most part in those trades least affected by the industrial revolution. Moving from town to town to perfect himself in his craft, the *compagnon* made the *tour de France*. He relied upon his local *compagnon-*

---

[22] For brief discussions of the Revolutionary and Napoleonic legislation, see Sée, pp. 115-119; and J. H. Clapham: *The Economic Development of France and Germany* (Cambridge, 1921), pp. 76-77.

nage to provide food and shelter, to find him work, to aid him in case of illness, and to cheer his leisure hours with good fellowship. But the *compagnonnage,* product of another age, was destined to decline under the onslaught of the new forces of the industrial era. Organizations by trades seemed more suited to the achievement of the workers' ends. New industries were arising which claimed workers who had never been members of the *compagnonnages.* The novices rebelled against the harshness and formalism of their seniors, and the dissidents formed separate organizations. Finally the railroad altered the conditions under which the migratory workman had thrived, and the second half of the century witnessed the definitive decline of the *compagnonnage.*

A second form of labor organization, encouraged by the government, although technically illegal, was the so-called mutual aid society — the *bureau de bienfaisance* or *caisse de secours mutuels.* Organized for the purpose of rendering aid to its members in cases of sickness, accident, retirement, or death, the local groups were controlled by the government through its intermediary, the central *Société philanthropique de Paris,* a creation of the reign of Louis XIV. The societies had become widespread before the July Revolution, and continued thereafter to expand under the friendly rays of governmental encouragement. In 1840 Paris alone had more than 200 of them, while there were eighty-two at Lyon and thirty at Roubaix.

The government was to discover, however, that it had acted with unwarranted complacency in many instances. For, behind an innocent façade, many of these organizations were nothing more than *sociétés de résistance,* collecting strike funds and laying plans for enforced wage increases. Despite the determined opposition of the government toward these organizations and the ample legal power of suppression which it possessed, the *sociétés de résistance* continued to multiply after 1830. Indeed the reign of Louis-Philippe witnessed the first general attempt of the working class to provide itself with effective organization.[23] The law of 1834,[24] however, dealt the *sociétés de résistance* a serious blow, and many of them were dissolved.

The years 1835 to 1840 witnessed a distinct lull in the labor movement, and workers' organizations seem to have made little progress. But the crisis of 1839-1840, and what amounted virtually to a " general strike " in Paris in the latter year, ushered in a period of vigorous revival. Despite the failure of the strike, it had done much to emphasize working-class solidarity. The expansion and strengthening of *sociétés de résistance* went on apace, in the face of determined governmental opposition. The *Chambre syndicale des typographes de Paris*, founded in 1839, had by 1843 succeeded in enlisting *half* of the workers in the typographical trades, and wages were fixed by a mixed committee of masters and workers. The ephemeral workers' press of the 'thirties was now replaced by a much more vigorous plant; but the workers continued to be interested more in political than in social questions, reflecting a typical working-class attitude which was to be prominent in the days of '48.

The workers also played a rôle in the more purely political organizations of the period. The secret societies languished after the affair of May, 1839, and the imprisonment of Barbès and Blanqui. But the *Société des saisons* was reorganized, and a number of workmen were members of the directing committee of the new society, the *Nouvelle saisons*. Prominent among the latter was Albert, later to become a member of the Provisional Government. A certain element in the *Saisons*, impatient of the moderation and inactivity of the committee, seceded and

[23] Sée points out that the beginnings of the movement seem not to be traceable directly to the more rapid industrialization of this period, since the workers who played the leading rôle at first (e.g., shoemakers, hatmakers, workers in the *de luxe* industries and the building trades) were precisely those least affected by these changes (p. 124).

[24] Under Articles 291-294 of the Napoleonic Penal Code, associations of more than twenty persons were forbidden. The law of 1834 forbade associations of even twenty persons, if such associations were parts of some larger whole. Otherwise the government seems to have felt that the Revolutionary and Napoleonic legislation was quite adequate as an instrument for the control of labor.

formed the *Société dissidente,* in 1847. This step was apparently a symptom of a reviving revolutionary activity in the years 1846-1848. But the history of the secret societies in this period is very obscure, and does not permit us to evaluate their influence upon the outbreak of the Revolution.

The workers' cause was likewise supported by various other groups. The *Réforme* had Louis Blanc as one of its editors, but in general interested itself more in political than in social questions. Its editors maintained relations with the revolutionaries of the secret societies. The system of Cabet was supported by the *Icariens* in the *Populaire.* A secondary rôle was played by Buchez and the *Atelier,* which was edited by workers. And there were the "socialists" of every *nuance,* winning converts to various schemes of reform, which invariably envisaged a society more happily arranged from the worker's point of view.

What has been said of the various types of workers' organization is sufficient to indicate that the period in question was one of transition. The changing industrial conditions of the 'thirties and 'forties witnessed the decay of the *compagnonnage,* antiquated survival of another day, and the progress of the societies of mutual aid and resistance, forerunners of the later labor unions. A new age posed new questions. The social critics replied with complete and tidy plans for the reorganization of society. The workers were more modest: their demands embraced wage-fixing, reduction of the hours of work, the right of association and of the strike, and the "right to work." But the fundamental outlines in the incipient struggle between capital and labor were as yet clear neither to the social critics nor to the workers. That problem awaited definition in the burning words of Marx.

II

To a large part of the proletariat, in a precarious position at best, the prolonged economic crisis of the years 1846-1848 dealt a severe blow. The accelerated industrial development of the late 'thirties and early 'forties had been accompanied by a less rapid expansion of commerce; desultory attempts to open certain foreign markets had been made by the government, but the fear of irritating the English was always present. Expanding industry had, therefore, found itself provided with inadequate markets and faced a crisis of overproduction, with its inevitable concomitants: falling prices, frozen capital, business failures, unemployment.

Railroad development, seriously hindered in the 'thirties by the fumbling policy of the Chamber and the crisis of 1839, had been given sudden impetus by the law of 1842. Railroad projects flooded the Chamber, and investors poured funds into the coffers of hastily chartered companies. A veritable orgy of speculation struck Paris.[25] Lavish investments in railroad and industrial issues and extensive expenditures on public works by the government resulted in a widespread condition of frozen capital.[26] This situation was seriously complicated by the bad harvests of 1845 and 1846, as a result of which large agricultural purchases abroad were necessary. Credit was severely constricted at the very moment when it was needed by infant industries and the railroads. The credit situation was further adversely affected by the crisis in England, with the accompanying sharp rise in the discount rate of the Bank of England. At the same time the crisis reduced the capacity of the English market to absorb French exports.[27]

The British crisis was not dissimilar in character from that in France. The rapid expansion of the railroads had given rise to the fear that a proper relationship between fixed and circulating capital had not been maintained. Stocks declined in the

---

[25] Everyone was speculating in 1845—men and women alike—and few even of the noble families were unaffected, says D'Alton-Shée (Edmond, Comte d'Alton-Shée: *Mes mémoires 1826-1848* [Paris, 1869, 2 vols.], II, pp. 304-305).

[26] Between 1840 and 1847 the railroads had absorbed 419,000,000 francs; in the same period of time the ministry of public works had expended a billion; the ministry of war, 260,000,000 (140,000,000 of which went into the fortifications of Paris); *chemins vicinaux* cost about 210,000,000 francs during the same period. Hence the total investment in seven years was 1,889,000,000 francs, of which about 600,000,000 had been expended in less than two years (Quentin-Bauchart: *Crise sociale*, p. 128).

[27] For a brief treatment of the French crisis, see Quentin-Bauchart: *Crise sociale*, pp. 127 ff.

summer of 1846. The previous year had seen a failure of Irish potatoes; the failure of 1846 was still more serious, and was accompanied by a similar deficiency in British potatoes and a short harvest in British wheat. With a seriously diminished harvest on the continent, it became necessary to ransack the world for sources of corn. And the price, although it remained fairly steady through 1846, rose sensationally in the first six months of 1847.[28] Meanwhile calls on foreign railway shares drained gold from England, and the Bank raised its discount rate to 3½ per cent, then to 4 and 5 per cent; finally, in April, the rate went to 5½ per cent, and only first-class bills due in May and June would be accepted. The failure of a number of prominent corn firms, followed by that of a series of banking houses, put severe stress upon the reserves of the Bank of England. A new crisis had been produced by autumn, and only the government's famous letter of October 25, 1847, promising a bill of indemnity for a possible infringement of the Bank Act of 1844, restored confidence and saved the situation. The Bank's reserve rapidly mounted, and during the following year of revolution " the purely banking and currency situation in Threadneedle Street was perfectly comfortable." [29]

The Bank of France also promptly felt the influence of the French crisis. Its reserve, which stood at 225,000,000 francs on January 1, 1846, had fallen to 80,000,000 a year from that date. Two weeks later it had declined to 59,000,000 francs.[30] The Bank promptly took measures to strengthen its reserves: it had demonetized coins (silver) refined, to the amount of

---

[28] For the three months ending May 29, 1847, it averaged 80s. 6d. May 29 it touched 102s. 5d. For the six months ending June 26 the average was 94s. 10d. By September 18 it was again at 49s. 6d. as a result of a better harvest, better potato prospects and heavy importation of corn (J. H. Clapham: *An Economic History of Modern Britain*. Volume I, *The Early Railway Age, 1820-1850* [Cambridge, 1926], p. 529).

[29] *Ibid.*, p. 534. For a succinct account of the whole crisis, see *ibid.*, pp. 526-535 and *passim*.

[30] Quentin-Bauchart: *Crise sociale*, p. 129. Cf. C. Juglar: *Des Crises commerciales et de leur retour périodique en France, en Angleterre et aux États-Unis* (Second edition, Paris, 1889), p. 417. Juglar gives the reserve as 252,000,000, July 1, 1846, and 80,000,000 January 1, 1847.

15,000,000 francs; secured between 4,000,000 and 5,000,000 francs in gold and silver in the provinces; borrowed 25,000,000 from the Barings, in effect from the Bank of England; and raised the discount rate from 4 to 5 per cent.[31] With credit contracting and markets shrinking, a wave of panic passed over the business world, and there followed a general depression in securities, extending even to government bonds.[32] The Bank gradually recovered its reserve, and by December, 1847, the discount rate was again reduced to 4 per cent. When the Revolution of 1848 broke out, the crisis " seemed to be expiring." [33] Meanwhile the working classes had suffered severely.

III

The proletariat was harassed at once by widespread unemployment and by a rise in the cost of living, resulting from crop failures at home and abroad.[34] And there is some evidence to indicate that rising food prices and unemployment were accompanied by declining wages.[35] Unemployment followed the general decline in the output of most plants and the failure of many businesses. The annual number of failures increased from 2,500 in 1842 to 4,762 in 1847. Some idea of the trend in unemployment is given by the figures for sentences for begging, which had increased during the same period from 3,500 per year to 10,646, and by the sentences for petty larceny, which had increased from 25,000 to 41,000.[36]

[31] *Ibid.*, p. 417; Clapham: *Early Railway Age*, p. 530. The discount rate exceeded 4 per cent for the first time in 27 years.

[32] Quentin-Bauchart: *Crise sociale*, p. 129.

[33] Juglar, p. 417.

[34] Crop failures had caused sharp rises in food prices, particularly in the case of bread, fundamental article of French diet (Quentin-Bauchart: *Crise sociale*, p. 129).

[35] The only figures available showing the general trend in wages are those discussed on pp. 6-8. The unsatisfactory character of these figures is there noted; they cannot be taken as demonstrating conclusively that there was a decline in the general wage level during these years, although they point in that direction. The whole question needs much further study.

[36] A. Cherest: *La Vie et les oeuvres de A.-T. Marie, avocat, membre du Gouvernement provisoire, etc.* (Paris, 1873), p. 171, and note 1.

The worsened condition of the workers was reflected in numerous proletarian disturbances toward the end of the year 1847. Riots, pillaging, even murders, were not uncommon, and the Departments of the Meurthe, Mayenne, Sarthe, Indre-et-Loire, Ille-et-Vilame, and Indre, and Nancy and Paris, witnessed stormy gatherings of the unemployed, demanding work and bread and forcing the bakers to diminish prices. Provision trains were held up on the roads, and in certain sections troops were necessary for the protection of wheat shipments.[37]

The distress of the workers was set in bold relief against a background of waste and corruption in political circles, and hatred for the upper classes was further enhanced by a series of public scandals at the end of the reign of Louis-Philippe. The unconcerned magnificence of the great world goaded the workers to desperation, while Lamartine thundered against corruption and indifference in high places and predicted the approach of the *révolution de mépris*. The realities of the crisis gave new vitality to the propaganda of the socialists, grown vigorous in the past decade; and the campaign of the political banquets, however little concerned with the lot of the workers, enhanced the revolutionary spirit among the proletariat. The vision of an almost universal opposition to the monarchy among the town dwellers, strengthened by the apathy of the peasants, gave renewed hope to the workers of a solution of their economic problems.

Yet the imminence of revolution was felt by few. Tocqueville's prescient warning to his colleagues of the Chamber that they were sleeping over a volcano was received by the jeering laughs of the great majority. And the speaker later admitted that he himself had exaggerated his anxieties.[38] The government little understood the widespread sympathy evoked by the campaign of the banquets, and the speech from the throne[39] referred in scathing terms to the "*passions ennemies*

[37] Quentin-Bauchart: *Crise sociale*, p. 129.
[38] A. de Tocqueville: *Souvenirs de Alexis de Tocqueville* (Paris, 1893), p. 21 and *passim*.
[39] December 28, 1847.

ou aveugles " of the parliamentary opposition. Nor did the
latter group understand or sympathize much more with the
demands of the workers. Questions political had a virtual
monopoly of the attention of the group which participated in
the banquets, and the social question was noticed almost not
at all. This exclusive absorption of the reform group in its
own political interests was destined to a rude awakening following the February Days. For the bourgeois party of reform
quickly discovered that its collaborators in the Revolution
(the workers) were intent on giving that movement a far different issue from that which they had themselves envisaged.

THE NATIONAL WORKSHOPS

CHAPTER I

POLITICAL OR SOCIAL REVOLUTION?

I. The Provisional Government a Triumph for the Moderates. II. The Radical Revolutionaries Forestalled by Concessions.

THE unstable history of the Second French Republic was implicit in its foundation. For the February Revolution was accomplished by two elements: the " moderates," who favored a political revolution pure and simple; and the radical republicans, who welcomed a political revolution as the vestibule to a profound reorganization of society, for which, however, the plans were numerous, vague, and inchoate. This dichotomy in the forces of the Revolution led to a struggle culminating in the June insurrection, which blasted the cause of the radicals — and subsequently that of the moderates as well. This struggle had its inception in the very hours in which the final defeat was being administered to the retreating forces of Louis Philippe.

I

The swiftness of the collapse of the July Monarchy found the moderates without plans for the assumption of power, and fearful that the social revolutionaries might quickly make themselves masters of the situation. To forestall this contingency was the purpose of an irregular meeting of moderates [1] held in the offices of the *National*, right wing republican organ, on the morning of February 24. Toward noon this group chose a *comité de direction*. The latter was only mildly republican, with strong leanings toward an Orleanist regency, as was clearly evident from its membership. Its moderate republican members included François Arago, the distinguished astronomer; Garnier-Pagès; Marie; and Marrast, editor of the *National*.

---

[1] The meeting was not convoked by the *National* editors, but appears to have been composed of a group generally sympathetic with the newspaper's views.

But the committee sought additional strength from the ranks of the Orleanists in the inclusion of Odilon Barrot, whose choice was explained as a " concession to the bourgeoisie "; and Lamartine, who was still believed to favor a regency. The left republicans and the socialists met a sharp rebuff when both Ledru-Rollin and Louis Blanc were refused places, the latter after a defence in person of the cause of the workers. It was clear from the beginning that the moderates intended to curb the radicals at all costs.[2]

The committee list was rushed from the offices of the *National* to the Palais Bourbon, where the historic final session of the Orleanist Chamber of Deputies was about to be convened. By now the *National* group bearing the committee list and headed by Emmanuel Arago was no longer talking of a *comité de direction* but of a " provisional government." The adherence of Marie to the plan was quickly won,[3] followed by that of Lamartine, who astonished his petitioners and gave events a new turn by a categorical declaration in favor of the Republic.[4] Odilon Barrot, whose acceptance might now have been a source of embarrassment, proved obdurate in his defence of the Regency.[5]

The dramatic events in the chamber are a matter of general knowledge. The President, Sauzet, having been refused the aid of General Bedeau, was helpless to protect the deputies against the force of the mob. The Duchess of Orleans and her sons arrived; the mother's *sang-froid* in the face of mounting dangers drew the acclaim of the chamber, but the attempts of her supporters, notably Odilon Barrot, to secure for her the Regency were fruitless. The revolutionary mob had slowly filtered in among the deputies. Demands for a provisional government grew louder and more urgent. Amid the din of the

---

[2] A. Crémieux: *La Révolution de février; étude critique sur les journées des 21, 22, 23, et 24 février 1848* (Paris, 1912). See Crémieux's completely documented account on the selection of the *National* committee (pp. 367-370).

[3] Cherest, pp. 106-107.

[4] A. de Lamartine: *Histoire de la Révolution de 1848* (Brussels, 1849, 2 vols.), I, pp. 121-128.

[5] Crémieux: *Révolution de février*, pp. 377-378, and sources there cited.

tumult Marie, Crémieux, Ledru-Rollin, and Lamartine in turn made impassioned pleas for the immediate constitution of a provisional government. Meanwhile a second invasion of the chamber had taken place. Sauzet declared the session adjourned, and Dupont (de l'Eure), patriarch of the republican cause, was summoned to the chair by the mob.

Lamartine, who was still on the tribune, now received lists from all sides, many of them improvised at the moment. On the basis of these, he dictated the names of the new provisional government *sotto voce* to the tellers. Presently the names were read out, the mob signifying its wishes by shouts of " oui " or " non." The new government was to include Dupont (de l'Eure), François Arago, Lamartine, Ledru-Rollin, Garnier-Pagès, Marie, and Crémieux. In fulfillment of the traditional revolutionary ritual, the members of the new government departed for the Hôtel de Ville, there to be " consecrated by the people." [6]

The most striking feature of the government thus chosen was its omission of any representative of the workers' cause. Why was it that a revolutionary mob, composed largely of *gens du peuple,* armed to the teeth and presumably favoring a revolution *social* as well as *democratic,* failed to insist upon the inclusion of a socialist element in the new executive? There is almost no evidence that Louis Blanc's name was even so much as suggested from the floor.[7] In the light of subsequent

[6] For the selection of the Provisional Government, see the stenographic report in *Le Moniteur universel. Journal officiel de la République française,* edition of February 25-26, 1848. Cf. also the documented account in Crémieux: *Révolution de février,* pp. 373 ff.

[7] There is no reference to such a demand in the account in the *Moniteur,* February 25-26. Cf. Lamartine (*Révolution de 1848,* I, p. 166), who declares that Blanc's name was called from the floor and actually included in some of the lists presented to him (Lamartine), but that he passed it over as unsuited to a government whose aim was the conciliation of all classes. Blanc's popularity is attested by his subsequent reception by the populace at the Hôtel de Ville, which ensured his acceptance by the moderates as a member of the Provisional Government. Cf. Quentin-Bauchart (*Crise sociale,* pp. 135-137), who insists that the socialists were passed over because none of them had sufficient prestige to have his name impose itself, that nothing was said of a " République

developments it must be admitted that this is an extremely curious fact, for which there is really no adequate explanation. To be sure the mob had no more definite program than that which crystallized in hysterical demands for a provisional government and a republic. But it may still be objected that, with the memories of 1830 before them, the workers would be expected to attempt to safeguard their cause by insistence upon inclusion in the government of an element favorable to them.[8]

The mob was of course obviously much influenced by " bourgeois " leadership. Lamartine was of the first importance. The poet admits that in selecting the names to be read out, he chose those most appropriate to the national emergency![9] The *National* group had prepared a list in advance, had won the adhesion of Lamartine and Marie, and appears to have been active on the floor of the chamber in behalf of its slate.[10] Its influence, directly and through Lamartine, was doubtless considerable. Indeed four members of the original *National* list were chosen: the elimination of Odilon Barrot was inevitable after his speech in support of the Regency, while the disappearance of Marrast's name may well have been due to Lamartine, who had no love for the editors of the *National*. The three additions are likewise intelligible. Dupont (de l'Eure), who commanded universal respect, was an obvious addition, more especially after his summons to preside over the assembly. Ledru-Rollin's selection was inevitable, by reason of his ardent and long-standing republicanism, upon which he had succeeded in focussing attention anew by his speech in behalf of a provisional government. Crémieux, but just returned from wishing

sociale " in the popular assembly at the Hôtel de Ville until Louis Blanc pronounced the words.

[8] Suspicions of the good faith of the new government appeared at once. Ledru-Rollin had scarcely finished speaking, toward the end of the session, when a student of the *École polytechnique* shouted: " Vous voyez qu'aucun des membres de votre gouvernement provisoire ne veut la République! Nous serons trompés comme en 1830 " (*Moniteur*, edition of February 25-26).

[9] The importance of Lamartine's influence is further attested by the fact that *all* of the names which he read out were approved.

[10] Cherest, pp. 114-115.

Godspeed to departing royalty, had changed ground with the address of a fencer. His plea for a provisional government was simultaneously an advertisement of his candidacy — and none of the four who made speeches in behalf of the new executive was refused a place therein!

*   *   *   *   *

The rebuff of the *National* at the hands of the right wing republicans that morning had only intensified Louis Blanc's determination to have the radical group included in any government which should be constituted. Blanc was, however, willing to support the *National* list with certain additions.[11] The debate early that afternoon at the offices of the *Réforme,* organ of the left republicans, resulted in the selection of a government composed of François Arago, Marie, Garnier-Pagès, Lamartine, Marrast, Ledru-Rollin, Louis Blanc, Flocon, and Albert. Thus the *Réforme's* list included five of the seven members chosen at the Palais Bourbon, but it included also Marrast, Louis Blanc, Flocon, editor of the *Réforme,* and Albert, a worker.[12] The last three would inevitably, as representatives of the popular cause, invite the opposition of the moderate republicans of the *National nuance*. Louis Blanc was above all the subject of suspicion by reason of his widely known schemes of social regeneration.[13]

[11] Blanc had no desire to compromise his own cause by opposing such popular names as those of Lamartine, Ledru-Rollin, and Arago.

[12] Albert (whose name was Alexandre Martin), " ouvrier mécanicien," had taken a prominent part in secret societies under the July Monarchy. He was also one of the founders and anonymous editors of the *Atelier*. The precise reasons for his selection as member of the government, as opposed to some other worker, are obscure (see Crémieux: *Révolution de février,* p. 422, note 6). He was condemned to deportation, 1849, for his part in the events of May 15, 1848, amnestied in 1859, and refused thenceforth to play a political rôle, although he was subsequently made a member of the *commission des barricades* by the Government of National Defence in 1870 (*Dictionnaire des parlementaires français,* I, pp. 28-29).

[13] On the selection of the government in the offices of the *Réforme,* see Crémieux: *Révolution de février,* pp. 421-422. Louis Blanc's own account is thoroughly untrustworthy (L. Blanc: *Histoire de la Révolution de 1848* [Fifth edition, Paris, 1880], pp. 63-68).

It was about eight o'clock that evening and the new government selected in the chamber had already installed itself in the Hôtel de Ville, when Louis Blanc, Flocon, and Albert arrived. Enthusiastic acclaim by the populace milling about the Hôtel de Ville and by a self-constituted popular assembly in the Salle Saint-Jean was followed by a cold reception from the new government. Surprise, mingled with irritation, greeted the three, when Louis Blanc defended their rights to inclusion in the government. A compromise was effected only when Garnier-Pagès pronounced the word "secretaries." The three yielded and agreed to act in that capacity, asking only the inclusion also of Albert, which was granted.[14]

II

The events of the day had shown clearly how sharp was the cleavage between the moderates, on one hand, and the radicals, on the other. The cleavage was to become increasingly more marked in the days that followed, both within and without the Provisional Government.

For the moment the moderates were pleased to yield because they were forced to yield: they were in no position to court the wrath of the popular assembly in the Hôtel de Ville nor of its hysterical supporters massed in the Place de Grève. But the two groups within the government were by no means of equal strength. Despite the fact that the new "secretaries" quickly attained to a position of equality with the other members, the

[14] It is not clear precisely what function the four new "secretaries" were to perform. Louis Blanc suggests that the title was connected with the fact that three of them were writers by profession. It appears that originally it was intended that they should have only a *voix consultative*. The whole incident is obscure (Crémieux: *Révolution de février*, pp. 451-452). It is clear, however, that the moderates were desperately opposed to the inclusion of Louis Blanc, and wished to relegate the four to an inferior place (*ibid.*; Blanc: *Révolution de 1848*, I, pp. 75 ff.; L. A. Garnier-Pagès: *Histoire de la Révolution de 1848* [Paris, 1861-1872, 11 vols.], V, pp. 320-321; *Rapport de la Commission d'enquête sur l'insurrection qui a éclaté dans la journée du 23 juin et sur les événements du 15 mai* [Paris, 1848, 3 vols.], I, p. 266). For Garnier-Pagès and Crémieux, at least, there was no objection to Marrast. Flocon also appears in a favorable light in Garnier-Pagès' account, while Albert figures as an unknown.

moderates possessed advantages which they hastened to capitalize.

In the period preceding the Revolution the moderates had interested themselves in parliamentary and electoral reform and had, in large measure, neglected social and economic questions. They were substantially united upon a program of universal suffrage. Here they possessed an advantage of first-rate importance: to the radicals' divergent and amorphous plans for social reform, the moderates opposed a simple and comprehensible, albeit highly revolutionary, program — universal suffrage and the expression of the popular will through a duly elected constituent body.

In the first days of the Revolution, therefore, the problem of the moderates took a simple form: they must at all costs control the course of the Revolution and prevent the radicals from gaining the upper hand until the constituent assembly should be convened.[15] The road to eventual success was to be paved by present concessions, essential to placate the popular party which had triumphed in the February Days and which stood ready to exert instant and decisive pressure upon a government which for the present lacked any effective means of protecting itself. Three such concessions were quickly yielded the radicals: the famous " guarantee of work," the establishment of the National Workshops, and the creation of the Commission of the Luxembourg.

*   *   *   *   *

The position of the new government on the morning of February 25 seemed precarious indeed. There were no armed forces at its command; meanwhile the mob surged all about the Hôtel de Ville and was so massed on the stairs and in the corridors of the building that it was virtually impossible for deputations to reach the government. Suddenly, about half-past twelve, the door of the council chamber was noisily opened and there appeared before the government a worker, gun in

---

[15] For an illuminating passage on the problem of the moderates, see the deposition of Garnier-Pagès (*Commission d'enquête*, I, p. 284).

hand, his face pale and excited from his exertions, his eye on fire — like a spectre, says Louis Blanc.[16] He struck the floor with the butt of his gun, thrust a petition toward the government, and in a loud voice demanded the "organization of labor . . . within the hour!"[17] And with an ominous gesture he pointed to the mob in the Place de Grève.

Like a clap of thunder the social revolution had burst upon the government. To refuse all consideration of this imperious demand was to court immediate disaster. The members of the government elected to temporize: Garnier-Pagès, Marie, Lamartine harangued the worker, Marche by name,[18] and urged him to see that society could not be reorganized in a day. What plans had *he* for the "organization of labor?" Marche faltered, and Louis Blanc summoned him to a window where, in the course of a brief discussion, Blanc drafted the following decree:

Le Gouvernement provisoire de la République française s'engage à garantir l'existence de l'ouvrier par le travail;

Il s'engage à garantir du travail à tous les citoyens;

Il reconnait que les ouvriers doivent s'associer entre eux pour jouir du bénéfice légitime de leur travail.

Le Gouvernement provisoire rend aux ouvriers, auxquels il appartient, le million qui va échoir de la Liste civile.[19]

[16] Blanc: *Révolution de 1848*, I, p. 126.

[17] The petition, drawn up by A. B. de Lancy, editor of the Fourierist organ, *La Démocratie pacifique*, was couched in the most vague and general terms, asking the "organisation du travail, le droit au travail," etc. (*Moniteur*, February 25-26).

[18] Marche appears only this once and then sinks back into the oblivion from whence he came, although his name appears on a list of candidates to the assembly whose election is urged by the *Père Duchêne* (May 30-June 1), and a letter from him is published in the *Vraie République* (May 26), in which he declares that the decree on the "guarantee of work," "rendu après mûre délibération, est fort loin d'être un décret *arraché*."

[19] *Moniteur*, February 25-26. The lack of agreement among the three principal accounts of the incident makes it impossible to present a definitive picture. There is fair agreement as to the rôle of Louis Blanc, but Marie's attempt to evade responsibility for the decree is unconvincing. He persists in maintaining that it was signed only by Louis Blanc and Garnier-Pagès and was never discussed by the government. (In the *Moniteur* the decree appears without the

The decree's most striking characteristic is its vagueness. The state undertakes to "guarantee" work to all its citizens, but nothing is said as to how this is to be done beyond the vague recognition of the coöperative principle. The petition Marche presented asked immediate adhesion to the "organization of labour." Louis Blanc had made the latter phrase famous in a book published nine years earlier.[20] No better commentary on Blanc's lack of a practical program with which to implement his general scheme is needed than his apparent inability to use this magnificent opportunity to force his plans upon the government.

The moderates had no sympathy with the utopian decree which circumstances had obliged them to accept. But the temper of the mob had convinced them that their own position was too precarious to permit vacillation, that their vague decree must at once receive some substantial fulfillment in a form calculated to allay the mounting suspicions of the populace.[21] The result was the establishment on the following day of the

names of any of the members of the government.) According to his own admission, Marie was present and took an active part in the discussion. He must inevitably have given his assent, at least tacitly. It is quite obvious that Marie, who was bitterly opposed to the decree (Cherest, p. 178, note 1, and *passim*) and who was anxious to escape responsibility for its adoption (*ibid.*, p. 139), was, like the others, acting under the influence of fear (*ibid.*, pp. 177-178). On the whole incident, see *ibid.*, pp. 136-141 and *passim*; Blanc: *Révolution de 1848*, I, pp. 126-128; Garnier-Pagès, VI, pp. 53-59; C. H. Phipps (First Marquis of Normanby): *A Year of Revolution, from a Journal kept in Paris in 1848* (London, 1857, 2 vols.), I, pp. 167-168; and the vague account of Lamartine: *Révolution de 1848*, I, pp. 329 ff.

[20] L. Blanc: *Organisation du travail* (Paris, 1839).

[21] Cherest, pp. 142, 147-148; cf. Garnier-Pagès, VI, pp. 106 ff. It will have been noted that the vigorous *démarches* before the government in this period were the work of revolutionary leaders. The populace itself was carried away by a delirium of fraternity ("une sorte d'anarchie bon enfant") in the days immediately following the Revolution. Count Apponyi, *attaché* of the Austrian embassy, reports that everything was in a state of inconceivable calm and that no city in the world was safer than Paris (Comte R. Apponyi: *Vingt-cinq ans à Paris* [*1826-1852*]. *Journal du comte Rodolphe Apponyi, attaché de l'ambassade d'Autriche à Paris* [Paris, 1913-1926, 4 vols.], IV, p. 153). This "honeymoon of fraternity" lasted but a few days, however (*ibid.*, IV, pp. 171 ff.).

all-too-famous National Workshops.[22] Nothing was said as to the character of the Workshops, but the name itself (*Ateliers nationaux*) was undoubtedly intended to suggest to the workers that this was a substantial concession to Louis Blanc, whose social scheme envisaged the establishment of *Ateliers sociaux*. The very absence of precise definition, however, and the clause attributing the execution of the decree to Marie, the minister of public works, are eloquent. Marie was a notorious opponent of socialist ideas and especially of the system of Louis Blanc.[23] He had no intention of seeing the National Workshops become a socialist experiment. Quite the contrary, he viewed the Workshops as a reservoir into which could be drained the unemployed and troublesome members of the Parisian populace. Thus he could remedy two ills at one stroke, assuaging the real and immediate need of the unemployed and immobilizing turbulent elements of the social revolution.

If Marie and the moderates were clear as to their object, they were much less so as to the method by which it could be accomplished. In general, it was intended that the Workshops should be simply *chantiers de charité*, in much the same form that this type of public relief for unemployment had been used at various times in the past.[24] The establishment of " open-air workhouses " was an old expedient, but in the past, notably in 1830, it had been well understood that the institution was

[22] *Moniteur*, February 27:

" Le Gouvernement provisoire de la République

" Décrète l'établissement immédiat d'Ateliers nationaux.

" Le ministre des travaux publics est chargé de l'exécution du présent décret."

[23] Blanc: *Révolution de 1848*, I, p. 219; Cherest, p. 178, note 1.

[24] For bibliography on the *chantiers de charité* prior to 1848, see G. Renard: *La République de 1848. Notes et références* (Paris, 1906), p. 2. " Chantiers de démolition et de terrassement " as a means of caring for the unemployed go back at least as far as the reign of Henry IV (G. Fagniez: *L'économie sociale de la France sous Henri IV, 1589-1610* [Paris, 1897], p. 78). For a case similar in many respects to that in 1848, see the description of the workhouses established in 1788 (F. Dreyfus: *Un philanthrope d'autrefois. La Rochefoucauld-Liancourt* [*1747-1827*], Paris, 1903, pp. 167-172). These *chantiers* were only closed in June, 1791, and then with some exceptions.

temporary and charitable in character. In 1848 for the first time the establishment of these *chantiers* followed a " guarantee of work." They were viewed, therefore, by the workers as more or less permanent and as representing in any case an obligation of the government toward its unemployed citizens.[25] With this general example in mind the immediate necessity was to find means of employing the workers. Public works, readily organized and requiring large numbers of unskilled laborers, seemed the logical answer. A series of acts of the government, drafted by Marie, immediately provided for the initiation of such works, considered sufficient in extent to employ some 10,000 workers, at that time believed quite adequate to meet the expected demand.[26] The work consisted of *terrassement*: excavation, "levelling," and "filling" projects, for the most part preparation for construction work.[27]

The new organization had scarcely made a beginning when the unexpected happened. In place of the moderate numbers which had been anticipated, a veritable deluge of workers presented themselves for admission to the newly created Workshops.[28] The responsibility for the ensuing confusion Marie attributes to the weakness of the mayors of the Paris arrondissements, who were entrusted with the machinery of admissions. Frightened by the clamor of the turbulent multitude seeking work, says Marie, the mayors hastened to disembarrass themselves of this flood of laborers by evading the strict instructions of the minister and granting admissions to the Work-

[25] See, e.g., Odilon Barrot: *Mémoires posthumes de Odilon Barrot* (Paris, 1875-1876, 4 vols.), I, pp. 58-59.

[26] *Moniteur*, February 28; Cherest, pp. 187-189, 198, note 1.

[27] Each worker was to provide himself with a certificate of domicile, signed by his landlord, attesting his residence in Paris. When the certificate had been given a visa by the commissioner of police, the worker presented it at the *mairie* of his arrondissement, where he was given an admission card to the National Workshops. He was subsequently accepted in that workshop in which there was a vacancy and paid at the rate of two francs a day. If no vacancy existed he was given a dole of one and a half francs (E. Thomas: *Histoire des Ateliers nationaux* [Paris, 1848], pp. 29-30).

[28] Cherest, pp. 189-190, 198, note 1; cf. Garnier-Pagès, VI, pp. 303-305.

shops indiscriminately and in great haste.[29]   Such inefficiency
on the part of the Paris mayors contributed in turn to the ease
with which workers from the suburbs and departments nearby
hastened to Paris and were admitted to the already over-
crowded Workshops.[30]   Within a few days angry mobs of unemployed workers, for whom no place could be found, were
surging about the various *mairies*, and the whole organization
was in a state of acute disorder.

It was under these conditions that Émile Thomas, a young
man of twenty-six, former student of the *École centrale des
arts et manufactures*, submitted to the minister of public works
a scheme for the reorganization of the National Workshops
along military lines. The project was enthusiastically received
and was put into operation at once.[31]

Meanwhile the moderates had been obliged to yield a third
concession to the radical element in the government. On the
morning of February 28 a procession of several thousand workers marched into the Place de Grève with banners bearing
demands for a " Ministry of Progress " and the " Organization
of Labor." While a delegation from the workers was waiting
to be admitted to the presence of the government, Louis Blanc
vigorously defended the workers' demands. The new ministry
was essential, he declared, if the " fraternal organization of
labor " was to be effected. The moderates energetically com-
batted their colleague's arguments. Blanc offered his resignation and that of Albert. The moderates recoiled before the
danger of civil war, and a compromise was reached in the
founding of the Commission of the Luxembourg, a parliament
to debate the workers' ills, presided over by Louis Blanc.

[29] P. de la Gorce: *Histoire de la seconde République française* (Paris, 1887, 2
vols.), I, p. 276. The initiation of such a system amid the confusion then prevailing in Paris must have been exceedingly difficult. Probably neither the ministry of public works nor the mayors of the Paris arrondissements functioned
very efficiently at first. On the other hand, the failure of the mayors to execute
orders respecting the Workshops was repeatedly the subject of complaint for
some months to come.

[30] Cherest, pp. 190-191.

[31] See Chapter II.

The concession was to prove illusory. Blanc later complained bitterly that, in place of a ministry with a budget and the *power to act,* he had been granted " une orageuse école où j'étais appelé à faire un cours sur le faim, devant le peuple affamé ! " [32] The moderates not only were opposed to the creation of a ministry of progress, which would have given Louis Blanc and socialism a powerful place in the new régime, but they hoped that the discussions before the workers' parliament would reveal the inanities of the workers' demands and at the same time would ruin the prestige of Louis Blanc.[33] On the other hand, there was perhaps no single moment during the course of these revolutionary months when Louis Blanc had a better opportunity to force the adoption of his views, to oblige the moderates to make far-reaching concessions to the social revolution.[34] Subsequent events were to show that his decision did great damage to the cause of the radicals. While the Luxembourg Commission consumed weeks in airing its views on the organization of society, the cause of the workers steadily lost ground; simultaneously the forces of the opposition were given time in which to arm themselves to crush the social revolution. Even more important, Louis Blanc had permitted the administration of the National Workshops, which would have been subject to his own direction as minister of

[32] *Moniteur,* February 29; Blanc: *Révolution de 1848,* I, pp. 133-138; Garnier-Pagès, VI, pp. 182-188; Cherest, pp. 179-182 (cf., Thomas, pp. 141-142). The Commission of the Luxembourg was so called because it held its meetings in the Palais du Luxembourg; its full title was the *Commission du gouvernement pour les travailleurs.* On its organization and history, see G. Cahen: " Louis Blanc et la Commission du Luxembourg (1848)," *Annales de l'École libre des sciences politiques,* XII (1897) ; and P. Loustau: *Louis Blanc et la Commission du Luxembourg* (Paris, 1908). On the desperate character of the situation faced by the moderates in the early days of the Revolution, see the statement of Arago to Circourt (Adolphe de Circourt: *Souvenirs d'une mission à Berlin en 1848, publiés pour la Société d'histoire contemporaine, par M. Georges Bourgin* [Paris, 1908], p. 91).

[33] Loustau: *Commission du Luxembourg,* p. 30 and *passim.*

[34] For Blanc's motives in yielding, see Garnier-Pagès, Cherest, and particularly Blanc: *Révolution de 1848,* I, pp. 133-138; and cf. Renard: *République de 1848,* p. 9; and Loustau, pp. 28 ff.

progress, to remain under the control of the declared enemy of his schemes.[35]

The subsequent relations of the Luxembourg Commission with the National Workshops are of sufficient importance to warrant a brief description of the activities of that interesting institution. Two hundred workers were summoned to the first meeting, March 1, in the Palais du Luxembourg.[36] Louis Blanc announced that the object of the commission was twofold: (1) to study labor problems in general and to prepare solutions to present to the constituent assembly; (2) to provide an immediate solution for the most pressing needs of the workers. In the latter connection it was decided in the same meeting that the practice of *marchandage* [37] should be eliminated and that working hours should be reduced from eleven to ten in Paris and from twelve to eleven in the provinces.[38] Louis Blanc, eager to achieve his ends through conciliation wherever possible, invited representatives of the Paris *patrons* to meet with him the following day. The employers agreed to accept the two changes voted by the workers, and on the same day, March 2, decrees to this effect were issued by the Provisional Government. This immediate and striking triumph for the new com-

[35] Quentin-Bauchart: *Crise sociale*, p. 238. It has been repeatedly stated that Blanc and Albert, who was made vice president of the Commission, necessarily absented themselves frequently from the meetings of the government and thus left unprotected the interests of the workers. But the *procès-verbaux* show only a dozen absences for Albert and the same number for Louis Blanc, and only three meetings from which both were absent (C. Seignobos: "Les procès-verbaux du Gouvernement provisoire et de la Commission du pouvoir exécutif de 1848," *Revue d'histoire moderne et contemporaine* VII, [1905-1906], p. 584).

[36] It is not known how the initial group was chosen. The Luxembourg Palace had been selected as a locus by the government as a means of giving the parliament the superficial appearance of greater prestige.

[37] *Marchandage* was of various kinds. As understood by the action of employers and workers on this occasion, it referred to the practice of subletting part of a project (it was used particularly in the building trades) to a *marchandeur* at a contract price. The latter then employed the workers at a wage which he fixed, but which it was obviously in his interest to make as low as possible.

[38] Working hours were of course not uniform, as the decision of the workers might suggest. They varied greatly.

mission made a great impression and at once enhanced the prestige of Louis Blanc.[39]

Subsequently the Luxembourg Commission was given a definitive organization. Each of the Parisian workers' *corporations* [40] was to send three representatives to the commission, a total of 242 coming for the first general session of March 10.[41] One of the three delegates from each *corporation* was to take part in the commission's daily deliberations, the other two to be present only at the general assemblies, where reports from the daily sessions would be discussed. Ten delegates were selected by lot to form a permanent workers' committee.

The *patrons* were likewise invited to elect three delegates from each industry. On March 17 there were assembled 231 *patrons*, representing seventy-seven *corps de métiers*. The employers likewise selected ten of their number by lot to form a permanent committee.[42] The two permanent committees (of workers and employers) discussed important questions in joint sessions, to which were also invited certain prominent economists of various *nuances,* whose coöperation Louis Blanc had asked. Through the coöperation of workers and employers, the commission accomplished its most valuable work, that of preventing a number of strikes by regulation of differences between *patrons* and workers. Beyond that, its work was embodied largely in decrees which were never executed or were subsequently suppressed.[43]

But the honeymoon of workers and masters was destined to be short-lived. It suffered the *contre-coup* of the events of the middle of March,[44] and presently the workers' delegates were

[39] Quentin-Bauchart: *Crise sociale,* p. 280.

[40] *Ibid.,* p. 274. The elections were not uniform in character since the Parisian " corporations n'existaient plus guère." Sometimes there were several groups of delegates from one trade.

[41] In the course of the month 454 additional workers' delegates were named (*ibid.,* p. 274).

[42] For details of organization, see Loustau, Ch. II. The employers were drawn from commerce, the building trades, transport, and *petite industrie,* but very little from *grande industrie* (Quentin-Bauchart: *Crise sociale,* p. 275).

[43] For a summary of the commission's work, see Loustau, Ch. XVI.

[44] See below, Ch. III.

devoting their energies to the problem of electing workers' candidates in the forthcoming elections. A *Comité central des ouvriers du département de la Seine* was chosen to organize the working-class vote and win its support for the Luxembourg candidates. The latter were to be chosen in plenary session of the delegates on the basis of a report prepared by a *Commission des élections* which was to investigate the eligibility of prospective candidates.[45]

The rebuff dealt the workers' cause in the events of April 16 [46] Louis Blanc sought to repair by further regimentation of the working-class vote. The *Comité central des ouvriers* was joined to certain other groups to form the *Comité révolutionnaire, composé des délégués de deux cents clubs, des corporations ouvrières, de la garde mobile, et de l'armée.*[47] Unfortunately, as Blanc himself complains, the final list of Luxembourg candidates omitted the names of any of the moderates in the government and thus compromised the workers' chances of success. Only five of the Luxembourg list were elected,[48] of a total of thirty-four deputies chosen in the Department of the Seine.[49]

The overwhelming defeat of the workers' cause presaged the early end of the Luxembourg Commission, for which the new assembly had little sympathy. Louis Blanc and Albert resigned the presidency and vice-presidency,[50] and the last

[45] Cahen: " Commission du Luxembourg," *Annales de l'École libre des sciences politiques,* XII (1897), pp. 372 ff. Cahen notes that the commission was given between 100,000 and 120,000 francs from the government, with which to send electoral agents into the departments to campaign for workers' candidates; the latter represented a concession of the government to induce the workers to accept the election date. [The workers desired postponement of the date. Cahen gives no source for the statement.]

[46] See below, Ch. IV.

[47] The formation of this committee is interesting primarily because it included the same groups precisely with which the delegates of the National Workshops were to coöperate, beginning the end of May. (See below, pp. 230 ff.)

[48] Caussidière, Albert, Ledru-Rollin, Flocon, and Louis Blanc.

[49] On the whole question of the election, see Cahen: " Commission du Luxembourg," *Annales de l'École libre des sciences politiques,* XII (1897), pp. 460 ff.

[50] Blanc: *Révolution de 1848,* II, p. 171.

meeting was held May 13.[51] Following the invasion of the assembly, May 15, the commission ceased to exist, without any decree having been pronounced to that effect.[52] But the *Comité central des ouvriers,* under the name of the *Comité des délégués du Luxembourg,* continued to function very actively.[53] It was this group that was influential in healing the long-standing breach between the Luxembourg and the National Workshops. The capital importance of this step will be considered subsequently.[54]

[51] *Gazette des tribunaux,* March 8, 1849. Actually the functions of the Luxembourg Commission had been superseded by those of the assembly's new committee to investigate the condition of agricultural and industrial laborers (*Moniteur,* May 11).

[52] Cahen: " Commission du Luxembourg," *Annales de l'École libre des sciences politiques,* XII (1897), pp. 469-470.

[53] *Ibid.,* pp. 474-475.

[54] See below, pp. 101 f.

CHAPTER II

THE NATIONAL WORKSHOPS MILITARIZED

I. Thomas' Plan Adopted. II. The Intricacies of Administration.
III. Work Projects Fail to Materialize.

I

EVEN before the appearance of Émile Thomas, the minister
of public works had taken measures to remedy the chaotic
condition into which the National Workshops had fallen. The
control of admissions had been centralized in two offices with
a view to the correction of abuses by the *mairies*, but the
remedy quickly proved inadequate. One of the two offices was
located opposite the residence of Thomas, and the future
director describes the crowds of angry workers in a state of
what he terms "perennial insurrection." Students of the
École centrale, whose services had been secured by the director, Higonnet, were soon disgusted with the inefficiency of the
whole system and brought their complaints to Thomas, who
had maintained close relations with the students since his
graduation at the *École*.[1]

Thomas never lacked self-confidence. He immediately
evolved a plan of reorganization for the Workshops and
secured an interview with Marie, March 3, through the intervention of a friend of his father who enjoyed the minister's
confidence.[2] Thomas hoped, by means of a semi-military organization and with the aid of students of the *École centrale,*
to reëstablish order among the workers through "moral influence," he told the minister. Marie greeted eagerly a scheme
which promised to restore order where anarchy now reigned.[3]

[1] Thomas, pp. 31-33.
[2] *Ibid.,* p. 33; Cherest, p. 204, note 1.
[3] Thomas, pp. 35-36; Cherest, p. 193.

Garnier-Pagès, mayor of Paris, added his assent, and it was agreed that Thomas should formally present his proposal for the consideration of the mayors of the twelve arrondissements on March 5.[4] The eager and offhand approval by Marie and Garnier-Pagès of a scheme by a young man about whom they knew almost nothing and their willingness to give into his hands the control of an army of laborers of dubious personnel and intentions, is apparently to be explained by the really desperate character of the situation.[5] It must be admitted, however, that the intrinsic appeal of Thomas' plan and the lucid and convincing manner in which he seemed capable of expounding it won instant support from all who heard him.[6]

Before the mayors of the arrondissements and other highly placed municipal officials, Thomas developed his plan at length on March 5. Since the government lacked the means of preserving order by *force,* Thomas urged the use of *moral influence,* exerted by students of the *École centrale* as officers of a semi-military hierarchy, in which the workers were to be organized in brigade and company units. Control was to be achieved through the establishment of a highly centralized administration. But Thomas warned the gathering that the success of the scheme must finally rest upon the regular provision of work projects adequate to employ those enrolled. Otherwise incalculable results might ensue.[7]

It is no exaggeration to say that Thomas' project was accepted with enthusiasm. There was nothing but praise for the plan; not an objection was raised, says Marie.[8] Indeed the mayors, eager to be rid of their heavy and perilous burden, urged immediate action. Thomas demurred, and it was agreed that the new director should have four days for organization. On March 9, the mayor of the eighth arrondissement, the most

---

[4] *Ibid.,* p. 192; Thomas, pp. 38-39.

[5] Cherest, p. 194 and *passim*; Thomas, pp. 32-33, 39-40, 48-50.

[6] Thomas, pp. 35-36, 38, 53-55; Cherest, pp. 192-193.

[7] Thomas, pp. 48-53.

[8] Cherest, p. 193, note 1.

seriously embarrassed, was to send to the central offices for enrollment all his workmen, some three thousand in number.[9]

II

The new director of the National Workshops addressed himself with vigor to the difficult task of actually initiating the new system, as yet existing only on paper. He won the ready adhesion of the students of the second and third years at the *École centrale,* as well as that of certain graduates and former students.[10] The central administration was soon located in the modest château at Monceau, in the northwestern part of the city, hence well removed from the proletarian sections.[11] A commodious riding school offered protection in inclement weather for the formation of the necessary military units, while other parts of the same building were to be made serviceable as offices. The château itself, although in a state of serious disrepair, was to be made habitable for the director, assistant directors, and their several staffs.[12]

Thomas had a passion for administrative organization and a profound conviction that even the minute details of a complicated system could be controlled by means of administrative regulation.[13] An elaborate central administrative machine was

[9] *Ibid.,* pp. 193-194; Thomas, pp. 53-54. The latter reports Garnier-Pagès as exclaiming after he (Thomas) had left the room: " 'Messieurs! voilà un homme d'état qui se révèle!' " (*Ibid.,* p. 55.)

[10] Thomas, pp. 77-78; E. Delessard: *Souvenirs de 1848. L'École centrale aux Ateliers nationaux* (Paris, 1900), pp. 12-13. The students entered upon their duties with genuine enthusiasm; quite aside from motives of patriotism and public service, it appears that for those who had not yet graduated the salaries as officers had a special appeal as the first money which they had earned.

[11] The grounds now form the attractive Parc Monceau, which owes its name to a village on the site of which it was laid out in 1778 by Carmontelle for Philippe d'Orléans, duc de Chartres, and father of Louis-Philippe. It formed part of the civil list under the July Monarchy.

[12] Thomas, pp. 40-41, 73-76.

[13] See La Gorce's caustic comment (*Seconde République,* I, p. 277): " Si les règlements minutieux suffisaient à faire les bons administrateurs, M. Émile Thomas eût été sans rival. Nul, en effet, ne fut plus prodigue d'arrêtés, nul ne s'ingénia davantage à créer des emplois, à organiser des cadres, à établir des moyens de surveillance; et c'est même, à proprement parler, le seul soin auquel il ne faillit jamais."

set up with three assistant directors, each the head of a department, and a fourth assistant director whose functions were somewhat miscellaneous.[14] The departments were in turn subdivided into numerous bureaus.[15] More important was the correspondingly complicated system which extended right down to the lowest unit, the newly enrolled worker. Ten men, together with a squad leader whom they elected, formed a squad. Five squads and a brigadier, also chosen by election, composed a brigade.[16] Four brigades were included in a *lieutenance*, commanded by a lieutenant, and four *lieutenances* in turn formed a company, commanded by a captain (*chef de compagnie*). Generally three companies were included in a *service*, commanded by a *chef de service*, who in turn was subject to a *chef d'arrondissement*. The officers, beginning with the grade of captain, were drawn from the *École centrale*.[17]

[14] The last named was Jaime, Thomas' trusted adjutant, who was charged particularly with the pacification of dissatisfied elements in the organization.

[15] The three departments embraced the following functions: (1) general maintenance of order, formation of military units, classification by occupation of all workers, distribution of provisions to necessitous workers; (2) accounting, *matériel*, police, pay of the administrative staffs; (3) surveillance of projects in course of construction and inspection of all projects submitted (Thomas, pp. 110-115).

[16] Squad leaders and brigadiers were originally appointed by the central administration. As a concession to the workers, election of these two grades was introduced, March 22 (Thomas, pp. 147, 151). According to Lalanne, Thomas' successor, the change resulted in a certain loss of control over these units by the central administration. The new system tended to increase enrollments: an ambitious worker, desirous of becoming a brigadier, would recruit fifty-five men whose suffrages he had obtained in advance. Lalanne also claims that it was easy to get brigadiers, chosen in this way, to shut their eyes to frauds connected with the payment of workers (L. Lalanne: " Lettres sur les Ateliers nationaux, III," *National*, July 19, 1848). Lalanne of course took a very critical, if not hostile, view of the Thomas regime.

[17] On the grades within the hierarchy, see Thomas, pp. 58-59, and Lalanne: " Lettres sur les Ateliers nationaux, III," *National*, July 19, 1848. On the basis of the organization outlined above, the numbers in each unit, including the commanders in each case, were:

Squad	11
Brigade	56
Lieutenance	225
Company	901
Service	2,703

*   *   *   *   *

The much elaborated system of the newly organized Workshops was given its initial trial the morning of March 9, when nearly 3,000 workers from the eighth arrondissement arrived at the Monceau headquarters. Measures had been taken to remedy the abuses in the enrollment method employed under the Higonnet régime, but the system remained complex and unwieldy. An applicant first presented himself to the mayor of his arrondissement, bearing a certificate of domicile, signed by his landlord and attesting residence in Paris.[18] The mayors then checked each certificate of domicile and sent daily to the mayor of Paris alphabetical lists of all registrations, thus making possible a comparison of the registrations in the various arrondissements and the prevention of double enrollments.[19] Cards of admission to the Workshops were issued by the mayors to the properly certified workers, and these in turn were presented at the Monceau headquarters. There the workers were assigned to squads and brigades.[20]

The same complexity was evident in the regulations providing for the functioning of the organization. The latter dealt with the hours of work, the calling of the roll, the fining of workers for breaches of the rules, authorizations for the use

This represents the organization as it finally existed. During the first month it was much simpler: the *lieutenance* did not exist, the company included only 225 men, and the *service* was composed of but 901. The *chef d'arrondissement* had a varying number of *chefs de service* under his command, depending upon the importance of the arrondissement.

[18] *Moniteur*, March 7. Buchez, deputy mayor of Paris, in a letter of March 27, 1848, urges that the mayors secure wherever possible a proof of Paris domicile extending back to February 24 (*Archives de la Seine. Mairies. Série* O²ᵇ, no. 4586, hereafter cited as *Arch. de la Seine. Mairies* O²ᵇ).

[19] There were constant complaints that this part of the system never functioned satisfactorily. The mayors were overwhelmed with demands for admission to the Workshops, and no serious attempts at verification of the certificates of domicile were made (Lalanne: "Lettres sur les Ateliers nationaux, III," *National*, July 19, 1848). On the failure of the mayors to obey instructions from the mayor of Paris, see *Arch. de la Seine. Mairies* O²ᵇ, no. 4585.

[20] On the rules governing the formation of the military units, see Thomas, pp. 59-61.

of tools, and the making of the daily pay. The pay was originally a function of the squad leaders, later of the brigadiers,
but no satisfactory system of checks was ever found.[21] In the
beginning the workers were paid at the rate of 2 francs for
days of actual employment and 1½ francs for idle days. The
latter dole was reduced to 1 franc, March 17. Officers were
paid correspondingly more: brigadiers, 3 francs a day; squad
leaders, 2½ francs for days of activity and 1½ francs for idle
days.[22]

In addition to the regular pay, provision was made for aid
to necessitous workers and their families in the form of a food
allowance. A central office was established for distribution of
bread, meat, and soup to properly certified members of the
National Workshops, and a sliding scale in kilograms was
devised, the allowance depending in each case upon the size
of the family.[23] Free medical aid was provided in a dispensary
to which twelve doctors were attached. The service included
free consultation at the dispensary, free medicines, house visits,
and supplementary monetary aid for those in serious need by
reason of illness. The service was in effect for forty-one days.
During that period more than 14,000 workers were treated,
4,000 in their homes, at a total cost of a little less than 9,000
francs, hence a cost of approximately 60 centimes per patient.
The doctors in charge urged the continuance of the service

[21] See Appendix II.
[22] On the subject of the pay, see Thomas, pp. 29-30, 62-63, 92-94, 135-137.
Lieutenants were paid 4 francs a day, all students or former students of the
École centrale, regardless of rank, 5 francs, the chef du cabinet and the assistant
directors, 10 francs. Thomas gave his services gratuitously, but was allowed an
expense account for his house.
[23] Thomas, pp. 173, 187-188; Arch. de la Seine. Mairies O²ᵇ, no. 4585. The
bureau de secours was aimed, above all, to care for workers who had received
admission cards from their respective mayors but who had not yet been inducted
into units of the Workshops; this process sometimes required several days.
Thomas consistently urged that the money dole for idle days be eliminated and
that aid in the form of provisions be substituted (Thomas, pp. 31, 93, 189,
349).

which was, they claimed, distinctly less expensive than that of the hospitals.[24]

*   *   *   *   *

The preceding sketch of the National Workshops presents essentially an *ideal* picture of the organization of this institution, based largely upon the apologia of the director himself. It portrays what Thomas *intended* the Workshops to be, had the organization functioned perfectly. It presents a contrast with the picture of the National Workshops as an army of indolent and dangerous wasters of the public moneys, a view created by the attacks on the institution during the campaign for dissolution, and subsequently by those of hostile historians of the right. The latter view also of course requires considerable rectification.

It is true that at no time was there sufficient work to employ more than 10,000 men, so that by June more than 100,000 workers were receiving what amounted to a dole on any given day.[25] Moreover, the descriptions of contemporaries indicate clearly that even those actively "employed" very often worked in a perfunctory fashion, came and went as they liked, interrupted their "work" to play at *buchon* or to pass the time in some cabaret nearby.[25a] This situation reflected to some extent no doubt the feeling that since a job was *guaranteed* every man by the state, the worker was justified in doing as little as need be. It is perfectly clear that this spirit did exist

---

[24] *Ibid.*, pp. 68-70, 133-135; *Procès-verbaux du Comité du travail à l'Assemblée constituante de 1848* (Paris, 1908. Forms No. 1 of the *Bibliothèque de la "Révolution de 1848"*), pp. 73-74. (The citation hereafter is *Proc.-verb. du com. du travail.*)

[25] It is evident that what actually happened was that those enrolled received 8 francs a week—i.e., 1 franc a day for four days (the "dole" rate) and 2 francs a day for two days (the pay for *jours d'activité*)—and that this was irrespective of the number that could actually be employed. Since not more than 10,000 could be given work, i.e., 30,000 for two days each in any given week, it is evident that a considerable number were receiving a 2-franc dole during part of each month. The daily pay figures given by Thomas (p. 390) can be made to show that this was the situation.

[25a] On such abuses, arising in part from the fact that there were only two roll-calls during the day, see *Commission d'enquête*, I, p. 275; II, p. 176.

among certain of the workers. On the other hand, it is equally clear that the government, in failing to provide work projects, encouraged idleness, poor workmanship, and even sabotage. Numerous cases evidenced the attempts of workers to " make the job last " by working slowly and badly, even by breaking tools.[26]

It is also true that a very large proportion of those enrolled made poor " terrassiers "; they came from occupations (especially from those in the luxury industries) which little fitted them for the rigors of manual labor. Moreover, as the months passed, the continued enforced idleness of a large proportion of the total Parisian working population (not to mention the large numbers of recruits from the provinces) tended to demoralize the workers. It seems to be a uniform experience with the dole that it steadily saps the morale of those who receive it.

But, despite all the evidence of the abuses within the Workshops,[27] it would patently be a libel on the French worker to accept at face value the numerous statements that the worker preferred idleness to employment of a serious nature. A large proportion of the members of the Workshops received an habitual wage in their several trades ranging from fifty to a hundred and fifty per cent higher than that which the government paid them.[28] The Workshops dole was indeed completely inade-

[26] As will be pointed out subsequently, the government's achievement in finding work was not an impressive one, when in the course of four months fewer than a tenth of the workers could be given any kind of employment. A letter from four engineer-members of the National Workshops' administration to the *Presse*, May 30, declared that the workers seemed lazy because they were convinced of the futility of the work they were obliged to do (Thomas, pp. 365-368). On the other hand, workers frequently threatened their comrades who worked well (*Commission d'enquête*, II, p. 178; A. Chenu: *Les Montagnards de 1848* [Paris, 1850], p. 117).

[27] The extensive abuses touching the question of the pay are considered in Appendix II.

[28] This is evident when the census of workers in the Workshops by trades (Thomas, pp. 376-378) is considered along with such wage statistics as those given by Louis Blanc for the Paris trades (*Organisation du travail*, pp. 34-35). Blanc of course has no interest in making wages appear too high. The fact of

quate for a man with a family living in Paris.[29] Under these conditions it is difficult to believe that serious workmen preferred to remain underpaid and in idleness simply to escape the rigors of work in their own trades.[30] Moreover, there is evidence to the contrary. Repeatedly the workers, especially through their delegates, asked that the government take steps to restore normal working conditions. The marble workers, as an example, asked to be permitted to form a coöperative for the execution of works in the Louvre and elsewhere, then being projected.[31] What seems to have given rise to the attacks on the workers and the claims that they sought to remain in idleness was the fact that the workers often insisted on posing conditions for their return to private industry. In many cases they refused to accept employment except with wage increases.[32] The demand was a quite natural one, for they believed that the Revolution had been fought to improve the workers' economic condition. This idea had of course subsequently been fostered by the socialists, and especially by the Luxembourg Commission.[33] On the other hand, there is no doubt that the demands were often exaggerated, especially when it is considered that many business men were in a precarious position, owing to the depression of 1845-1848, followed and reënforced by the Revolution.

this difference in the habitual wage of the workers in question and that received in the Workshops is so obvious that it needs no elaborate statistical demonstration.

[29] See above, p. xvi.

[30] This does not of course account for the abuses by such workers as those who worked in their own homes and at the same time managed through fraud to receive a second wage in the National Workshops. This group naturally wanted the Workshops to be continued. (See the statement of Falloux in the *Moniteur*, June 24.)

[31] *Vraie République*, June 14.

[32] See, e.g., letter of delegates to Thomas (*Père Duchêne*, May 28-30).

[33] Charges were general that the delegates of the Luxembourg Commission, particularly after the latter was dissolved, exerted influence on the workers to induce them to leave their places, to remain temporarily in the National Workshops, and thus to exert pressure on their employers in the interest of higher wages (*Commission d'enquête*, II, pp. 167, 169, 174). The existence of the National Workshops of course made this manœuvre much more feasible.

Despite their inefficiency, the National Workshops per-
formed certain works of real value. The *chemins de ronde,*
which were in a serious state of disrepair, were macadamized.[34]
Efficient work was done in the levelling of the Champ-de-Mars,
where night shifts were apparently used successfully for a
time, possibly in order to prepare for the *Fête de la Concorde.*[35]
It was also expected that the clearing of the Place de l'Europe
would materially enhance the value of property in that
section.[36]

It must of course be admitted that the National Workshops
system cannot be defended from an economic point of view.
The huge expenses were altogether disproportionate to the
results accomplished. Considerable sums were lost through the
frauds of brigadiers, squad leaders, and workers, and through
various other abuses.[37] And the thinly disguised dole caused
unfortunate repercussions in the provinces where the peasants
objected that they were taxed excessively to keep the Parisian
workers in idleness.[38]

III

At the outset Thomas had laid his finger on what was to
prove the fundamental weakness in the Workshops. He had
cautioned the mayors on March 5 that the provision of adequate public works must be kept abreast of the steadily
increasing enrollments. The director's prediction was destined
to gloomy fulfillment. By the middle of March some 12,000
men were daily receiving the inactivity dole, and by June 22
this figure had reached more than 100,000! The failure of the
government to provide projects adequate to the employment

[34] Regnault, pp. 176-177. The *chemins de ronde* ran along the top of the
walls surrounding Paris, between the parapets on either side.

[35] See report of Peaucelier *fils* to the director of the National Workshops, May
24 (Thomas, pp. 368-370). On the efficacy of piece-work, subsequently instituted, see *République,* June 23.

[36] *Peuple constituant,* June 9.

[37] See below, Appendix II.

[38] See, e.g., *Liberté,* June 21. Peasant protests on this score were numerous,
and some of them violent.

of at least a large proportion of these men was unquestionably one of its most costly mistakes.

In the beginning it had been agreed that Marie should provide the director with daily reports on the number of workers who could be employed by various members of the state engineering corps.[39] Despite this promise, no new sources of employment were forthcoming, and in despair Thomas was obliged to employ his first brigades as best he could, in transporting tools and in replacing on the boulevards trees broken during the February Days.[40] By the middle of March the situation was desperate. Marie summoned a meeting of government engineers-in-chief for March 15. Thomas complained that he must have the loyal coöperation of the engineers which had been promised, or resign forthwith. The tactics of the engineers were denounced in forceful terms by Marie and by Trémisot, head of the Paris department of street paving. But the engineers replied evasively, and the meeting's only result was the acceptance of projects suggested by Trémisot and Thomas, designed to employ between 8,000 and 10,000 men. It appears that even these projects were executed only in part.[41]

Various forces contributed to this embarrassment of the new Thomas administration. Of first importance was the failure of the government engineers to coöperate with the administration of the Workshops. The latter situation reflected to some degree the bad feeling existing between the *École polytechnique,* from which the government engineers came, and the *École centrale* — hostility notorious and of long standing.[42] When the Polytechnicians played a prominent rôle in the February Days, the jealousy of the members of the *École centrale* was at once

---

[39] Thomas, p. 79. The engineers referred to are those of the *Ponts-et-chaussées*. The *services* of the *Ponts-et-chaussées* were subject to the control of the minister of public works, except " l'hydraulique agricole " and " l'assèchement des marais." The two latter *services* were subject to the minister of agriculture. See article, " Ponts-et-chaussées," *La grande encyclopédie,* vol. 27.

[40] Thomas, pp. 79-81.

[41] *Ibid.,* pp. 87-92; Cherest, pp. 196-197.

[42] Thomas, pp. 42-43; Cherest, p. 201.

evident,[43] and the latter welcomed the National Workshops as an outlet for their patriotic energies. And when the Workshops were established and it was evident that the members of the two corps would be called upon to coöperate, Thomas insisted upon a compromise which would save the *amour propre* of the engineers of the *École centrale*.[44] More solid reasons than mere vanity, however, appear also to have influenced the government engineers. They feared that the introduction of units from the National Workshops would seriously affect the severe discipline which obtained among their own workmen.[45] Moreover, it is pretty obvious that the government engineers had very little sympathy in general with the National Workshops as a scheme of relief and that helpful initiative from this source was scarcely to be anticipated.[46]

Lack of unity within the Provisional Government further handicapped the achievement of a sound public works' program. Marie early conceived a plan for the construction of a railroad encircling Paris and providing thus, at some distance from the populous quarters, a whole series of workshops, separated one from the other and easy to control. This project was actually approved by the government engineers, but the Provisional Government rejected it, primarily for financial reasons. Marie viewed the rebuff as so serious that he considered immediate resignation.[47] Lamartine charges the government with vacillation in the execution of its plans; Marie in particular temporized with unpromising projects, the poet

[43] Thomas, pp. 31 ff.

[44] Thomas, pp. 43-46. When units from the National Workshops were employed on projects being executed by government engineers, the members of the *École centrale* were to act merely as *officers* in command of the workmen and were to have nothing to do with the technical direction of the works; on all other projects the members of the *École centrale* were to function simultaneously as *officers* and *engineers*. Both Thomas and Marie appear to have irritated the government corps by favoring projects for its reorganization (*ibid.*, pp. 233-234; Cherest, p. 202).

[45] *Ibid.*, p. 197.

[46] Thomas, p. 233.

[47] Cherest, pp. 209 ff.

claims, while he, Lamartine, and certain others favored the organization of reclamation projects on a large scale.[48]

But, however seriously others may be charged with contributing to the failure of the public works' program, a large share of the burden of responsibility must be borne by Marie himself. The minister's acts seemed to reflect alternately a lack of resolution and unwarranted precipitation. He lectured the government engineers like schoolboys on March 15, but no important results followed. He vigorously supported his pet project of a railroad to encircle Paris, but when the plan was rejected by the government, he did not resign. Perhaps even more seriously compromising his ability to act with the required promptitude was his firm belief that only the recovery of private industry could bring relief to the unemployment situation. Such was undoubtedly the case, but the convalescence of private industry was necessarily a slow process. Meanwhile, because the minister viewed the Workshops not as a means of accomplishing the " organization of labor " but as a temporary expedient to meet an emergency situation, his attempts to secure adequate employment for the workers appear to have been half-hearted at best. In any event it is difficult to see how the government engineers, forming an element in the very administration over which Marie presided could have successfully and consistently thwarted the minister's orders, had they

---

[48] Lamartine: *Lettre aux dix départements* (Paris, 1848), p. 31; *Révolution de 1848*, II, pp. 90-91. As usual Lamartine's charges and remedies are distinguished by an easy vagueness and generality. Cherest defends Marie with vigor: the project to which Lamartine referred was the canalization and clearing of the Sologne, declares Cherest, a plan projected *after* Marie had left the ministry of public works; the treasury had insufficient funds in any case for so wholesale an emigration; the government lacked the armed force to oblige Parisian workmen and their families to leave for distant and unpromising work, and when a similar step was taken later it precipitated the June Days (Cherest, pp. 207-209). Regnault, *chef du cabinet* to Ledru-Rollin, notes that the Paris *mairie* spent more than 15,000,000 francs on public works between March and July, 1848, but he does not say why these were not used as a means of employing a part of the workers in the National Workshops (E. Regnault: *Histoire du Gouvernement provisoire* [Paris, 1850], pp. 177-179).

been issued with the requisite energy.[49] How serious a problem was presented by the presence in Paris of a hundred thousand idle members of the Workshops will appear in the subsequent chapters.[50]

[49] On the subject of Marie's responsibility, see Cherest, pp. 197, 202, 214 ff., and *passim*.

[50] About 30,000 men a week, in two-day shifts of 10,000 each, was the maximum number actually given employment at the time of the greatest enrollment in the Workshops. (See report of Peaucelir *fils* to the director of the Workshops, May 24, 1848 [Thomas, pp. 368 ff.])

CHAPTER III

THE SOCIAL REVOLUTION IN THE BALANCE
MARCH 16 – APRIL 16

I. March 16 and March 17. II. The Workshops Subjected to Political Influence. III. The National Guard again a Bourgeois Instrument.

I

THOMAS' reorganization of the National Workshops was still in its inception when Paris became prey to new alarms. Superficially directed at the achievement of quite other ends, the demonstrations of March 16 and March 17 had fundamental implications for the future of the social revolution, and hence eventually also for the National Workshops.

The conservatives became thoroughly exercised by the policy of the Provisional Government in the early days of March, when monarchical opportunities seemed to be fading fast. As minister of the interior, Ledru-Rollin's instructions to subordinates assigned them " unlimited powers " in assuring the election to the National Assembly of representatives of unquestioned republican convictions.[1] The suspicions of the " right " were further aroused by a semi-official intimation that the government was considering postponement of the general elections and would thus lengthen its tenure of office.[2] Another and more immediate blow to the conservatives was seen in the *Moniteur's* announcement of March 14 that the crack flank

---

[1] *Commission d'enquête*, II, pp. 216-217, prints a police report for March 14, reflecting the fright of the bourgeoisie. Apponyi (IV, p. 170) notes that the circular " dépasse toute la tyrannie républicaine de 93, aussi a-t-elle inspiré une terreur générale." Cf. Regnault, p. 194. See also Crémieux, A., and Génique, G.: " La question electorale en mars 1848," *Révolution de 1848*, III (1906-1907), pp. 206-212, 252-263.

[2] An " address " of Blanqui to the people of Paris, urging the adjournment of the elections to a future date if the return of reaction were to be avoided, was allowed to appear in the semi-official *Bulletin de la République*, March 15.

companies of the National Guard, composed of well-to-do members of the bourgeoisie, would be dissolved and their members redistributed among the new units of the reconstituted Guard, to membership in which all citizens were now to be eligible.[3] The aim of the government was to democratize the Guard, but the companies affected, distinguished by their striking uniforms and highly developed *esprit de corps,* and forming within the Guard a sort of " bourgeois aristocracy," were exasperated by this attack upon their prerogatives.[4] The decrees reorganizing the National Guard meant nothing more nor less than that this instrument of the bourgeoisie, often used in the past to combat the lower classes, was to be "proletarianized." The crack companies resolved on a swift and forceful protest in defence of their ancient privileges.[5] A demonstration was organized for March 16, and on that day a considerable representation of the National Guard marched to the Hôtel de Ville. But a delegation of their members was received coldly by the government and lectured by Marrast on the regrettable character of such a demonstration, which might very well provoke others of a contrary nature. The government held its ground, and the companies were duly dissolved.[6]

Plans for a counter-demonstration, the reply of the proletariat to the bourgeoisie, had been brewing for some days. On

---

[3] A natural complement to the decree granting universal suffrage was the decree of March 13, admitting all electors to the National Guard, formerly reserved to the bourgeoisie through the requirement that all must provide their own equipment. Henceforth the government was to equip all members of the Guard.

[4] The crack companies (*compagnies d'élite*) were the *grenadiers* and the *voltigeurs,* occupying, respectively, the right and left flanks of each regiment. The third element in the Guard was the *chasseurs,* who occupied a place between the other two. The distinguishing feature of the uniform of the crack companies was the high, bearskin hat, hence the sobriquet, applied to the March 16 demonstration, " manifestation des bonnets à poil." A contemporary caricature depicted a delegation of brown bears coming to thank the government for a decree so favorable to their kind (Renard: *République de 1848,* p. 32).

[5] D. Stern: *Histoire de la Révolution de 1848* (Second edition, Paris, 1862, 2 vols.), II, pp. 54-55.

[6] Renard: *République de 1848,* pp. 31-33; C. Seignobos: *La Révolution de 1848. Le second Empire (1848-1859)* (Paris, 1921), pp. 50-57; Regnault, pp. 211 ff.

the evening of March 16 a joint committee of delegates from the revolutionary clubs and from the workers of the recently organized Commission of the Luxembourg placarded a summons to a manifestation for the following morning.[7] The government was to be asked to dismiss the troops from Paris and to postpone to May 31 the general elections,[8] and to April 5 the election of the National Guard officers.[9] The workers sought postponement of the general elections on the theory that more time was necessary adequately to "republicanize" the country through propaganda. In the case of the election of National Guard officers, it was felt that, unless the workers newly inducted into the organization were given time to become acquainted with their fellows, the elections would result simply in returning the well-known bourgeois officers of the old Guard.

More than 100,000 men gathered on the morning of March 17 in the spacious Place de la Concorde and marched thence in perfect order to the Hôtel de Ville. A delegation was duly admitted to the presence of the government and read its petition. At this critical moment, when the precise character of the demonstration was unknown and when a violent *coup d'état* seemed a not unreasonable possibility,[10] Louis Blanc saved the day for the government by insisting that its members be given

---

[7] The participation of the Luxembourg raises the question of the part played by Louis Blanc. Did he actually arrange the demonstration as a means of bringing pressure to bear on the government? Stern (II, p. 54) declares that Blanc was responsible for arranging the demonstration; his own repeated references to the threatened celebration, before the government, lend weight to this view (Blanc: *Révolution de 1848*, I, pp. 307 ff.). Marie is obviously accusing Louis Blanc of having instigated the delegates of the Luxembourg, in his statement before the *Commission d'enquête* (I, p. 318; cf. E. Renard: *La Vie et l'oeuvre de Louis Blanc* [Toulouse, 1922], pp. 78-79). Blanc gives the impression that, although he was sympathetic with the aims of the demonstration, he took no actual part in planning it (Blanc: *op. cit.*, I, pp. 306-307). See further Seignobos: "Procès-verbaux du Gouvernement provisoire," *Revue d'histoire moderne et contemporaine*, VII, pp. 589, 592.

[8] The elections had been set for April 9.

[9] Officers of the reconstituted National Guard were to be elected by their commands, colonels and generals excepted. The elections had been set for March 18, then postponed to March 25 (Seignobos, pp. 55-56).

[10] Blanc: *Révolution de 1848*, I, p. 311.

time to deliberate, that no answer could be given which might seem a response to a threat of force.[11] Despite the dissatisfied murmurings of the adherents of the revolutionary agitator Blanqui,[12] the delegation finally yielded. The government appeared on the steps of the Hôtel de Ville, and the huge throngs of workers slowly passed in review amid shouts of "Vive la République! Vive le Gouvernement provisoire!"

Émile Thomas, warned in advance of the approaching demonstration,[13] took prompt and effective measures to prevent participation of the members of the National Workshops. The latter numbered about 14,000, and Thomas had sufficient work for only 1,000. He resolved nevertheless to employ the entire 14,000 on March 17. Accordingly all were summoned to appear at Monceau at 6 o'clock in the morning to receive tools and to proceed to the various workshops. More than 10,000 had been equipped when, about 11 o'clock, large red posters announcing the demonstration appeared. A small-scale revolt was produced, the remaining workmen loudly asserting that the administration sought to isolate them in order to effect a *coup de main* on Paris. The workers were finally persuaded to take up their tools and depart for the workshops. "The fourteen thousand men under our direction," Thomas confidently declares, "can prove a perfect alibi."[14]

---

[11] *Ibid.*, pp. 311-312.

[12] Blanqui was a "professional revolutionary" without any other visible occupation. His career as agitator began under the Restoration, and he fought behind the barricades of July. After being twice imprisoned for his ceaseless revolutionary activity, he was amnestied in 1837 but at once undertook the formation of the famous *Société des saisons*, secret revolutionary organization of wide ramifications. As a result of the failure of the revolt of May 12, 1839, Blanqui remained in prison until the Revolution of 1848. Following the Revolution he dominated the *Société républicaine centrale*, was suspected of numerous intrigues aiming to overthrow the government, and was finally arrested as a result of his alleged connection with the *coup* of May 15. (See S. Wassermann: *Les clubs de Barbès et de Blanqui en 1848* [Paris, 1913], especially bibliography; *Dictionnaire des parlementaires français*, I, pp. 343-344.)

[13] Thomas, p. 95. The director was doubtless warned by the government, which knew of the demonstration on March 13 (Blanc: *Révolution de 1848*, I, pp. 307 ff.; Garnier-Pagès, VI, pp. 390-391).

[14] Thomas, pp. 95-98; *Commission d'enquête*, I, p. 352.

*   *   *   *   *

The demonstration of March 17 was a turning point in the Revolution of 1848. Like its successors, the manifestations of April 16 and May 15, its general purpose was to exercise pressure upon the government.[15] Whatever its aims, however, whether to strengthen the authority of the radicals within the government or to "purge" the government of its moderate majority[16]—the results of the demonstration were far-reaching. The "fearful solemnity" of this procession of a hundred thousand proletarians of Paris left an indelible impression upon the minds of the bourgeoisie. What might not this unorganized mass become, if it were once submitted to discipline and given a program?[17] The apprehension of the bourgeoisie was increased in the days that followed when it became evident that the authority of the radicals in the government had been strengthened by the movement.[18] Louis Blanc described March 17 as "perhaps the greatest of all historic days in the memory of man," and Ledru-Rollin lent his ear increasingly to those of his entourage who envisaged a *coup d'état* with Ledru as dictator. Both men had misread events, and while Paris had apparently thrown its weight convincingly in the scales in favor of the social revolution, other and more potent forces were at work: (1) news was already filtering in from the provinces indicating that the elections would yield a triumph for the

[15] Not that the masses of workers who participated were aware of this. Their naïve adhesion was won by the plea that it was fitting to felicitate the government on its bold front of the previous day (Stern, II, pp. 67-68, 77).

[16] Cf. Renard: *République de 1848*, p. 33.

[17] Stern, II, 77-78, 153.

[18] The National Guard elections were finally postponed until April 5 and the national elections until April 23. Both changes were obvious concessions to the demands of the Parisian proletariat, despite the fact that the government attempted to conceal this fact in order to save its face (Seignobos: "Procès-verbaux du Gouvernement provisoire," *Revue d'histoire moderne et contemporaine*, VII, pp. 589, 592). A further concession was made in the removal of the drink tax; and the government consented to make an official appearance before a session of the Commission of the Luxembourg. On the latter occasion Louis Blanc's sense of personal triumph is obvious in his address to the delegates (L. Blanc: *La Révolution de février au Luxembourg* [Paris, 1849], pp. 37-42).

moderates;[19] (2) within the government itself the moderates were feverishly active in an attempt to stem the tide of radicalism in Paris. Subsequent events were to reflect the degree of success of their efforts. One thing is clear: the social revolution had *not* triumphed, despite superficial appearances. Indeed it was to be seriously undermined in the succeeding weeks, before the national elections finally administered the *coup de grâce* to all aspirations for a fundamental reformation of society.[20]

II

The events of March 17 resulted in the initiation of a new policy toward the National Workshops, or perhaps more precisely a shift of emphasis in the earlier policy of the minister of public works. Heretofore Marie had viewed the Workshops as primarily an economic expedient, a solution for the pressing problem of unemployment. But the manifestation of March 17, engineered by the clubs and the Luxembourg, revealed how desirable it was to develop a counterweight to the growing influences of radicalism. In short, the minister now envisaged the possibility of employing the Workshops as a political instrument.[21] The "loyal" members of the Workshops were to

[19] Cf. Léon Faucher: *Léon Faucher* (Paris, 1888, 2 vols. See bibliography for separate titles of volumes), I, pp. 212-213.

[20] March 17 marked a crisis for the social revolution, and Louis Blanc again occupied a key position. Never again did the radicals have so favorable an opportunity to turn the tide in their own favor (P. J. Proudhon: *Les confessions d'un révolutionnaire pour servir à l'histoire de la Révolution de février* [Third edition, Paris, 1851], p. 88). Louis Blanc's pacific attitude saved the moderates. Why did he take such a stand? Were his convictions entirely opposed to a violent *coup*; i.e., did the pacific nature of his social philosophy paralyze his capacity to act? Did he fear that the movement would get beyond his control and that he, in turn, would be swept aside by more radical leaders? (Cf. La Gorce, I, p. 146.) Did he fear to loose civil war, with all its dangers to the Revolution itself, as he himself declares? (Blanc: *Révolution de 1848*, II, pp. 1 ff.) Or was he temperamentally more fitted to write and to speak than to act, as his hesitations in a number of important crises suggest? Perhaps Blanqui on this occasion saw more clearly than Louis Blanc where the interests of the social revolution lay. (Cf. Renard: *République de 1848*, p. 33.) For a penetrating portrait of Blanc, see Stern, II, pp. 40 ff.

[21] Cherest, pp. 231-232.

be used to combat and counterbalance the influence of the socialist workers of the Luxembourg and the " seditious " elements in the radical clubs.[22] To split the Parisian proletariat, to combat the people by means of the people, to neutralize the socialists by workers rendered docile and obedient — such was the program of the government, says Renard.[23]

Marie was obviously influenced not merely by the participation of the workers of the Luxembourg in the events of March 17 but by the growing influence of Louis Blanc's labor parliament, an influence which he believed to be in the highest degree pernicious — dangerous to the cause of order and inimical to the recovery of industry.[24]   In his plans to combat the Luxembourg, Marie found in Thomas a willing *aide,* firm friend of the cause of order and implacable opponent of Louis Blanc and all his works.[25]   If complete credence may be given Thomas' report of a conversation with Marie, March 23, the latter's plans had larger scope than that of the mere exercise of salutary political influence: the minister actually envisaged

[22] Cherest, pp. 228-229; Lamartine: *Révolution de 1848,* II, p. 91.

[23] Renard: *République de 1848,* pp. 59-60.

[24] Cherest, p. 218, note 2; Thomas, pp. 141-142; cf. *Commission d'enquête,* II, p. 174; and Cherest, pp. 219-228.

[25] *Commission d'enquête,* I, p. 352. In this connection it should be noted once again that the historical error which attributed the foundation and control of the National Workshops to Louis Blanc has long since been interred. A rapid inspection of the evidence on this point can leave no doubt as to the original error:

Thomas, pp. 142-143, 156-157, 200-201, 207, and *passim; Commission d'enquête,* I, pp. 240, 352-353; Blanc: *Révolution de 1848,* I, pp. 217 ff.; Cherest, pp. 177-180, 217 ff. and *passim;* Lamartine: *Révolution de 1848,* II, p. 91. J. A. R. Marriott (*The French Revolution of 1848 in its Economic Aspect* [Oxford, 1913, 2 vols.], I, pp. xciv-xcv) insists that Louis Blanc must bear a " moral responsibility " for the National Workshops, due to his " persistent propagation of the doctrine of the *droit au travail."* But the *droit au travail* is a *general* principle, like the " right of revolution." As an outworking of this general principle, Louis Blanc envisaged the establishment of *ateliers·sociaux* (see Blanc: *Organisation du travail,* pp. 102 ff.). His opponents, however, succeeded in establishing the *Ateliers nationaux,* a totally different conception, in order to render the general principle of the *droit au travail* nugatory. To lay the responsibility for the *Ateliers nationaux* at the feet of Louis Blanc is justified in about the same degree as to charge Karl Marx with Bismarck's social legislation.

the possibility of employing the Workshops' organization as an army to combat the radical proletariat in the eventuality of a further insurrection. In the course of that conversation Marie asked Thomas if the members of the Workshops could be relied upon. The director replied that he thought so, but that the increasing numbers made it more difficult to exercise the requisite control. " Don't worry about the number," Marie reassured him; " if you can control them, it will never be too great. . . . Spare no money; if necessary it will be provided for you from the secret funds." When Thomas questioned him further, the minister replied: " Perhaps the day is not far distant when we shall have to summon them into the street." [26]

On March 28 Marie addressed representatives of the workers, and the officers and members of the administration of the Workshops. He assured the workers of the unwavering solicitude of the government for their interests and its intention to extend the Workshops' system as rapidly as possible.[27] The minister's speech was cleverly concluded on a political note. " The elections are at hand. The Government desires that in the ranks of the officers, as in the assembly, you should be in large measure represented by men chosen among yourselves." [28] The minister's speech was enthusiastically received. Indeed Marie, who had come to the meeting in an anxious frame of mind, was deeply impressed with the discipline and pacific atti-

---

[26] Thomas, pp. 146-147; cf. Cherest, p. 232. Thomas is the sole source for the conversation, but Cherest admits that the substance of his report is probably correct. Thomas says that on another occasion the minister suggested the advisability of arming the workers, but the director insists that he personally had no faith in a policy of force (Thomas, p. 158).

[27] That Marie envisaged an expansion of the Workshops at this time, perhaps of considerable proportions, is borne out by what he said to Thomas, March 23. For this expansion, which later became a problem of the most embarrassing character for the government, Marie must bear a share of the responsibility, although other factors beyond his control were also at work. If he really planned the development of a pretorian army, then his responsibility is serious indeed, for the size to which the Workshops had grown by June made it difficult, if not impossible, to dissolve the organization without bloodshed.

[28] *Moniteur,* March 29; Thomas, pp. 147-148, 152-156.

tude of the workers, which he attributed in large measure to the influence of Thomas.[29] When, therefore, the director urged the establishment of a workers' club, the minister lent an attentive ear. Thomas emphasized the advantages of exercising salutary influence upon the workers by means of periodical meetings of their representatives. He admits frankly that he envisaged the creation of a platform from which he could combat the " pernicious influence " of the Luxembourg.[30] Despite his aversion to anything in the nature of a political club, Marie gave his consent. His biographer defends the minister's act with the statement that the members of the Workshops, despite the excitations of the Luxembourg, refused to take part in the demonstration of April 16 and, by answering the National Guard *rappel*, contributed to the defeat of the projects of the radicals.[31] Thomas goes further and claims that, thanks to the newly created club, he was able to prevent the demonstration of May 15 from assuming the proportions of that of June 22.[32]

The announcement of the formation of the club appeared March 30. The word itself was carefully avoided in the name of the club: *Réunion centrale des Ateliers nationaux.* The new organization was " to concern itself with the interests of the unemployed worker," and was to be composed of workers' representatives, one elected by each two brigades, hence one for every 112 men. To the 400 workers' delegates, who were themselves all to be *workers*, were to be added the student officers of the *École centrale.*[33]

The delegates were summoned to the first meeting of this

[29] Cherest, p. 233. Marie's own words evidence his surprise and pleasure at the situation which he found. Absorbed by his duties as minister, he had visited the Workshops only once before, in the very beginning. Marrast, who was to have accompanied Marie but who arrived later, was also very favorably impressed with the results achieved (Thomas, p. 158; cf. also the very favorable police report of April 7 — *Commission d'enquête,* II, pp. 178-179).

[30] Thomas, pp. 156-157.

[31] Cherest, pp. 234-235.

[32] Thomas, p. 157.

[33] Thomas, pp. 159-160; *Commission d'enquête,* II, pp. 142-143. On the days of the meetings of the central club the workers' delegates were excused from work and received a total pay of 2 francs, 75 centimes.

newest " workers' parliament " on Sunday, April 2. They were harangued at length by Thomas and Jaime, his trusted adjutant, upon their duties toward a benevolent Republic which, though revolutionary in origin, now required above all the loyal coöperation of all citizens in the preservation of order! Although the workers were henceforth to be " consulted " regarding all decrees affecting the Workshops, it was clear from Thomas' remarks that it was the purpose of the administration to extend a conciliatory but none the less firm tutelage over these " enfants de l'Atelier national." [34] Thomas pointed out that the Workshops had had a practical object from the beginning. While certain misguided souls were seeking the key to the workers' felicity in utopian schemes for the " organization of labor," he (Thomas) and his assistants had turned to the practical problem of caring for the unemployed. So, too, the new club was to give attention, not to the abstract problems of " our social rights and duties " but to the concrete realities of the workers' needs. Above all else the club was to avoid all concern with questions political. [35]

The newly elected delegates to the National Workshops' club henceforth met regularly, twice a week, to hear the didactic harangues of their director. [36] The activities of this interesting organization will be noticed from time to time in the course of the subsequent history of the Workshops, in which it played no unimportant rôle.

III

Not content with the exercise of direct political influence upon the Workshops, Marie resolved further to assure the loyalty of the workers to the cause of order by enrolling them in large numbers in the National Guard. An extreme figure

---

[34] It is clear, however, that the influence of the club was at times very considerable and a source of embarrassment to the administration. (See, e.g., p.——.)

[35] Thomas, pp. 174-178.

[36] There were also twelve " branch clubs," one for each arrondissement. They appear to have had the same general functions as the central club, but almost no mention is made of them (see Thomas, p. 192).

places the numbers of the Workshops' representation in the Guard during the first part of April at 60,000.[37] This figure is undoubtedly too high, since the total enrollment in the Workshops did not reach that number until nearly the middle of April.[38] But there is good reason to believe that the representation from the Workshops was large.[39] The significance of this fact for the future of the social revolution is further emphasized by the statement of Thomas that three quarters of the Workshops membership later participated, as members of the National Guard, in repressing the rising of May 15.[40]

The enrollment of members of the Workshops in the Guard was only one feature of a much larger program of defence which was being carried out by the moderates within the government. At the time of the demonstration of March 17 the government, helplessly impelled in this direction and that, was still casting about for the support of armed force, which it had consistently lacked since the first days of the Revolution. The events of that day crystallized the fears of the moderates and induced them to seek with energy the forces requisite to the prosecution of their policies.

Influenced by his revolutionary studies and predilections, Lamartine inclined to the Girondin policy of summoning up the provinces to overwhelm the Parisian radicals. The tremendous opposition of the Parisian populace to such a policy rendered it impracticable for the moment, and it yielded place to the ideas of Marrast, who sought, in the tradition of the Convention, to strengthen the government's hand within Paris

[37] Stern, II, p. 164, note 1.

[38] See Appendix I.

[39] Regnault (p. 257) puts the number at " nearly 40,000 " for the first part of April. The Paris National Guard totalled 190,299, as of March 18, as contrasted with the figure of 56,751 for February 1, 1848 (J. B. Duvergier: *Collection complète des lois*, Paris, 1824-   See bibliography for full title. Vol. 48, p. 104). The workers, therefore, must have been in a substantial majority (Stern, II, p. 164; cf. Renard: *République de 1848*, p. 38).

[40] Thomas, p. 184, note 1. As a special inducement to workers to enroll in the Guard, they were given the same pay for days of duty with the militia as they received for " jours d'activité " in the Workshops.

itself.[41] Marrast's policy was twofold. He aimed to win the loyalty to the cause of order of the now proletarianized National Guard and simultaneously of the newly established *Garde mobile.*

No efforts were spared to assure the rapid arming of the National Guard, which was to be completed for the *Fête de la Fraternité* on April 20.[42] Measures were taken to accustom the recruits to the new service in the interest of promoting " fraternity " (and incidentally of preparing them for the eventualities of combat).[43] Meanwhile the general staff lectured the Guard on its duty, as a " pacific army," to protect the fruits of the Revolution against all who attempted to disturb the Republic by " projets insensés." [44]

The *Garde mobile,* established by the government in the first days of the Revolution, was nothing more nor less than a professional army recruited from the gamins of Paris. Uniforms, good pay, and barrack-life contributed to the rapid development of *esprit de corps* and to the weaning of this group from its proletarian sympathies. The government, as Karl Marx later remarked, had cleverly opposed one part of the proletariat to the rest.[45] In command of the *Garde mobile* was General Duvivier. Marrast succeeded in winning the coöperation of the latter, whose wrath at the moment was directed at Ledru-Rollin, whom he accused of being responsible for the delay in clothing his men.[46]

Marrast and his associates achieved a very considerable measure of success in this preliminary campaign for armed

[41] Regnault, pp. 246-247, 255-256.

[42] *Moniteur,* April 15 (see also March 24, April 4 and 14) ; Seignobos: " Procès-verbaux du Gouvernement provisoire," *Revue d'histoire moderne et contemporaine,* VII, p. 587. Care was exercised lest offence be given to the sensibilities of the workers, unable to equip themselves as the bourgeoisie had done in the past.

[43] *Moniteur,* March 20.

[44] *Ibid.,* April 4.

[45] Marx: *Lutte des classes,* p. 28. (See bibliography for title.)

[46] Regnault, p. 258; Stern, II, pp. 163-164; cf. the decree of the government authorizing the minister of war to aid in equipping the *Garde mobile* (*Moniteur,* March 21).

support, as subsequent events were to attest.[47] The National
Guard played a decisive rôle in the demonstration of April 16
in aid of the bourgeois cause, and the *Garde mobile* distinguished itself for bravery and ferocity in overwhelming the
barricades of its brother workers during the street fighting in
June.

[47] At the same time service in the regular army was made more attractive by
a reduction in the length of the term of enlistment to two years and by the
announcement that promotions would henceforth be made solely on the basis
of merit (*Moniteur*, March 18, April 1).

CHAPTER IV

THE DEFEAT OF THE RADICAL CAUSE, APRIL 16–MAY 15

I. April 16.   II. *Fête de la Fraternité.*   III. The Easter Elections.
IV. Origins of the Demonstration of May 15.   V. May 15.   VI. Rôle
of the Workshops.

APRIL 16 and May 15 are termini of a period which witnessed
the rapid discrediting of the workers' cause. Within the brief
space of a month the radicals met three stunning defeats:
twice, on the occasion of the demonstrations of April 16 and
May 15, the workers met a brutal rebuff at the hands of the
National Guard, while the elections to the National Assembly
yielded an immediate victory for the moderates and paved the
way for the eventual triumph of the " reaction."

I

As the national elections drew nearer, the radicals became
more and more alarmed at the prospects of a possible landslide
of moderate republicans and monarchists, returned by the
bourgeoisie and rural France. Indeed it was primarily the fear
that the aims of the social revolution would be overwhelmed
by the opposition of an unfriendly assembly that provoked the
demonstration of April 16.

The Luxembourg again played the leading rôle. Louis Blanc
admits that he considered the election by the workers of staff
officers of the National Guard an opportune moment for a
repetition of the demonstration of March 17: the attention of
the government must once again be forcibly focussed upon the
social question.[1] The petition of the manifestants presented to
the government clearly reflects the influence of the Luxembourg, concluding with demands for the " democratic republic,"

---

[1] Blanc: *Révolution de 1848*, II, p. 12. The reconstituted National Guard
staff was to include members elected by the workers. The latter were to assem-
ble in the Champ-de-Mars, April 16, for the election of fourteen officers.

the abolition of the exploitation of man by man, and the " organization of labor." [2] Repeatedly before his colleagues of the government Louis Blanc emphasized the pacific nature of the demonstration. None the less it is clear that he wished to have pressure exerted upon the government in the interest of strengthening the position of the minority and thus forcing action on his social program. Blanc apparently realized that his glowing panegyrics of distant utopias before the Luxembourg parliament were carrying less and less conviction; that, if he were to maintain his prestige, his predictions must be realized in concrete enactments.[3]

The rôle of Louis Blanc and the Luxembourg is more or less obvious. But other and more sinister elements appeared in the demonstration or had a hand in its preparation. Naturally, innumerable accusations were levelled at the radical clubs at a time when nearly everyone of prominence was accused of plotting.[4] Rumors reached the government that its moderate majority was forcibly to be eliminated and that it was to be succeeded by a committee of public safety.[5] There is some reason to believe that Blanqui may have entertained such a project, although definite proof is lacking. Barbès' relations with Ledru-Rollin were ambiguous, but both appear to have been influenced to serve the cause of the moderates primarily because of their fear and distrust of Blanqui. In any case their precise intentions cannot be determined.[6]

[2] *Moniteur*, April 17.

[3] Blanc: *Révolution de 1848*, II, pp. 12-13; La Gorce, I, pp. 188-189; cf. Stern, II, pp. 48-49.

[4] See, e.g., Stern, II, pp. 168-173; La Gorce, I, pp. 187 ff.; Wassermann, pp. 121 ff.

[5] Thomas, p. 201 (reporting a conversation with Marie the evening of April 16); Blanc: *Révolution de 1848*, II, pp. 13 ff.; Garnier-Pagès, VII, pp. 369 ff.

[6] For the whole question of the manœuvres of Barbès and of Blanqui, and of the *Club de la Révolution* and the *Société centrale républicaine*, see Wassermann, pp. 121 ff. See also Quentin-Bauchart: *Crise sociale*, pp. 296 ff. Cahen (" Commission du Luxembourg," *Annales de l'École libre des sciences politiques*, XII, pp. 376-377) notes that Louis Blanc, always influenced by ideas of legality, did not seek to overthrow the government, but that the Luxembourg delegates were doubtless in close touch with those clubs that did favor *épuration*.

A third, and very minor, element in the manifestation was composed of a group of workers from the National Workshops, whose rôle will be considered in another connection.

*   *   *   *   *

The government had been warned in advance of the approaching demonstration by Louis Blanc and Albert, who declared themselves powerless to prevent it. By the evening of April 15 it was evident to the government that it was faced by a serious crisis. Upon the minister of the interior, charged with the preservation of public order, rested the responsibility of calling to arms the National Guard. During the night and early part of the morning the moderates were in a state of extreme agitation while they awaited action by Ledru-Rollin. The latter, after apparent indecision, ordered the *rappel* to be beaten.[7] Like Louis Blanc on March 17, Ledru-Rollin in turn became the " savior of society."

Meanwhile the workers had assembled in the Champ-de-Mars, grouped by trades, each carrying its banner. The National Guard staff officers were duly elected, and a collection, destined as an offering to the government, was completed. On the previous day Émile Thomas had been warned by Buchez, deputy mayor of Paris, doubtless in concert with Marie, of the expected demonstration, his purpose being to have the director prevent the National Workshops from participating.[8] Thomas at once commissioned his assistants from the *École centrale* to appear in the Champ-de-Mar and to dissuade the Workshops' members from entering the procession. At the same time he drafted a proclamation directing the workers to give immediate response at all times when the call to arms was sounded by the National Guard.[9]

[7] The problem of Ledru-Rollin's hesitations is rather obscure. Various hypotheses have been suggested; unfortunately the evidence is inadequate. See, e.g., La Gorce, I, pp. 191-198; Wassermann, pp. 125 ff. and *passim;* A. R. Calman: *Ledru-Rollin and the Second French Republic* (New York, 1922), pp. 150-156.

[8] Thomas, pp. 194-195; cf. Garnier-Pagès, VII, pp. 372-373; La Gorce, I, p. 194.

[9] Thomas, pp. 195-196.

The next morning Thomas' assistants arrived in the Champ-de-Mar to find gathered there some 13,000 non-members of the Workshops, from 12,000 to 15,000 men from the Workshops, and from 700 to 800 delegates of the Luxembourg. The students mingled with the various groups, and, according to Thomas, were successful in persuading their workers to furl the National Workshops' banners and to repel the advances made by the delegates of the Luxembourg on behalf of the theories of Louis Blanc. Subsequently, when the *rappel* sounded, almost all of the Workshops' members, says Thomas, obedient to the spirit of his proclamation, retired to join their National Guard companies.[10]

The National Workshops' units gathered in the Champ-de-Mar were not the only members of that organization concerned in the demonstration, however. It appears that a considerable number assembled at the Hippodrome on the morning of April 16 in a meeting convoked possibly through the influence of Caussidière, the enigmatic prefect of police, whose rôle in the demonstration is still obscure.[11] It was agreed that the Hippodrome manifestants should form a second column which should join that from the Champ-de-Mars, the two then proceeding together to the Hôtel de Ville. But when the *tambour* was heard, the majority of those present hastened to join their respective National Guard units. Here again it appears that the Workshops' members were persuaded that the delegates of the Luxembourg, campaigning for the support of Louis Blanc's program, were acting contrary to their interests.[12]

A representation of considerable size from the Hippodrome meeting, however, continued on to the Hôtel de Ville. For, when the delegates of the Luxembourg presented a vigorous protest to the government (April 17) against the perversion of the pacific aims of the manifestation, certain " delegates of

[10] Thomas, pp. 200-201; cf. Garnier-Pagès, VII, p. 395.

[11] Stern, II, p. 174; cf. Garnier-Pagès, VII, pp. 374-375.

[12] Stern, II, pp. 174 and 177, note 1. Doubtless Thomas' assistants were despatched to this meeting also, although he makes no mention of it. See also the account of Garnier-Pagès, VII, pp. 374-375.

the National Workshops " added a protest in behalf of those Workshops' members present at the Hippodrome.[13] Despite the heated counter-protest of Émile Thomas that the Hippodrome document was without official authorization and that " our workers . . . formally disapproved " the demonstration,[14] it is evident that there was present a sympathetic element from the Workshops, whose participation Thomas had been unable to prevent.[15] The numbers of this group cannot be ascertained, but the *fact* is symptomatic: despite the strenuous efforts of the government to combat the doctrines of the Luxembourg, the influence of that body was already beginning to permeate the ranks of the National Workshops. Very gradually the workers of the latter were being persuaded that their interests lay, not in the support of a government which was slowly drifting in the direction of reaction, but in the constitution of something amounting to working-class solidarity in the face of the attacks on the workers' cause. This process was to continue gradually and almost unnoticed until the end of May,[16] when events rapidly accelerated its completion.

*   *   *   *   *

The *rappel* once sounded, the units of the National Guard formed quickly. General Duvivier was likewise instructed to despatch to the Hôtel de Ville such battalions of the *Garde mobile* as were sufficiently equipped. General Changarnier, arriving by chance to take his leave of the minister of foreign affairs,[17] was charged by Lamartine with the protection of the

---

[13] *Moniteur,* April 18. " Les délégués des ouvriers des ateliers nationaux protestent également, au noms de leurs frères assemblés hier à l'Hippodrome, contre les calomnies dont leur réunion de famille a été l'objet, et joignent leurs voix à celles de tous les délégués au Luxembourg."

[14] *Moniteur,* April 19.

[15] Cherest denies that the National Workshops participated (p. 235).

[16] This process was considerably influenced by the presence in the National Workshops of considerable numbers of Luxembourg delegates (*Vraie République,* May 3; E. Picattier: *Les Ateliers nationaux en 1848* [Saint-Etienne, 1899], pp. 101-102). See also Renard: *République de 1848,* p. 63.

[17] Changarnier had just been named ambassador to Berlin, which post, however, he never assumed.

Hôtel de Ville, which he energetically put in a state of siege. The result was that when the workers' procession reached the Place de Grève, it was greeted by a sea of bayonets closely massed about the Hôtel de Ville. A delegation of the two Guard corps was received by the government and warmly thanked by Lamartine, in behalf of " the whole of France," for having assured the inviolability of the Provisional Government. The workers' delegation, on the other hand, was received only by Deputy Mayor Adam, who listened coldly to the reading of their petition and then severely lectured the workers for a manifestation which appeared to aim at the imposition by force of acts contrary to the government's will.[18] Abashed and angered, the delegates retired, harassed by repeated cries from the National Guard: " À bas Blanqui! à bas Louis Blanc! à bas Cabet! à l'eau les communistes!" [19]

Presently, finding the workers' procession completely blocked in the Place de Grève, the delegates sought out Louis Blanc and remonstrated angrily about the ill-treatment accorded them. Blanc finally succeeded in having measures taken to permit the procession to pass, but the workers were obliged to march in a narrow line between the serried ranks of the National Guard and at such a distance from the steps of the Hôtel de Ville that their *vivats,* drowned by the cries of " À bas les communistes! " failed to reach the government's ears. The workers' humiliation complete, the National Guard regiments were reviewed.[20]

Whatever may have been the precise object of the radicals in organizing the demonstration of April 16, the collapse of their plans involved a defeat of the first magnitude for the workers' cause. One historian is willing to describe the débâcle as the " definitive defeat of the party of social reform." [21]   If

---

[18] Garnier-Pagès, VII, pp. 397-403.

[19] Stern, II, p. 178; Seignobos: *Révolution de 1848,* p. 70: " L'accueil différent fait aux délégués des deux manifestations marqua le sens de cette journée."

[20] Blanc: *Révolution de 1848,* II, pp. 21-22.

[21] Seignobos: *Révolution de 1848,* p. 70. The radicals generally viewed it as a triumph for the reaction. The workers of the Luxembourg protested with great vigor against the counter-demonstration of the National Guard and the misin-

it be objected that such a characterization is too sweeping, it is none the less clear that the miscarriage of the radicals' plans assured the election in legal form of a constituent assembly which would, to all appearances, be inimical to their program,[22] and that above all it crystallized the sentiment of opposition to socialism. Fear and hatred of the advocates of the social revolution were gradually forming a basis for coöperation between the moderate republicans and the monarchists. The time for judicial thinking on social reform was past: henceforth socialists, regardless of the *nuances* of their views, were classed together as fomenters of disorder, men of violence willing that the solid bases of a " well ordered bourgeois society " should yield place to the " chimeras " of socialist prophets. The class which had basked in the friendly rays of the bourgeois monarchy and which had been amused or bored by the " innocuous dreams " of a Fourier or a Saint-Simon, now recoiled in horror before the menace of far-reaching socialist experiments, initiated under the threat of violence.[23]

The defeat of the forces of the social revolution involved also a weakening in the position of the moderates. In adopt-

terpretation of their aims (*Moniteur*, April 18). Barbès, who distrusted the machinations of Blanqui, regretted that, in answering the *rappel* as colonel of the Twelfth National Guard Regiment, he had unwittingly served the cause of reaction (Wassermann, pp. 134-135). And Blanqui deplored the misguided devotion of his fellow proletarians to the citizen militia, arm of the bourgeoisie (*ibid.*, pp. 184-185).

[22] Barrot: *Mémoires*, II, p. 139. " . . . la journée du 17 avril avait produit ce grand résultat, que l'élection de l'Assemblée constituante était désormais assurée; les partis les plus violents eux-mêmes, désespérant de pouvoir l'empêcher, s'apprêtaient, au milieu de toutes leurs vociférations et de leurs menaces, à transporter un instant la lutte dans la lice électorale."

[23] Proudhon (*Confessions d'un révolutionnaire*, pp. 97-98) has a penetrating paragraph on this point: " C'est à partir du 16 avril que le socialisme est devenu particulièrement odieux au pays. Le socialisme existait depuis 1830. Depuis 1830, saint-simoniens, phalanstériens, communistes, humanitaires et autres, entretenaient le public de leurs innocentes rêveries; et ni M. Thiers, ni M. Guizot n'avaient daigné s'en occuper. Ils ne craignaient point alors le socialisme, et ils avaient raison de ne le pas craindre tant qu'il n'était pas question de l'appliquer aux frais de l'état et par autorité publique. Après le 16 avril, le socialisme souleva contre lui toutes les colères: on l'avait vu, minorité imperceptible, toucher au gouvernement ! "

ing an energetic policy toward the radicals on April 16, the moderates inevitably assumed, for the moment at least, the program of the reaction. They were henceforth holding a perilous course between the Scylla of reaction and the Charybdis of social revolution.[24] The events of May 15 aligned them dangerously close to the reaction, and the June Days shipwrecked the hopes of the *juste milieu*.

Notwithstanding the humiliation of the workers on April 16, the week between the demonstration and the national elections witnessed a whole series of apparent concessions to the radicals. The government's proclamation of April 17 was couched in words which seemed to announce a victory for the popular cause: it declared that the manifestation had "consecrated anew what the demonstration of March 17 had so potently begun. Like March 17, April 16 has revealed how unshakable are the foundations of the Republic."[25] In favor of the poorer classes, the *octroi* duties on meat were abolished and those on wine were reduced, while the consequent losses to the treasury were to be recovered by progressive and luxury taxes falling upon the well-to-do.[26] Felicitations were voted the clubs ("pour la République un besoin et pour les citoyens un droit");[27] the minority won the assent of their colleagues for an investigation of the events of April 16;[28] and Louis Blanc drafted a proclamation disparaging "tout cri provocateur," an obvious reflection on those who had joined in the shouts of "À bas les communistes!"[29]

---

[24] That this is no exaggeration is evident from a careful reading of the events of the days following (see, e.g., Garnier-Pagès, VIII, Chapters I and II). Rumors were prevalent that the extremists planned a *contre-coup,* and the National Guard and the *Garde mobile* were again called out in force early on the morning of April 18 (*ibid.,* VIII, pp. 28-32; *Moniteur,* April 19; see also *Journal des Débats,* April 20, for attitude of the conservatives with reference to the necessity of vigorous action in repressing the radicals).

[25] *Moniteur,* April 18.

[26] Decree of April 18 (*Moniteur,* April 19). The progressive taxes were levied on owners and renters of large houses, the luxury taxes on dogs, *de luxe* carriages, and male servants.

[27] *Ibid.,* April 20.

[28] *Ibid.,* April 18; cf. Renard: *Louis Blanc,* p. 85.

[29] *Moniteur,* April 19; Renard: *Louis Blanc,* p. 85.

These and other acts of the government [30] seem, on superficial examination, to denote a decided swing to the left following the demonstration of April 16. The better view would seem
to be that the moderates, sensing a victory for their cause in
the elections, considered conciliation of the popular movement
the wiser course at the moment:[31] the radicals could be more
readily controlled by the Constituent Assembly, in which they
would have little influence.[32] Doubtless the desire to win popular support in the elections was also a potent factor.[33] Moreover, some of the concessions granted proved, as probably was
intended, to be illusory or of ephemeral importance: nothing
came of the proposed investigation of the events of April 16,[34]
and the clubs of course were closed following the June Days.[35]

II

" With such a record of service," La Gorce dryly comments
in reference to recent concessions to the radicals, " the dictators

[30] Stern, II, pp. 182-183; cf. the bitterly ironic passage in La Gorce, I, pp.
199-201.

[31] Threats of resignation by one or another member of the minority or by
the whole minority seem to have been frequent at this time (Stern, II, p. 182).
The confidence of the minority is indicated by the fact that another attempt
was made to force acceptance of the red flag, but the move was vigorously
opposed, especially by Arago (*ibid.*, II, p. 183; on the original rejection of the
red flag, see Seignobos: *Révolution de 1848*, pp. 12-14).

[32] Cf. Renard: *République de 1848*, p. 39; Lamartine: *Révolution de 1848*, II,
pp. 257-258; Renard: *Louis Blanc*, p. 86. Of course it must be remembered
that the moderates were actuated also by fear of the " reaction " — fear that the
right groups might greatly strengthen themselves as a result of the defeat of
the radicals. Certainly the violence of the attack of the conservatives upon the
government at this time could not have been reassuring to the moderates.
Ledru-Rollin was accused of presiding at bacchanalian orgies at Versailles.
Crémieux had purchased a forest for himself out of state funds. Louis Blanc
and his acolytes were sumptuously dined at the Luxembourg. Albert was becoming a millionaire (Blanc: *Révolution de 1848*, II, Ch. XVII; Stern, II, pp.
180-182. The safest course for the moderates in any case was to maintain the
status quo and mark time until the elections arrived, making as few concessions as possible to either side (cf. Garnier-Pagès, VIII, pp. 23-24, 47-48).

[33] Normanby, I, pp. 329-330.

[34] Renard: *Louis Blanc*, p. 85.

[35] Wassermann, p. 219.

of the Hôtel de Ville considered the time ripe to mount into the Capitol and bear thanks to the gods." [36] A grand review of the military forces of the Republic was announced for April 20. It was to be known, ironically enough, as the *Fête de la Fraternité*. The review was to consecrate the "concord" and "sincere fraternity" existing between the army and the people of Paris. For fourteen hours the troops filed past the government stand at the Arc de Triomphe. Their garlanded cannon and lilac-bedecked rifles were intended to bespeak the spirit of harmony. But what was perhaps most lacking in this *fête* to fraternity was fraternity itself. For the bitter emotions aroused by the events of recent weeks would not be allayed by declaring that they did not exist. The government indeed profited by the occasion to retain in Paris five regiments of the regular army.[37] "La guerre civile couvait sous les fleurs et sous les sourires du printemps." [38]

The celebration witnessed an event, of minor importance in itself, but which nicely illustrates the antagonism existing between the National Workshops and the Luxembourg and the covert attempts of the latter to extend its influence to its "alienated brother proletarians." Émile Thomas had arrived and seated a group of delegates and officers from the Workshops in the reviewing stand, when he was informed that they were occupying places reserved for the Luxembourg representatives. Thomas refused to move his men, declaring that "delegates of peaceful workers would not retire before agents of disorder." The Luxembourg group then took seats below those occupied by the delegates of the Workshops, but later a compromise was reached and the two groups mingled.[39]

Subsequently the two groups received together a flag from the hands of the government and were passed in review. When,

[36] La Gorce, I, p. 201.
[37] Seignobos: "Procès-verbaux du Gouvernement provisoire," *Revue d'histoire moderne et contemporaine*," VII, p. 586.
[38] Renard: *République de 1848*, p. 39; *Moniteur*, April 21; Blanc: *Révolution de 1848*, II, pp. 44-48.
[39] Thomas, p. 210; *Moniteur*, April 21.

however, Rouvenat, Louis Blanc's secretary, wished to disband the group, Thomas captured the procession, led *all* the delegates to Monceau, and there lectured them for two hours on the "mad and pernicious doctrines" by which they allowed themselves to be influenced! If Thomas' story is to be credited, the delegates agreed that they disapproved these theories in large measure. They were even willing to proceed to the Hôtel de Ville and express themselves in that sense to the government. They were warmly congratulated by Deputy Mayor Buchez for having recognized their errors and having had the courage to admit it! [40]

III

Thomas and the administration of the Workshops played an important part in the elections of April 23 in behalf of the candidates of the moderate republicans. The director refused all coöperation with the Luxembourg,[41] and projected a monster review of the units of the Workshops, whose purpose was obviously to win the workers to the side of the moderates. The members of the Workshops were to be given a holiday and a bonus for the occasion, and were to be reviewed by Marie and Marrast. The day selected was April 22, on the eve of the elections. The baldness of the manœuvre and the vigorous

[40] Thomas, pp. 211-212. The story is doubtless colored: it is not sufficiently explained why the Luxembourg delegates should allow themselves to be thus humiliated. Lagarde, president of the Luxembourg delegates, offered to include Thomas' name on the Luxembourg's official list of candidates for the national elections in return for the support for that list of the National Workshops. Thomas refused. It is only upon the basis of the supposition that Lagarde really believed that Thomas would seriously consider some such course that the events above can be made intelligible.

[41] See above, p. 127, note 1. The Luxembourg list of candidates included the names of none of the moderates in the government. When Marie learned of this he replied by preparing a list from which the names of Louis Blanc, Albert, Flocon, and Ledru-Rollin were excluded. A "million" copies of the latter were printed and distributed under the direction of the mayor of Paris. Apparently the list was sponsored by Marie and Marrast, rather than by the moderates as a group (Cherest, p. 239; Normanby, I, p. 339; Thomas, pp. 216-217).

protests of Louis Blanc and Albert secured postponement until
" after the elections." [42]

More direct influence was brought to bear on the individual
workers by means of the brigadiers.[43] Marie likewise agreed
to the use of 500 members of the Workshops to distribute voting lists at the polls, including only the names of moderates.
For this task they were to receive five francs a day each.[44]
Finally, while the elections were actually in progress, Thomas
employed his organization to oppose wherever possible the
influences of the radicals. He commissioned his assistants from
the *École centrale* and students of certain of the other schools
to prevent meetings of workers where concerted action was
being attempted in favor of radical candidates. He was particularly anxious about a mass meeting of workers summoned by
the Luxembourg delegates for the early morning of April 23
in the Champ-de-Mar. The prompt intervention of the director's *aides* resulted in the dispersing of the workmen and the
failure of the meeting. The student campaigners also found
plenty of action elsewhere, one of their number even invading
the enemy's territory — at the gates of the Luxembourg — in
complete disregard of the threatening crowd of Luxembourg
delegates surrounding him.[45]

Thomas himself had ambitions to membership in the assem-

[42] Thomas, pp. 213-223; Cherest, pp. 236-239; Garnier-Pagès, VIII, pp. 277-
278; Blanc: *Révolution de 1848*, II, pp. 52-54. Doubtless Louis Blanc was irritated by the recent humiliation of Lagarde and the Luxembourg delegates at
the hands of Thomas and welcomed an opportunity to return the courtesy. But
a much more influential motive was obviously his desire to prevent the government from exercising any further influence on the workers unfavorable to
socialist candidates.

[43] M. Caussidière: *Mémoires de Caussidière, ex-préfet de police et représentant du peuple* (Paris, 1849, 2 vols.), II, p. 214. Caussidière comments upon
the use to which Thomas put the Workshops in securing the adoption of the
electoral list of the Hôtel de Ville. But cf. Thomas' statement to the contrary
(pp. 218-219).

[44] *Ibid.*, pp. 217-218; *Moniteur*, April 26, 1849, the report of Ducos on the
accounts of the Provisional Government.

[45] Thomas, pp. 223-227; *Commission d'enquête*, II, p. 179; cf. Garnier-Pagès,
VIII, p. 279; V. Pierre: *Histoire de la République de 1848* (Paris, 1878, 2 vols.),
I, pp. 235-236.

bly, as his activities prior to the by-elections of June 4 clearly proved. Why he did not come out in the open at this time cannot be determined. His candidacy was solicited by a group of delegates of the Workshops, he says; but he refused to be a candidate, fearing to be accused of using his official position to further his own interests. It is altogether possible that his immediate superiors had indicated to Thomas that any active candidacy would injure the moderate cause, especially when it was already compromised by other electoral activities. It was doubtless also felt that Thomas as a deputy, with an army of nearly a hundred thousand under his command, might prove a source of real embarrassment to the government. Notwithstanding his ostensible opposition to a candidacy, Thomas received 28,166 votes in the Department of the Seine.[46]

*　　　*　　　*　　　*　　　*

The tremendous increase in the number of voters greatly complicated the counting process, and it was not until ten o'clock on the evening of April 28 that the mayor of Paris was able to announce, before the Hôtel de Ville, illuminated for the occasion, the results of the election in the Department of the Seine. The returns there, as elsewhere, revealed a decisive defeat for the radicals. The candidates of the Luxembourg were routed, as were the heads of the clubs and the socialists generally. Louis Blanc and Albert seem to have been successful only by virtue of their enhanced prestige as members of the government and their resultant adjunction to the Central Committee's list.[47] Even so, their margin of safety was not impressive.[48] Of the thirty-four representatives elected from the Department of the Seine, the seven members of the govern-

---

[46] Lamennais, who was last on the list of thirty-four successful candidates, received 104,871 votes. On Thomas' candidacy, see Thomas, pp. 218-220, 322-327; Cherest, p. 230, note 1; *Moniteur*, April 29 (on the number of votes polled by the various candidates); and *Commission d'enquête*, II, p. 298. On his candidacy in the by-elections of June 4, see below, p. 91.

[47] Stern, II, p. 205. Blanc and Albert, as members of the government, were included in the slate prepared by the *Comité centrale*, controlled by the party of the *National*.

[48] Albert had 133,041 votes and Louis Blanc, 120,140.

ment's moderate majority occupied places one to seven, while the four members of the minority were in places twenty-one (Albert), twenty-four (Ledru-Rollin), twenty-six (Flocon), and twenty-seven (Louis Blanc)! [49]

Some of the predispositions of the members of the assembly with reference to the social question can be gathered from their professions.[50] Of the 880 members, ninety-nine were officers or former officers of the regular army. More than 325 were from the legal profession,[51] and fifty-three were doctors of medicine. Landed proprietors numbered 160,[52] while commerce contributed fifty-three members and industry sixty-five. When it is considered further that there were but six foremen (*contremaîtres*) and some eighteen workers elected, the overwhelmingly bourgeois character of the assembly is apparent.[53] But,

[49] *Moniteur*, April 29. For an elaborate analysis of the members of the assembly with reference to age, profession, education, etc., see A. Chaboseau: "Les constituants de 1848," *La Révolution de 1848*, VII (1910-1911), VIII (1911-1912), and Seignobos, who has consulted an unpublished *mémoire* on the subject (*Révolution de 1848*, pp. 82-84).

[50] Statistics from Chaboseau: "Constituants de 1848," *Révolution de 1848*, VII, *passim*.

[51] Including "magistrats, notaires, avoués, et avocats." The figure cannot be determined precisely because, of seventy-seven former members of the legal profession cited by Chaboseau, a considerable number had since become public magistrates.

[52] Many of these were, however, also former army officers, magistrates, etc. Only ninety-seven of them had, in the exploitation of their lands, their exclusive or principal interest.

[53] It is interesting to note that the *scrutin de liste,* adopted for the purpose of diminishing the influence upon the country population of the *curés* and great landowners, gave the same kind of results as the *scrutin d'arrondissement,* which prevailed during the two preceding reigns. Of the 880 members elected, 676 were "hommes de terroir"; that is, they were born in the department from which they were elected. Of 200 of the "non-originaires," Chaboseau says that the majority were also elected for the same reason; i.e., although not born in a given department, they were in some way prominently identified with it. This situation explains in a measure the failure of the radicals. Where local celebrities were being overwhelmingly favored, what chances in the provinces had the prominent radicals, most of whom came from Paris and the few other large towns? It is also to be noted that other groups were often successful in stealing the radicals' fire and themselves posing as the upholders of the workingman's cause (see the very interesting section on this subject in Stern, II, pp. 195 ff.).

however bourgeois in character the new assembly was to be, the election was no immediate triumph for the reaction. It was a repudiation of the monarchy of Louis Philippe and a victory for the moderate republicans of the *National* "party." Henceforth the left group perforce fastened their hopes upon the radical influence which revolutionary Paris was expected to exert upon a chamber sitting in its midst.

IV

From the point of view of the radicals of Paris the history of the period from the national elections to the fateful demonstration of May 15 is one of rapidly accumulating grievances and a growing consciousness of the magnitude of the defeat of their cause. The organs of the left were bitterly disappointed by the results of the elections,[54] but in general were still inclined to await patiently the convening of the assembly in the hope that measures favorable to the workers might be adopted.[55] Meanwhile the sanguinary news from Rouen, where a rising of workers, alleging frauds in the elections, was suppressed with bloodshed by the National Guard and troops of the line, was greeted by a storm of angry protest.[56]

While the fate of the left groups had plunged them in gloom or driven them to frenzied agitation, the reviving hopes of the conservatives encouraged them to come more and more into the open. The monarchist press denounced the "plots" of the communists on April 16 and delivered crushing replies to the demands of the clubs touching the rising in Rouen.[57] When the assembly was convened, the conservatives marshalled im-

---

[54] " Nous comptions sur de bien mauvais élections," wrote the *Réforme*, April 29, " mais l'événement, il faut l'avouer, a depassé notre attente."

[55] *Ami du peuple*, April 30; *Commune de Paris*, April 30 ff.; cf. *Peuple constituant*, May 2.

[56] See, e.g., *Ami du peuple*, April 30; *Vraie république*, May 2: " L'ordre s'est retabli au milieu des cadavres. Le calme de la terreur règne dans cette ville." For the reactions of the clubs of Blanqui and of Barbès, see Wassermann, pp. 143 ff.

[57] Wassermann, pp. 151-153; Garnier-Pagès, VIII, pp. 2 ff.

pressive strength, both in numbers and in distinction.[58] Berryer, Falloux, la Rochejaquelein were among a brilliant representation of legitimists, which included also Montalembert, "lay pope of France." From the former *tiers parti* and the *centre gauche* came Dufaure, Billault, Vivien, de Rémusat, and de Tocqueville, while the *gauche dynastique* reappeared in the persons of Odilon Barrot, Duvergier de Hauranne, de Malleville, and Gustave de Beaumont. Indeed, if the former ministers of Louis Philippe and Thiers and Molé are excepted,[59] it will be seen that *all* of the well-known members of the two chambers under the bourgeois monarchy had been recalled to take part in the Constituent Assembly.[60] The sentiments of these men toward the reforms urged by the radicals were notorious. It is little wonder that the revolutionary press exercised itself in vituperative tirades against the " reaction."

The parties of the right, despite their strength, were condemned in the beginning to a policy of watchful waiting. Fearful of the excesses of the Parisian populace and the possible triumph of the social revolution through violence, they were obliged to accept whatever anti-socialist measures the moderates were willing to support, until events should impel a large section of the latter to take their view of things. They had not long to wait.

The moderate republicans were in a substantial majority. They did not form a " party " but were, in general, proponents of a middle course, committing them neither to the " excesses "

[58] The right included about a hundred legitimists and something fewer than 200 Orleanists. Of the remaining members of the assembly of 880, some 500 were moderate republicans, while the radicals mustered fewer than a hundred seats.

[59] Both were soon to be returned in by-elections.

[60] See La Gorce, I, p. 212; Stern, II, p. 209; and especially Chaboseau: " Constituants de 1848," *Révolution de 1848*, VIII, pp. 67-69. Of the 880 members of the assembly, 165 had represented the same department during the Hundred Days, or during the reigns of Louis XVIII, Charles X, or Louis Philippe; twenty-five had been deputies during the same period from other departments than those by which they were elected in 1848; and seven had been peers. Dupont (de l'Eure) was the only deputy in 1848 whose membership in a deliberative body antedated 1815: he had sat both in the Council of Five Hundred and in the *Corps législatif*.

of the radicals nor to the " follies " of the reaction. Lamartine, whose prestige had been further enhanced by his election in ten different departments, was the recognized leader of this bloc.[61] He enjoyed great prestige for the moment with the monarchists also, for it was believed that he could and would exercise a restraining influence upon those moderates, such as Ledru-Rollin, who exhibited strong " leftist " tendencies.

The supporters of the " révolution démocratique et sociale," numbering fewer than a hundred, were virtually reduced to the position of impotent spectators, forced to witness the crushing defeat of the causes for which they believed the revolution had been fought. Such parliamentary impotence of their representatives would not long be tolerated, however, by the Parisian populace and its leaders. Even before the convening of the assembly there existed a widespread feeling that another conflict in the streets was approaching.[62] In the light of the mounting antagonism between the radicals and their adversaries, it is difficult to see how it could have been avoided. The humiliating reverses of the radicals in the week following merely added fuel to the fire.

*　　*　　*　　*　　*

The newly elected assembly was formally convened on May 4 in the temporary [63] structure erected in the court of the Palais Bourbon. The radicals were soon given a clear view of the intentions of the moderates and their allies when the new constituent body was organized. The leaders of the left were entirely excluded. Buchez, deputy mayor of Paris, was elected president. Among the vice presidents were Deputy Mayor

[61] See Lamartine's exaggerated estimate of his own popularity at the moment (*Révolution de 1848*, II, pp. 263-264).

[62] See, e.g., Normanby, I, p. 354, entry of May 1: " . . . the language of all classes is now that it is impossible affairs should settle down without another conflict in the streets."

[63] *Ibid.*, I, p. 359. The British ambassador ironically comments: " The old Chamber of Deputies being quite inadequate to contain 900 members, a new building professing to be temporary (who knows that it may not survive much which it would now be treason to call temporary) has been raised." For a brilliant picture of the first session, see Stern, II, pp. 210 ff.

Recurt, soon to be minister of the interior; Cavaignac, future victor of the June Days; and Sénard, author of the repression in Rouen.[64]

The selection of the executive to succeed the Provisional Government was now at hand. The question of the form which the executive should take had agitated the various political factions for some time past. There had been rumors of a presidency, which Lamartine would logically have been summoned to fill. Odilon Barrot and the right supported a ministry selected by the assembly and subject to its control.[65] The radicals warmly advocated a proposal to continue in power the Provisional Government, thus assuring their group representation in the persons of Louis Blanc and Albert.[66] For the same reason, this motion was overwhelmingly rejected by the moderates and the right. The moderates finally had their way in the adoption of an Executive Commission of five members, to be chosen by the assembly. The commission was in turn to appoint and recall the ministers.[67]

A bitter struggle followed. The right and a large number of the moderates were determined to exclude Ledru-Rollin from the Executive Commission. Only the loyal support of Lamartine won Ledru a weak fifth place on the final ballot,[68] which included also the names of Arago, Garnier-Pagès, Marie, and Lamartine. The radicals, rebuffed in the formation and election of the new executive, were no better pleased with the announcement of the ministry. The names of all the moderates of the Provisional Government, except that of Dupont (de l'Eure),[69] appeared in the ministry or the Executive Commission. Only Flocon and Caussidière could be considered in any sense "left wing." Recently Flocon had won the confidence

---

[64] *Moniteur,* May 6; Stern, II, p. 215.

[65] Barrot, II, pp. 176 ff.

[66] Garnier-Pagès, IX, p. 36; cf. G. Bouniols: *Histoire de la Révolution de 1848* (Second edition, Paris, 1918), pp. 151-152.

[67] Garnier-Pagès, IX, p. 40 and *passim*; *Moniteur,* May 10. The Executive Commission was *not* permitted to name its own members as ministers.

[68] Stern, II, p. 217; Calman, pp. 172-177.

[69] Dupont had asked leave to retire, pleading his great age.

of the moderates of the Provisional Government by his frequent support of their views,[70] and Caussidière was well thought of even by many of the conservatives for his successful administration of the Paris police.[71]

On the very day of the election of the Executive Commission —stern rebuff to socialist ambitions—Louis Blanc mounted the tribune to urge once again the formation of a ministry of labor and progress. The moment was obviously ill chosen, and it was believed that Blanc was seeking to create a position which he was to be selected to fill.[72] The speaker managed, moreover, to irritate his auditors by seeming to pose as the sole defender of the workers' cause. The discussion took an ironic turn when a Catholic worker, Peupin, rose to combat Blanc's proposal and to expose the work of the Luxembourg Commission (of which he was a member) to the derision of his colleagues. The proposal was overwhelmed, and in its place the assembly created a committee of thirty-six to undertake an investigation of the conditions of agricultural and industrial laborers.[73]

This latest demonstration of hostility was only the last of a series of acts which convinced the left press that nothing was to be expected from the assembly in the way of a thorough-

[70] See, e.g., Garnier-Pagès, VII, p. 365-366.

[71] Stern, II, p. 299. The reappointment of Caussidière as prefect of police doubtless recognized a situation which the Executive Commission did not feel it was in a position to change at the time. The Provisional Government had been obliged to accept Caussidière, who had taken possession of the prefecture February 24 and refused thereafter to be dislodged. He was finally forced to resign as a result of his ambiguous activities during the demonstration of May 15.

[72] Blanc: *Révolution de 1848*, II, pp. 71-73; Stern, II, pp. 237-238. Blanc had resigned the presidency of the Luxembourg Commission, May 9, and had declared that he would accept no public office for the duration of the assembly. But the hostility of the assembly toward the socialists and the consequent inopportuneness of his motion must have been obvious to Blanc. Was his proposal a mere bid for popularity with the workers, or did he desire to unmask the intentions of the assembly regarding the social question and thus to invite the support of the populace of Paris for his program?

[73] *Moniteur*, May 11. Three days later this committee was fused with the assembly's Labor Committee. For a defence of the assembly's action in rejecting Blanc's proposal and appointing its committee of investigation, see the *National*, May 12.

going labor program, as they understood it. The *Vraie République* declared the Republic "pervertie" unless God or the
people should intervene.[74] The *Commune de Paris* warned that
the assembly's indefinite postponement of aid to the workers
might evoke "tomorrow" the eloquent petition of the Lyon-
nais: "*Vivre en travaillant, ou mourir en combattant!*"[75]
Even the patience of Lamennais was finally exhausted, and he
painted a dark picture of the forthcoming struggle between the
"tendance rétrograde" and the "tendance franchement républicaine."[76]

The first ten days of May form a watershed in the history
of the Revolution of 1848. The workers, influenced largely by
such leadership as that of Louis Blanc, had in the beginning
put their faith in the reform of the suffrage. Then successively
they had been alarmed by the "defection" of the provinces in
March and April, disillusioned by the results of the elections,
and finally outraged by the "deceptions" of an assembly
which had "betrayed" the popular cause.[77] The indignation
of the workers now awaited only a favorable occasion to vent
itself against the assembly and the government. The latter had
long planned a *Fête de la Concorde*, sequel to the *Fête de la
Fraternité*,[78] but agitation among the proletariat had reached
such serious proportions that the government, on May 13, postponed the *fête*, scheduled for the following day. At the same
time it took protective measures in anticipation of the popular
demonstration, which had now been announced for May 15.[79]

[74] May 10, and days following.

[75] May 11, cf. May 9.

[76] *Peuple constituant*, May 15; cf. numbers for May 2, 10, 11.

[77] This change in sentiment becomes readily evident from a reading of the
principal organs of the Paris press devoted to the workers' interests.

[78] Garnier-Pagès, VIII, p. 388.

[79] *Commission d'enquête*, II, p. 39. The *fête* had originally been announced for
May 4, but was postponed until May 14, because the government feared a *coup
de main*, connected with the suppression of the proletarian risings in Limoges
and Rouen (Garnier-Pagès, VIII, p. 388). After the defeat of Louis Blanc's
proposal for a ministry of progress, the delegates of the Luxembourg, obviously
acting under Blanc's influence, refused (May 11) to participate in the *fête*
(*Moniteur*, May 11; Blanc: *Révolution de 1848*, II, p. 73). The same stand

V

The demonstration of May 15 was presumably in favor of Poland. The recent news of the courageous defence of the Poles against heartbreaking odds had quickened again the perennial enthusiasm of the French for the cause of Polish freedom.[80] Poles returning to Paris from the scene of action had, through the medium of the clubs, acted upon the workers' sympathies.[81] In the assembly Wolowski, one-time Polish officer, read to his colleagues a petition from a Polish delegation and invoked the immediate intervention of France.[82] There were even those who, relying upon a time-tested tradition, frankly favored a foreign war as the means of solving domestic difficulties.[83] The discussion of the Polish question was set for May 15.

As in the case of its predecessors, the " journées " of March 17 and April 16, those contributing causes of the demonstration of May 15 about which we should like most to know are obscure. It seems clear that a very large element of the workers participating was sincere in its interest in Poland,[84]

was taken by the committee representing the former political prisoners (*Détenus politiques,* Caussidière, II, p. 109). A sharp protest against the assembly's action came from the *Club de la Révolution* (Wassermann, p. 162). These events, possibly also the abortive popular demonstration of May 13 — symptoms of the agitated state of Paris — convinced the government of the inopportuneness of the projected *fête.* The reason given, that the preparations were not complete, is not convincing (Caussidière, II, p. 110; cf. L. Lévy-Schneider: " Les préliminaires du 15 mai, 1848. La journée du 14, d'après un document inédit," *Révolution de 1848,* VII [1910-1911], p. 223).

[80] Stern, II, pp. 240 ff. On the government and the Polish question, see Apponyi, IV, p. 187, and especially Bourgin's introduction to the *Souvenirs* of Circourt, pp. lxxiv ff.

[81] Lamartine: *Révolution de 1848,* II, pp. 192-194, 312-313. One member of a delegation urging French intervention declared threateningly that the Poles " avaient quarante mille hommes des ateliers nationaux enrôlés pour se joindre à eux le lendemain, et pour marcher ensemble sur l'hôtel de ville . . ." (*ibid.,* II, p. 193).

[82] Speech of May 10 (*Moniteur,* May 11).

[83] *Liberté,* May 15: " Nous répétons, nous, après avoir été les premiers à le dire dans la presse, que la guerre à l'étranger, pour la sainte cause des peuples, est seule capable de comprimer les dissensions intestines."

[84] See, e.g., Stern, II, p. 252; the same impression is given by Thomas' account (p. 257); cf. also *République,* May 15.

but the events which took place after the invasion of the assembly revealed a very different spirit: certain elements were not averse to forcing their "agents" (*commis*) to do the "will of the people." In short, the aims of the social revolution were to be forced upon the assembly: the theory of popular sovereignty was given the crude interpretation that the will of the people of Paris represents the will of the people of France.[85] A third element, certainly a very slight minority, aimed at the dissolution of the assembly and the reënactment of the events of February 24. The latter was precisely what happened, with this difference, that the *coup d'état* of May 15 was abortive.[86] Why then did events take a course desired only by a small minority? The answer probably lies in the fact that, once again, a popular demonstration lacked acknowledged leaders and definite aims.

  *   *   *   *   *

On the morning of May 15 the manifestants duly gathered in the Place de la Bastille. Present were the numerous workers' trade groups, delegations of the clubs, some 14,000 members of the National Workshops, a considerable number of the National Guard from the provinces (in Paris awaiting the *Fête de la Concorde*),[87] and others. The procession, passing along the boulevards, reached the Pont de la Concorde, where

[85] Representing an attempt to renew the "right of petition" as exercised at the time of the Convention.

[86] The elements in the demonstration can be distinguished in the *Moniteur's* account (May 17) of the events in the assembly. On the origins of the demonstration, see the report of Carlier, chief of the ministry of the interior's police, May 14 (*Commission d'enquête*, II, pp. 227-228). The demonstration was organized by the *Club centralisateur*, successor to the *Clubs des clubs*, of which Huber was president. An announcement of the demonstration was placarded on May 14. Neither Barbès nor Blanqui favored it. But, whereas Barbès succeeded in persuading the *Club de la Révolution* to abstain, Blanqui was unable to overcome the enthusiasm for the cause of Poland of his auditors in the *Société républicaine centrale*. The latter voted to participate. Blanqui yielded and was drawn perforce into the demonstration himself (Wassermann, pp. 164 ff.). Louis Blanc declares that he also opposed the demonstration and expressed his fears of its possible results to Barbès (Blanc: *Révolution de 1848*, II, p. 81).

[87] Lévy-Schneider: "Les préliminaires du 15 mai," *Révolution de 1848*, VII, p. 231 and *passim*.

General Courtais was stationed in command of units of the National Guard. Exactly what happened is not clear, but presently the mob was pressing across the bridge toward the Palais Bourbon. The National Guard and the *Garde mobile* withheld their fire. At this point, and perhaps considerably earlier, certain elements in the procession deserted, disapproving the character the demonstration was assuming.[88] The remainder forced their way into the court of the Palais Bourbon, and presently into the public galleries and on to the floor of the assembly. Tumult followed. The official account in the *Moniteur* and the statements of eyewitnesses establish a strong impression that the leaders were quite unable to control events but were swept along in their course. Certain of them harangued the audience, but their words were audible only a short distance from the tribune. Louis Blanc and Barbès, while commending the people for exercising their " right of petition," implored them to leave the assembly to the dignified discussion of the popular demands. Blanqui spoke. Although he let it appear that the immediate reconstitution of Poland was the burden of his plea, he adverted in scathing terms to the " massacres " of Rouen and the sufferings of the unemployed.[89] Barbès, possibly fearing that his hated rival, Blanqui, would make himself master of the day, and doubtless intoxicated by the revolutionary fervor of the mob, suddenly demanded that the assembly take immediate revolutionary action: that it authorize at once the departure of an army for Poland, a tax of a billion on the rich, the interdiction of the *rappel,* and the dismissal of the troops from Paris.

The tumult was at its height when the distant sound of the

[88] Among these was the representation from the National Workshops, the members of which were drawn away from the demonstration by their commanders as a result of Thomas' orders (Thomas, pp. 260-261; cf. Stern, II, pp. 269-270). Certain of the National Guard from the provinces also deserted apparently and offered their services to the Paris Guard to suppress what began to look like a seditious rising (Lévy-Schneider: " Les préliminaires du 15 mai," *Révolution de 1848,* VII, p. 231 and *passim*).

[89] There were frequent demands from the floor for the " organization of labor," a " ministry of labor," etc.

drums was heard — the *rappel*. President Buchez, threatened by violence, was forced to give a counter-order.[90] The tumult continued. Presently Huber, revolutionary leader of dubious loyalty, possibly *agent provocateur*, mounted the tribune and declared the assembly dissolved![91] A provisional government was quickly improvised and accepted, and, to complete the revolutionary ritual, the mob set out for the Hôtel de Ville, headed by Albert and Barbès, there once again to " consecrate the new government." Presently the deputies, most of whom had remained in their places until Huber declared the assembly dissolved, began to return to the hall. The session was resumed. Lamartine and Ledru-Rollin set out at the head of the National Guard for the Hôtel de Ville. There the insurrection promptly collapsed, and the leaders were arrested.[92]

VI

The connection of the National Workshops with the events of May 15 had results of capital importance for the future of that organization. Notwithstanding the unremitting activities of revolutionary agitators in the first half of May, the weight of the evidence indicates that Thomas continued to have the workers well in hand. The great majority of them were loyal to the cause of order and remained so until well after May 15, when they were finally estranged for other reasons. No better evidence of this spirit can be adduced than the fact that they

[90] Which, however, had no effect, for the units of the National Guard began to arrive a short time afterward.

[91] Despite numerous objections from the floor, among them that of Barbès. It was believed by some that Huber was acting as an *agent provocateur* for Marrast. Such a popular demonstration, suppressed by the government, would strengthen the position of the moderates by eliminating certain radical leaders and simultaneously revealing to the monarchists the value of the moderates as their protectors against the radicals. The ambiguous character of Huber's career lent color to this story (Stern, II, pp. 248-249; Blanc: *Révolution de 1848*, II, pp. 78-80; Garnier-Pagès, IX, p. 88, note 1). Huber subsequently assumed entire responsibility for his act (*Commission d'enquête*, II, p. 110).

[92] For the events in the chamber, see *Moniteur*, May 17, which needs to be supplemented by the accounts of eyewitnesses, especially as contained in the report of the *Commission d'enquête*.

offered to assist in the suppression of the rising of their brother workers in Rouen.[93] The director likewise induced the workers not to participate in a demonstration on May 12, whose object was to felicitate Lamartine for his support of the candidacy of Ledru-Rollin for the Executive Commission.[94] It was only too obviously Thomas' place to discourage a demonstration which might strengthen the hand of Ledru, opponent of Marrast, from whom the director took orders. But already there was evidence within the Workshops of that defection which later became widespread. For on May 13, while inspecting units of the fifth arrondissement, Thomas was advised that there was a plot on foot to murder him a short distance further along the line of inspection.[95] Presently he was greeted by cries of "Vive Louis Blanc! Vive la République sociale! À bas Émile Thomas! Etouffez-le!" Thomas kept his head and cowed the disturbers by a warm speech denouncing all such revolutionary agitation. The director attributed the disturbance to *provocateurs* from the Luxembourg and Blanqui's club, but there is evidence to indicate that *bona fide* members of the Workshops were also implicated.[96]

[93] Thomas, pp. 245-246.

[94] Thomas, pp. 252-253. The director was also successful in dissuading the workers from joining the abortive demonstration of May 13, precursor of that of May 15 (*ibid.*, p. 247).

[95] Thomas had begun a general inspection of all the workers on May 9, taking the arrondissements in turn, hearing and redressing complaints and appealing to the loyalty of the workers. He says that he sought to dissipate rumors that he was afraid to appear among them; doubtless he desired above all to sound the disposition of the workers and to determine to what extent the current revolutionary agitation was making itself felt in their ranks. The *fact* of a general inspection at this time evidenced the director's disquietude; on the other hand, with the exceptions noted, he declares that he was everywhere well received (Thomas, pp. 252 ff.).

[96] Thomas, pp. 253-255. The director is attempting to picture a situation favorable to himself with "ten thousand protectors" rising to defend him against plotters from outside (cf. *ibid.*, pp. 358-361). There can be no doubt that agitators from the Luxembourg and the revolutionary clubs were attempting at this time to influence the members of the Workshops. But that some members of the Workshops were actually implicated in the disturbance is indicated by a letter to Thomas from one of the brigadiers of the fifth arrondissement: " . . . le citoyen Hédouin, chef de notre première escouade, a été brutalisé en cherchant

*   *   *   *   *

Thomas had been successful in preventing the workers under his direction from participating in the demonstrations of March 17 and April 16. He was not so fortunate on May 15. The Place de la Bastille was dotted with banners of the National Workshops at ten o'clock in the morning, the hour appointed for the rendezvous.[97] The representation from the Workshops numbered some 14,000, according to the careful estimate of Thomas' own assistants.[98]

On that morning the director was continuing his series of inspections, interrupted by the disorders of the Saturday previous, when the workers' delegates requested the termination of the inspection so that they might not miss the demonstration in favor of Poland.[99] Thomas declares that he attempted to persuade the workers that the *fête* might have other than patriotic objects, but to no avail. He was obliged to content himself with sending his subordinates to survey the situation. Some time later the officers despatched by Thomas reported to the director that at the head of the procession they had observed, among others, the banners of certain of the revolutionary clubs, and had also made out the delegates of the Luxembourg.[100] Thomas at once despatched a letter to Buchez, president of the assembly, warning him of the possible danger,

à faire rentrer quelques hommes dans de meilleurs sentiments" (*ibid.*, p. 360). An article in the *Réforme* for May 15 attributes the disturbance to the fact that the workers, kept waiting in a hot sun for four hours, had lost patience. The article unfortunately is highly satiric.

[97] *Journal des Débats*, May 16; *Réforme*, May 16; cf. Garnier-Pagès, IX, pp. 147-149, 286-287.

[98] Thomas, p. 258. Thomas' figures are often unreliable; elsewhere he gives the number as 10,000 (*Commission d'enquête*, I, p. 352). Thomas notes the total number of manifestants as 25,000 (Thomas, p. 262).

[99] Thomas, p. 257. " Des émissaires se répandaient parmi nos rangs et sollicitaient les ouvriers pour cette noble cause. Ils ne les y trouvèrent pas sourds, et bientôt tous crièrent: *Vive la République! Vive la Pologne! Vive l'Assemblée nationale!* "

[100] *Ibid.*, pp. 258-259. The members of the National Workshops were apparently sincere in their interest in Poland, for, in the procession, they mingled with members of the National Guard, and their units were in many cases commanded by officers of the Guard (*Liberté*, May 16).

which, however, he (Thomas) minimized.[101] Edmond Adam, deputy mayor of Paris, informed at the same time, shared Thomas' view that there was no reason to become unduly alarmed; he advised keeping the workers occupied in the workshops, however.[102]

Meanwhile Thomas commissioned his subordinates and the Workshops' delegates to take measures to separate members of the Workshops from the demonstration and to have all workers who were members of the National Guard join their companies immediately the *rappel* was beaten. Both missions were successful, declares Thomas. The workers' units were induced to withdraw and not a single banner from the Workshops was seen in the invaded hall of the assembly.[103] Subsequently, three-quarters of the workers took part in the repression of the movement as members of the National Guard.[104]

Perhaps the most significant aspect of Thomas' entire account is what he fails to mention. In contrast to the elaborate measures he had taken to prevent the participation of the workers in the two previous demonstrations,[105] the director appears this time to have neglected to take any advance precautions whatever. The manifestation had been given wide publicity by means of posters on Sunday, May 14.[106] Thomas admits that he knew of it.[107] Indeed the general state of agitation and unrest in Paris at the time, with which he was only too well acquainted,[108] must have convinced him that a popular demonstration could readily become a pretext for violence.[109] And

---

[101] Thomas, pp. 258-259: " C'est une seconde édition du 16 avril, mais je la crois encore plus dangereuse. Toutefois, il n'y a rien à craindre avec quelques précautions ; les meneurs sont évidemment peu nombreux, deux à trois mille tout au plus ; quant aux ouvriers, ils sont de bonne foi, et ne pensent qu'à la Pologne."

[102] *Ibid.*, pp. 260-261.

[103] *Ibid.*, pp. 260-262 ; cf. Stern, II, pp. 269-270.

[104] Thomas, p. 184, note 1.

[105] Thomas, pp. 95 ff., and 194 ff.

[106] Stern, II, p. 250.

[107] Thomas, p. 257.

[108] *Ibid.*, pp. 244 ff.

[109] Cf. *ibid.*, pp. 257-258.

yet Thomas took no precautions.[110]   To what motives is his
course of action to be attributed?

It is possible to interpret Thomas' apparent inertia as reflecting the shaken condition of his nerves as a result of numerous
threats of violence which had been proffered him during the few
days past.[111]   Some days later he told Falloux that he had
risked his life, that he did not wish to risk it again, that he
feared a revolt among the workers, and that he could do nothing (in the way of taking dissolution measures) without the aid
of government and assembly.[112]   Fear may well have been an
element influencing Thomas; yet subsequently he acted with
resolution and succeeded in withdrawing the units of the Workshops from the procession. There are, moreover, other and
more weighty explanations than fear.

Thomas' actions probably reflected above all personal pique
— arising from the cavalier treatment he had recently received
at the hands of Marie and other members of the government —
and opposition to the government's program for dissolution of
the Workshops, about which he had already received plain
indications. The attitude of the government toward the Workshops had certainly undergone a fundamental change following the national elections. It became impossible to interest
any of its members in the institution, Thomas complains; [113]
as to the review which had been promised, there was no longer
any possibility of that.[114]   To the repeated proposals of the

[110] His failure to make a claim that he *did* is probably equivalent to an
admission that he *did not*.

[111] The director's life had been threatened on May 13, and further warnings
reached him on the following two days (Thomas, pp. 253-257). Had the extremists' *coup* been successful, May 15, doubtless Thomas, notorious as the opponent
of Louis Blanc and the radicals in general, would have fared badly.

[112] *Arch. nat.* C. 928. *Min. sténog. du com. du travail*, May 25.

[113] He did not see Marie from May 3 until June 23, Thomas declares (p. 244).
He was of course no longer director of the Workshops after May 26.

[114] *Ibid.*, p. 248. The review was to have been an electoral manoeuvre, and
Thomas' reference to it *after the elections* may seem naïve. But it is altogether
reasonable to believe that the director had continued to urge it and that the
miscarriage of the plan was a distinct blow to his vanity. What youngster of
twenty-six would willingly forego a parade of a hundred thousand troops of
whom he was the commander!

director, aimed at the amelioration of the general economic situation, Marie turned a deaf ear—or at best he temporized.[115] And his successor in the ministry of public works, Trélat, seemed little inclined to take the director's advice.[116] In short, Thomas, who until recently had been allowed to feel that he was performing a function of the greatest importance, now found himself quite neglected.[117] Indeed there is no evidence that the director, to whom the government had appealed so frequently in the past, received any official notification of the demonstration of May 15 or any orders in connection therewith.[118]

The accumulation of these grievances was very possibly sufficient to cause such resentment on Thomas' part that he would show distinctly less than his usual enthusiasm for the cause of the government.[119] It is perfectly conceivable that this state of mind induced him to allow events to take their own course, with only such a perfunctory discharge of his duty as was

[115] *Ibid.*, pp. 238-244. Thomas was highly indignant that his plans for economic reorganization and remedies for the situation in the National Workshops received scant attention. His most comprehensive plan, with its loans to industry by the state, the construction of communal workers' dwellings, the "unions" of workers and employers, etc., is strongly suggestive of Louis Blanc's conception. Blanc accuses Thomas of plagiarism (Blanc: *Révolution de 1848*, II, pp. 130-132).

[116] Thomas, pp. 262 ff.

[117] This feeling was only enhanced by the omission of the Workshops from the program for the *Fête de la Concorde*. Thomas was obliged to protest in order to secure the inclusion of the Workshops (Thomas, pp. 266-268). In this connection it is worth noting that the *fêtes* lay within the province of the director of the fine arts, Charles Blanc, brother of Louis Blanc.

[118] It may be objected that Marie had already warned Thomas, May 12, of the demonstration projected for May 13 and had instructed the director to prevent the Workshops from participating. But there is no evidence that these instructions were repeated. Moreover, the government's attitude toward Thomas may have changed considerably in these three days: on May 12 Trélat discovered Thomas' attitude of opposition to the government's general plan for dissolution of the Workshops; on May 13 the government proceeded secretly to take the first step in that program, giving Thomas no hint of its nature.

[119] Thomas' resentment is obvious in his apologia, although his attitude had doubtless been embittered by his removal from office (see, e.g., Thomas, pp. 244, 248-252).

involved in mildly attempting to dissuade a small group of workers from participation.

Thomas' attitude was doubtless also influenced by his perfectly sincere opposition to any brusque dissolution of the Workshops. The director's attitude was later made clear in his refusal to execute the government's radical dissolution program of May 24, a refusal which resulted in his removal from office. In his first interview with Thomas, on May 12, Trélat insisted that the Workshops must be dissolved as quickly as possible.[120] Thomas' unalterable opposition to such a policy may well have rendered him willing to see the workers enter the demonstration in considerable numbers, in order (by means of a veiled threat) to allow both the Executive Commission and the assembly to perceive the strength of the Workshops and more especially of their leader, in the hope that such a display of force might discourage any precipitate solution of the problem. There were those who believed the director capable of such a policy.[121] Thomas was fortified by a strong sense of his own power,[122] and influenced by a rapidly mounting disgust with what he considered the dilatory and ineffective policy of the government.

*   *   *   *   *

Thomas' negligence on May 15 suggests the complementary problem of the government's policy. Did the failure of the latter to send the director instructions reflect merely a loss of

---

[120] Thomas, p. 263; for the date, see the statement of Trélat before the assembly, May 29 (*Moniteur*, May 30).

[121] See, e.g., Garnier-Pagès, X, p. 114.

[122] Thomas, p. 252 and *passim*. " Et si mécontent que je puisse être d'un état de choses gouvernemental, quand je n'aurais qu'à lever la main pour l'anéantir ainsi, je ne le ferais pas; . . ." Cf. Trélat's statement (*Commission d'enquête*, I, p. 355): " Je dirai un mot d'une affaire grave pour moi; je parle du départ d'Émile Thomas. Je lui dit où il devait aller: ' Ah! celà ne serait pas arrivé, s'écria-t-il, si j'avais accepté les propositions de Louis Blanc.' Lesquelles? lui dis-je. Si elles étaient mauvaises, vous avez bien fait. Je ne sais si j'ai eu raison, repondit-il. J'avais une armée de cent mille hommes. Si elle avait agi, les choses aurait peut-être tourné autrement au 15 mai." This statement was alleged to have been made to Trélat on the evening of May 26, when Thomas was removed from office. Cf. the statement of Boulage, who was present (*Commission d'enquête*, I, p. 242).

confidence in Thomas, or was it by chance part of a precon-certed plan to discredit the whole institution, which the govern-ment had already determined to destroy? Events of the days both before and after May 15 reveal that the director no longer possessed the government's confidence, while they strongly suggest that the government may have sought to discredit the Workshops.

The Executive Commission had already embarked upon a program looking to the dissolution of the Workshops. May 13, on a motion of Garnier-Pagès, it was decided that enrollments were to come to an end, that unmarried workers eighteen to twenty-five years of age were to be invited to enlist in the army, and that those refusing to enlist were to be dismissed from the Workshops and returned to their homes.[123] This decision, apparently known only to the government, indicates clearly that it was prepared to proceed with radical measures *prior* to the events of May 15.[124] The members of the Execu-tive Commission had always viewed the Workshops as a tem-porary measure.[125] The severe drain on the treasury and the potential danger to the cause of order made it evident to them now that prompt action was necessary.[126] Moreover, with the elections past, the political usefulness of the Workshops was at an end.[127]

The government knew that its program would incur serious opposition and began preparations in case the final settlement should involve the use of force.[128] The government also knew, at least after Trélat's initial conference with Thomas, May 12,

---

[123] *Commission d'enquête*, II, p. 161. The provision returning workers to their homes had, by May 15, been changed to read that those refusing enlistment were to be dismissed (Caussidière, II, p. 124).

[124] Cf. Garnier-Pagès, IX, p. 80.

[125] Cherest, pp. 177-178; Lamartine: *Révolution de 1848*, II, pp. 342-344; Gar-nier-Pagès' account can leave no doubt that he held the same view, as did also Arago. Ledru-Rollin interested himself but little in the question.

[126] Lamartine: *op. cit.*, II, p. 343.

[127] Renard: *République de 1848*, p. 63.

[128] Lamartine: *Révolution de 1848*, II, pp. 343-344.

that this opposition would include Thomas.[129] Just how far
the Executive Commission believed the director's opposition
would go is not clear, but Garnier-Pagès says that it was feared
that he might cause an insurrection among the workers.[130] It
is not difficult, therefore, to understand why the government
had lost confidence in Thomas, and may have considered it
useless to rely upon him in this crisis.[131]

Beyond this lies the more difficult question of whether the
Executive Commission actually *planned* to discredit the Workshops. It is obvious that if the Workshops could be associated
in the public mind with the radical revolutionaries, the government would win adherents for its dissolution plans. The fact is
that this is precisely what happened: the events of May 15
were followed by a concerted attack upon the institution by
the government, by large elements of the press, and subsequently by the assembly.[132] Moreover, the government's actions during the day of May 15 also point in the direction of a
conscious policy aiming to discredit the Workshops.

The Executive Commission met at eight o'clock on the morning of May 15. Reports of the growing demonstration reached
the government uninterruptedly.[133] It is certain that its members knew of the large participation of the Workshops, ren-

---

[129] Thomas, p. 263 and *passim*.

[130] Garnier-Pagès, X, p. 114. The statement was made, however, in justification of Thomas' arbitrary removal from office. Cf. Cherest, p. 230, note 1.

[131] If this hypothesis is not adopted, it is difficult to explain why orders were
not sent Thomas to prevent the Workshops from joining the demonstration.
There is no question but that the government was alarmed at the prospect of the
demonstration; the military and other preparations of May 14 indicate that
clearly (*Commission d'enquête*, II, pp. 39-40; Seignobos: " Procès-verbaux du
Gouvernement provisoire," *Revue d'histoire moderne et contemporaine*, VII, p.
595; cf. Lamartine: *Révolution de 1848*, II, p. 313).

[132] See, e.g., *Journal des Débats*, May 18; *Constitutionnel*, May 25, 26; *Lampion*, May 28; and the answer to the " reaction " in the *Réforme*, May 20.

[133] Garnier-Pagès, IX, pp. 147-148. In the face of the statements of Garnier-
Pagès and the fact that the participation of the Workshops was notorious, the
report of the Executive Commission on the events of May 15 (published in the
Univers, June 1, and elsewhere) is lacking in frankness. The only reference to
the Workshops is the following: " Les ateliers nationaux sont sur leurs chantiers
et ils travaillent." (The latter is part of a report on the Bastille gathering).

dered notorious by their banners. Before two o'clock the Executive Commission had learned of the invasion of the assembly and had ordered the *rappel* to be beaten. At this point an order signed by Garnier-Pagès and Arago was despatched to the minister of the interior directing him to *execute immediately* the decision of May 13 respecting enlistments in the army for those of eighteen to twenty-five and the dismissal of those refusing to enlist! [134] Such precipitation in the execution of so radical a measure certainly implies that the government was merely awaiting a favorable opportunity. The opportunity presented was none other than the participation of the Workshops in the demonstration, already seriously compromised by its unfortunate invasion of the assembly. Without waiting to determine the *character* of this participation, without so much as consulting Thomas regarding the measures contemplated, the government launched its order. Such a situation cannot be made to demonstrate conclusively that the Executive Commission had *planned* to discredit the Workshops, although it certainly suggests it. But it does reveal that the government was determined to proceed with a radical dissolution policy; that it distrusted Thomas, feared his opposition, and was ready to act without his knowledge or coöperation; and that it was prepared to seize the first situation unfavorable to the Workshops as a pretext for the execution of its initial dissolution measures.[135]

[134] Caussidière, II, pp. 123-124; Garnier-Pagès, IX, p. 287, cf. IX, p. 153.

[135] Garnier-Pagès' defence of the government's hasty action is very lame and neglects to mention that the units of the Workshops left the procession before the invasion of the assembly (Garnier-Pagès, IX, pp. 286-287).

CHAPTER V

TOWARD DISSOLUTION

I. The Government Undertakes Dissolution: Trélat's Committee; Dismissal of Thomas; Disaffection of the Workshops. II. Assembly's Law of May 30; *volte face* of the Government; the Problem of a Census. III. The Assembly Takes the Helm; the Approaching Storm.

THE attack upon the assembly on May 15 discredited the radical cause and seriously damaged the prestige of the Executive Commission. Henceforth the government occupied an unenviable position from which it was subject to assault from two directions. Where previously the radicals had denounced its perfidy toward the *révolution démocratique et sociale,* a chorus of indignation now arose from the right: not only had the government failed to protect the assembly, but it had subsequently shown far too great leniency in its attitude toward the elements which had provoked the rising.[1] Meanwhile the government's moderate support progressively weakened as the conviction grew that its policy was vacillating and inconsequent. In a situation where a policy at once strong and consistent might have triumphed over the really tremendous obstacles facing the Executive Commission, its acts were now precipitate and now dilatory — and invariably inadequate to the difficulties presented. This weakness is notably evident in the case of the National Workshops, the problem which dominated the period separating the events of May 15 from the insurrection in June. For it was on the

---

[1] See, e.g., Barrot: *Mémoires,* II, pp. 206 ff.; A. Quentin-Bauchart: *Études et souvenirs sur la deuxième République et le second Empire (1848-1870). Mémoires posthumes publiés par son fils* (Paris, 1901-1902, 2 vols.), I, pp. 17-18; the results of the attacks of the right can be judged from a bitter attack on Charles Dupin, for his speech of May 16 denouncing " les ouvriers qui ne sont pas de bon Paris " (*Père Duchêne,* May 23-25). See also E. V. S. P., Maréchal, Comte de Castellane: *Journal du maréchal de Castellane, 1804-1862* (Paris, 1895-1897, 5 vols.), IV, p. 68.

question of the National Workshops that the government eventually foundered.

Despite the fact that the Workshops had hitherto been an instrument of the moderates used to combat the radicals, it is none the less true that the organization was widely associated in the public mind with the rising of May 15. The innocuous character of the workers' participation was unknown or disregarded. The bourgeoisie recoiled in horror before a proletariat which could so readily lend itself to acts of violence. The mere presence of an army of 100,000 idle workers in Paris constituted an intolerable menace.[2] That an early solution for the Workshops' problem was essential, both government and assembly agreed. Conflicts between the two arose, not from a difference of opinion as to the desirability of dissolution, but from opposing views as to the means to be employed and the speed with which the transformation should be accomplished. The complexities of the problem may be somewhat simplified by considering successively three phases, more or less well defined, through which the question passed. During the first, from May 15 to about May 24, the Executive Commission accelerated its plans, already defined, for a radical solution of the problem. The second, from May 24 to June 14, was marked by the adoption of the assembly's dissolution plan of May 30, by the growing disaffection of the workers, and by a brusque *volte face* by the government, now apparently alarmed by the dangers of precipitation. In the third, June 14 to June 22, the assembly, wearied by the dilatory tactics of the government in the execution of its laws of May 30, brought the Workshops' problem effectively under its own control through the appointment of a special committee, and pronounced its adherence to the policy of immediate dissolution.

I

The precipitate action of the government on May 15, ordering the minister of the interior to execute at once its decree on

[2] Barrot: *Mémoires,* II, p. 234; *Journal des travaux publics,* May 18 and May 21.

enforced enlistments, was without result.[3] It is significant that this decision, as well as the radical measures which followed, were shrouded in the most profound secrecy. Neither the assembly nor the public had any precise notion as to what the government planned to do until the end of the month, when the government's plans had already been superseded by the assembly's law of May 30.[4] Had the character of the government's plans become known to the workers at once and had they received immediate execution, the June insurrection would probably have been precipitated some weeks earlier.

The government had determined then, prior to May 15, that the Workshops must go. The events of that day merely strengthened its determination to act promptly. Orders were given for the immediate cessation of enrollments, May 17,[5] and the same day witnessed the creation of an extra-parliamentary committee of " experts " to examine the whole question of the Workshops and to advise the government in the matter of their dissolution.[6] The committee was appointed upon the proposal of Trélat, who had only a few days previously succeeded to the difficult portfolio which Marie relinquished upon his election to the Executive Commission.

[3] Orders were given by the minister of the interior to the mayors of Paris in this connection (*Arch. de la Seine. Mairies* O²ᵇ, no. 4594), but obviously they remained unexecuted. Marie later stated that it had proved impracticable to induce the workers to enlist, but he does not say why those refusing were not dismissed (*Archives nationales*, C 928. "Minutes sténographiques provenant du Comité du travail . . ." [see bibliography for full title], May 27. Hereafter cited as *Arch. nat. c 928, Min. sténog. du com. du travail*).

[4] See, e.g., the *Liberté*, which as late as May 30, declared: " On assure que le Gouvernement a formé le projet de donner une nouvelle organisation aux ateliers nationaux."

[5] *Commission d'enquête*, II, p. 161. The mayor of Paris gave prompt orders in this connection (*Arch. de la Seine. Mairies* O²ᵇ, no. 4593). Difficulties at once arose (letter of Adam to Pagnerre, May 18, *Archives nationales* BB³⁰, 312, *liasse* 1). The attempt to stop enrollments was never completely successful: 3,100 were enrolled, May 16 to May 31, and 1,200, June 1 to June 15. Yet these figures are to be compared with those of the previous month: 34,530, April 16-30, and 13,610, May 1-15 (Lalanne: " Lettres sur les Ateliers nationaux. I," *National*, June 14, 1848).

[6] *Commission d'enquête*, II, p. 161; Lalanne: " Lettres sur les Ateliers nationaux. I," *National*, July 14, 1848.

The selection of Trélat, physician, philanthropist, head of the Salpêtrière institution for the indigent and feeble-minded, was an obvious reward for long service to the republican cause. His republican activities had even won him a prison sentence under the July Monarchy; moreover, the sincerity of his sympathies for the plight of the workers appears to have been unquestioned. But, as minister of public works in a crisis demanding abilities of a high order, Trélat was seriously handicapped by a lack of experience of public affairs.[7] His policies constantly reflected irresolution and an unhappy inability to see and accept the realities in a situation. It should be said in Trélat's favor, however, that his vacillation was no more serious than that of the government. In the beginning he shared the Executive Commission's view that the Workshops should be dissolved as expeditiously as possible.[8] The appointment of the extra-parliamentary committee of experts was part of this program.

The precipitation which characterized both the appointment of this commission and the execution of its allotted task reflects the spirit in which the government attacked the whole Workshops' problem.

The members chosen — three government engineers and four " civil engineers " [9] — were first summoned to meet at noon, May 18. In the course of this session, which lasted until six-thirty o'clock in the evening, the committee interviewed Émile Thomas and Boulage, who continued to fulfill under Trélat the functions of *secrétaire général* of the ministry of public works. Unfortunately both were called away to other engagements, with the result that Boulage was questioned for two hours, Thomas for only half an hour. On the basis of this

---

[7] Stern, II, p. 233; *Dictionnaire des parlementaires français*, V, pp. 442-443; cf. the prejudiced but interesting appreciations of F. A. P., Vicomte de Falloux: *Mémoires d'un royaliste* (Paris, 1888, 2 vols.), I, pp. 329-330; Tocqueville: *Souvenirs*, p. 187; and Blanc: *Révolution de 1848*, II, pp. 133-134.

[8] Thomas, p. 263.

[9] The term used to designate those not forming part of the government corps and engaged in the private practice of their profession.

meagre investigation a report, which subsequently occupied twenty-four printed pages, was drafted in the course of the night and submitted to the committee at eight o'clock the following morning.[10]   Certain changes were made, and at four o'clock in the afternoon the completed report was placed in the hands of Trélat, who immediately authorized its printing.   At two o'clock on the following afternoon, May 20, 1,200 copies of the report were delivered to the minister.[11]   It has seemed important to insist upon the details of the preparation of the report — especially upon its superficial character — for it was on the basis of this document that the government proposed to undertake the dissolution of the Workshops!   It should be said in defence of the committee, however, that the speed with which the report was prepared doubtless reflected the government's orders.

In its printed form the report was to have been distributed at once to the members of the assembly.[12]   But at this point it mysteriously disappeared, obviously suppressed by the government, but for what reasons only conjectures could be offered at the time.   Léon Lalanne, the committee's secretary, later declared that the report had been destroyed, only a few copies escaping.[13]   In any event it had not been seen from that day to

[10] No attempt was made by the committee to familiarize itself with the functioning of the institution by an investigation *on the ground* of its administration. No attempt was made to obtain the views of workers themselves, although the June Days were a protest in part against certain of the measures proposed. No attempt was made to determine whether adequate finances existed for the execution of the committee's proposals, which would have entailed extensive outlays.

[11] On the preparation of the report, see Lalanne: " Lettres sur les Ateliers nationaux. I," *National*, July 14, 1848; and the *Rapport fait au nom de la Commission instituée par décision ministérielle du 17 mai 1848 pour l'examen de diverses questions relatives aux Ateliers nationaux* (Paris, 1848), pp. 5 ff. (hereafter cited as *Rapport de la Commission du 17 mai 1848*).

[12] Lalanne: *loc. cit.*

[13] L. Lalanne: *Rectification historique sur les Ateliers nationaux* (Paris, 1887), p. 4. Lalanne defends the moderation of the committee: " Ces voeux [of the report] . . . n'étaient dictés que par un amour sincère pour la classe laborieuse . . . ; ils étaient émis, à l'unanimité, par une réunion d'hommes expérimentés et rompus à la pratique des travaux: MM. Mary, inspecteur général des ponts et chaussées; Reynaud, le célèbre directeur des phares; Flachat, Faure, Grouvelle,

this.[14] As a matter of fact, however, a single copy had found its way into the *Bibliothèque nationale,* sometime between the founding of the Third Republic and the year 1879, but its entry in a supplementary volume of the *Catalogue de l'histoire de France* had remained unnoticed until the writer found it there recently.[15]

Why was the report suppressed? The document itself permits us to draw certain further inferences which offer reasonable certitude. In the first place, it may be noted that it was *accepted* by Trélat[16] and subsequently *rejected* by the Execu-

Polonceau, ingénieurs civils d'une rare distinction et nullement suspects d'esprit révolutionnaire" (*ibid.,* pp. 3-4).

[14] Kept secret at that time, " il l'est demeuré jusqu'à nos jours," notes Georges Renard, " si bien que nous sommes réduits à des conjectures sur sa terreur mystérieuse" (*République de 1848,* p. 65). In October, 1929, Renard again mentioned the report to the writer as worthy of search.

[15] Actually the title was first noticed under Lalanne's name in the *Catalogue général des livres imprimés de la Bibliothèque nationale. Auteurs,* Vol. LXXXVI, p. 901. The latter was published only in 1925. The report was traced thence to the *Catalogue de l'histoire de France,* Vol. XI (*Supplément*) (1879), p. 344. The report bears the stamp " RF." Since it does not appear in the *Catalogue de l'histoire de France,* Vol. IV (1857), which lists all books received up until that time, the stamp refers, not to the Second, but to the Third Republic. Hence it was received some time between September 4, 1870 and the publication, in 1879, of Volume XI of the *Catalogue.* Possibly Lalanne gave the *Bibliothèque nationale* a copy. The reasons for its suppression had long since disappeared. We know that he had at least one copy in July, 1848, from which he produced a *résumé* and a long quotation in his letters to the *National* (see numbers for July 14, 15, and 19). He still had a copy at the time of the debates on the combination laws in 1884, for he read a section of the report before the Senate, January 18, 1884 (*Journal officiel. Sénat. Débats parlementaires,* 1884, Vol. I, pp. 34-35). Curiously enough Lalanne on this occasion attributed the work of the commission to the initiative of the assembly: " . . . je vous demande la permission de vous lire quelques lignes, quelques pages si vous voulez d'un écrit qui fut ordonné par l'Assemblée nationale de 1848 et que, malgré son sincère désir de pacification, elle n'a pas eu le courage de publier " (cf. Lalanne's statement, made just after the events, attributing correctly the intiative to the government [" Lettres sur les Ateliers nationaux. I," *National,* July 14, 1848]).

[16] Proudhon: *Confessions d'un révolutionnaire,* p. 122; Lalanne: " Lettres sur les Ateliers nationaux. I," *National,* July 14, 1848; cf. statement of Trélat before the assembly, May 20 (*Moniteur,* May 21). Differences between the policy favored by Trélat and the decisions of the Executive Commission will be noted consistently in the succeeding weeks.

tive Commission.[17] By the latter it was *not* suppressed by reason of its superficial character, for a number of its suggestions were promptly adopted by the government and made part of its dissolution program. In execution of the latter, Trélat, on May 24, sent instructions to Émile Thomas, prescribing drastic measures for the dissolution of the Workshops. Four of the five measures were taken, in substance at least, from the report of the special committee: (1) A census of the workers was to be taken at once; those resident in Paris less than six months, prior to May 24, were to be dismissed.[18] (2) Workers refusing to accept employment in private industry, when offered, were likewise to be dismissed. (3) Workers' units were to be formed, on a semi-military basis, and directed to public works' projects in the provinces. (4) Piece-work was to be substituted for work by the day for those workers who should remain, during a transition period, in the National Workshops of Paris.[19]

It was believed at the time in certain quarters that the government's action reflected particularly its dissatisfaction with the formal recognition of the "right to work."[20] And it is true that the report not only recognized the "right to work" as a general principle,[21] but urged its extension to include adequate provision, in the form of state aid, for the care of those unable to avail themselves of the state's offer of work (the aged, the sick, orphans, *et al.*).[22] It is highly probable that the Executive Commission had no desire to prejudice its position with the assembly, a large number of whose members were

[17] Cf. Marie's statement before the Labor Committee of the assembly, May 27, 1848 (*Arch. nat.* C 928, *Min. sténog. du Com. du travail*).

[18] The report was more severe in this connection than the government's instructions, the former requiring six months' domicile in Paris prior to February 24.

[19] Thomas, pp. 271-273.

[20] See, e.g., Blanc: *Révolution de 1848*, II, p. 132; Proudhon: *Confessions d'un révolutionnaire*, pp. 122-123. The latter declares that he was informed on this point by Lalanne himself. On the other hand Lalanne denied that he knew the motives of the government (" Lettres sur les Ateliers nationaux. I," *National*, July 14, 1848).

[21] *Rapport de la Commission du 17 mai 1848*, p. 13.

[22] *Ibid.*, pp. 23-24.

known to be very hostile to the " right to work." [23] What reason was there to precipitate a debate on an abstract principle, with which the Executive Commission itself was not sympathetic? The government's prime interest lay in the preparation of an efficacious plan for dissolution. It were better to let sleeping dogs lie.

The report suggests other reasons also for its suppression. It envisaged indeed the dissolution of the Workshops, but it provided also for the concurrent revival of business and the extensive development of public works. Among these " mesures réparatrices " were loans to private industry for the payment of wages, orders by the state to idle industry, absorption of the unemployed belonging to the building trades in such projects as the completion of the Rue de Rivoli and the building of *Halles centrales* (with extensive indemnities of course for those whose property was affected), the provision of drawbacks for exporters during a limited period, and so on.[24] With certain of these ideas the government was sympathetic, but the immediate problem was the dissolution of the Workshops, and the Executive Commission was doubtless impatient of the delays which would have been imposed by the endorsement of the committee's elaborate project *as a whole*. The distribution of the report to the assembly would have implied the approbation by the government of the measures which it proposed. Furthermore, the vast expenditures which the plan envisaged doubtless met opposition, especially from Garnier-Pagès, who, having held the portfolio of finance under the Provisional Gov-

---

[23] Marie's statement to the Labor Committee, May 27, may very well reflect this sentiment (*Arch. nat.* C 928, *Min. sténog. du Com. du travail*):

" Voici le rapport de la Com. dont je vous ai parlé. Ce rapport est de 24 pages fort detaillées que votre Com. appréciera. Je ne présente pas encore un travail définitif, mais jusqu'à présent un travail d'aperçu. Il ne vous a pas encore été distribué quoique imprimé depuis q.-q. jours parce qu'il y a là q.-q. passages sur lequels [sic] nous voulions que l'on n'insistât pas: c'était une proposition faite qui selon nous ne devait pas être acceptée. . . . " It is to be noted that Marie speaks of " une proposition " — was it that touching the " right to work " ?

[24] *Rapport de la Commission du 17 mai 1848*, pp. 15 ff.

ernment, was well aware of the financial insufficiencies of the young Republic.

In the latter connection there should be noted particularly the extraordinary proposal to erect an enormous " people's Colosseum " opposite the Champ-de-Mar and on the site where Napoleon had projected a vast palace for his son, the King of Rome. The hill in question, which commands the Seine, is now occupied by the *Palais du Trocadéro*. This huge structure, which was to seat between 100,000 and 120,000 persons, was to provide a suitable *locus* for the " grandes fêtes " so necessary to a " democratic republic." It was to follow the general lines of the Roman Colosseum, with the exception that it was to be covered.[25]

This proposal must have appeared somewhat fantastic to the government, and would have appeared even more so to the assembly. Lalanne himself omitted all mention of it in his letters to the *National*, which include a *résumé* of the report. The expense of the structure would have been great, its utility dubious. A large part of the assembly, in whose memories the events of May 15 were only too fresh, had no desire to furnish any further occasion for " grandes fêtes républicaines." Moreover, the strongly republican flavor of the language of the report would scarcely have recommended the project to a majority of the deputies:

> Thanks to its position, this edifice would dominate all Paris and would worthily proclaim the capital from a distance. The towns of the middle ages stood beneath the Aegis of their great cathedrals, symbols of their religious faith; our monument will be the symbol of the right of meeting, of the majesty of the people, and of the dignity of labor.[26]

It is clear, then, that there were any number of reasons why the government was unwilling to have the report distributed to the assembly. It preferred instead to extract certain of the ideas which the report contained, and to frame from them a concrete program, susceptible of rapid execution. If this program could

---

[25] *Rapport de la Commission du 17 mai 1848*, pp. 17-18.
[26] *Rapport de la Commission du 17 mai 1848*, p. 18.

be carried into effect immediately, the problem of the dissolution of the Workshops would remain in the hands of the government. A successful issue to the whole question would go far to reëstablish its shaken prestige.

*   *   *   *   *

Simultaneously with the appointment of the committee of experts, Trélat appeared before the assembly, May 17, to make the first statement of governmental policy toward the Workshops. A sympathetic reception awaited the frank pronouncement of the minister in favor of dissolution. The Workshops were a "temporary organization," declared Trélat. The workers were receiving "disguised charity" for the execution of "useless projects"; the organization "must be made an end of as quickly as possible," and no one desired the accomplishment of this more than the government. Trélat tempered the severity of his remarks with a plea for funds for the inevitable *period of transition*.[27] None the less it seemed apparent to the assembly that the government had set for itself an unequivocal course. In the same session Duclerc, minister of finance, introduced a measure for the repurchase of the railroads by the state, essential element in the government's dissolution plan, which envisaged sending large numbers of workers from Paris to railroad projects in the provinces, where the necessary National Workshops were to be organized.[28]

Actually the government was preparing to adopt much more specific measures than it was yet ready to share with the assembly. For presently the unexecuted order of May 15, providing for obligatory enlistments of young, unmarried workers, was revived. To it were added a series of measures inspired by the suppressed report of Trélat's committee of experts. And the whole formed the subject of peremptory instructions from the minister to Émile Thomas on May 24. The instructions prescribed drastic measures for the dissolution of the Workshops:

[27] *Moniteur,* May 18.
[28] *Ibid.,* May 18; Garnier-Pagès, IX, p. 318.

(1) Unmarried workers, eighteen to twenty-five years of age, were to be given the option of enlistment in the army or dismissal from the Workshops.[29]

(2) A census of the workers was to be taken at once. Those resident in Paris less than six months prior to May 24, were to be dismissed.

(3) From lists provided in a placement bureau employers might require whatever number of workmen they needed. Those refusing to accept such offers were to be dismissed.

(4) Those who remained temporarily (*transitoirement*) members of the Workshops were to be paid on a piece-work basis.

(5) Workers' units were to be organized and sent to the departments, there to be employed on public works under the direction of government engineers.[30]

The director of the National Workshops was informed that these sweeping measures were to be executed without delay![31] The radical nature of the instructions becomes more apparent when they are analyzed. One group of workers was faced with unemployment, perhaps starvation, or an uncongenial enlistment in the army. Those without Paris domicile were to be thrust out on the street provided only with the scant means of returning to their homes in the provinces but without any assurance of work when they arrived. Those with legitimate Paris domicile might be subjected to the caprices of employers virtually empowered to fix wages.[32] The workers who remained "temporarily" members of the Workshops were to be paid on a piece-work basis; the hardship that this measure would work is apparent when it is remembered that a considerable proportion of the workers came from crafts which little fitted them

[29] But they were to be given a transportation allowance with which to return to their homes, according to the *procès-verbal* of the Executive Commission (*Commission d'enquête*, II, p. 161).

[30] The government's instructions to Thomas were sent in a letter signed by Boulage (Thomas, pp. 271-273; also published in *Journal des Débats*, May 30, and elsewhere). The *procès-verbal* of the government curiously makes no mention of Provision 1 (*Commission d'enquête*, II, pp. 161-162), although it is certain that it formed part of the instructions.

[31] Boulage warned Thomas " que cette mesure est d'une urgence extrême, et qu'il ne faut pas perdre un seul instant pour l'exécuter " (Thomas, p. 273).

[32] The obvious tendency to pay low wages under these conditions and even to dismiss higher paid workmen in favor of those newly employed from the National Workshops, needs no comment.

for the rigors of manual labor (e.g., the jewellers and "luxury" groups generally, hard hit by the financial crisis). Finally, another group was faced with the prospect of deportation from Paris to distant projects in the provinces.

The instructions to Thomas are characteristic of the government's fitful policy, now energetic, now vacillating. It is very likely, however, that Trélat saw also in these instructions a means of driving Thomas into the open and of preparing the way for his dismissal, which followed two days later. Unquestionably the director had recently become a very serious problem for the government. He had frequently been a source of embarrassment to Marie by reason of his independence and his tenacious tendency to give advice. The substantial participation of the Workshops in the demonstration of May 15 doubtless shook the government's faith in his ability to control the workers, if it did not actually cause them to suspect the director's good faith. Garnier-Pagès believed Thomas quite capable of using his influence with the workers to oppose the government by force, if occasion should arise.[33] The Executive Commission, moreover, had no desire to see Thomas elected to the assembly, and the director admits that he hoped for success in the by-elections of June 4 and planned to oppose the government's Workshops' policy.[34] It was also believed that Thomas was acting in the interests of the candidacy of Louis Napo-

[33] Garnier-Pagès, X, p. 114; see also his statement to the Commission d'enquête (I, p. 285), and the statements of Trélat (ibid., I, pp. 355-356) and Trouvé-Chauvel (ibid., II, p. 316), and cf. Thomas, p. 252. Thomas of course denies that he had any such intentions (ibid., pp. 322-323).

[34] Thomas, pp. 324-325. Thomas denies that he intended to abuse his influence as director: he planned to resign, if elected to the assembly. Both Recurt and Adam encouraged him in his ambitions, he declares. This fact and others indicate that the latter were not in sympathy with the government's dissolution program (ibid., pp. 263, 274). Thomas' candidacy was supported by the Liberté, which included his name on its list of recommended candidates (May 31); Thomas' declaration of political faith also appeared in the Liberté (June 1), and is reprinted in the director's apologia (pp. 385-387). See further the support of his candidacy by the Workshops (ibid., pp. 381 ff.). Arago later accused Thomas of augmenting the numbers in the Workshops in the interest of additional electoral support (Commission d'enquête, I, pp. 228-229).

leon.[35] But, above all, the government's attitude toward Thomas reflected the director's determined opposition to the official plans for the immediate dissolution of the Workshops.[36] Thomas had opposed Trélat's plans from the beginning. In his first interview with the minister, the director had raised serious objection to Trélat's view that dissolution was urgent and that a census of the workers was, therefore, essential.[37] Thomas of course suspected that strong measures were preparing, and, if we are to give his story full credence, he finally determined to forestall the government by a bold *coup*. When, on May 22, Thomas was summoned before the Labor Committee of the assembly to inform its members of the situation in the National Workshops, he threw a bombshell into the meeting. The anarchic condition of the Workshops, he declared, was due to the lack of unity of control from above. Unity could be achieved by transferring the control of the Workshops to a *special committee of the assembly*, given for that purpose "une sorte de dictature"! The director would then become merely the "responsible agent" of the committee. Trélat was among those present. Naturally the minister was by no means flattered or reassured when his subordinate suggested that the Workshops be removed from his control.[38] Indeed the minister had had ample opportunity to observe the director's growing spirit of opposition; his latest act amounted virtually to a declaration of war upon the government. It was scarcely to be expected that Trélat could tolerate such insubordination.[39] Apparently there remained merely the question

[35] A. Lebey: *Louis-Napoléon Bonaparte et la Révolution de 1848* (Paris, 1907-1908, 2 vols.), I, p. 306. Lebey doubts that this was a reason: Trélat, Garnier-Pagès, the exiles of December 2 would have said so later (see below, p. 125).

[36] Cherest, p. 230, note 1; Thomas, pp. 262 ff. and *passim*; letter of Thomas to his mother, May 27 (*Vraie République*, May 30).

[37] Thomas, pp. 263-264; Trélat's statement to the assembly, May 29 (*Moniteur*, May 30).

[38] Thomas (pp. 268-271) is the sole source for Thomas' coup. The *procès-verbaux* of the Labor Committee make no mention of Thomas' startling suggestion.

[39] Thomas frankly admits (p. 330) that he refused to take responsibility for the government's orders of May 24, by reason of their provocative character. There

of how the dismissal of Thomas could be accomplished with the least possible disturbance.

When Thomas received Trélat's radical instructions regarding the dissolution of the Workshops, he objected strenuously that the measures were utterly inconsistent with the " guarantee of work " and that their execution would imperil public order. Although the minister appeared convinced and yielded a delay of twenty-four hours,[40] he had obviously decided to make an end of Thomas' influence. For on the next day the director was advised of the appointment of a " National Workshops' Commission," subject to which Thomas and his associates were to act merely as subordinate agents.[41] Faced even with these humiliating conditions, Thomas did not resign.[42] Finally, on May 26, Trélat took his troubles to Garnier-Pagès. The latter's self-confidence was quite equal to the occasion. Of his own volition he authorized Trélat to request Thomas' resignation, and, if it were not forthcoming, to dismiss him.[43] Trélat promptly despatched a note to Thomas summoning the director to his office at nine o'clock the same evening.[44]

The dramatic interview between Thomas and Trélat[45] is described by Alexandre Dumas, who subsequently came to the defence of the director in a series of articles for whose accuracy

is every reason to believe that he was alarmed at the government's precipitation; he was advised by Desfossés, one of his *inspecteurs de travaux,* that the article on enforced military enlistments alone was sufficient " pour bouleverser tout Paris " (*ibid.,* p. 362).

[40] Thomas, p. 273. Thomas also consulted Recurt, whom he quotes as saying: " ' Mais ce n'est pas possible, c'est de l'aberration, c'est l'insurrection pour demain ! ' " (*ibid.,* p. 274).

[41] *Ibid.,* pp. 280-282; Lalanne: " Lettres sur les Ateliers nationaux. IV," *National,* July 23, 1848. The new commission was the product of the enlargement of Trélat's earlier extra-parliamentary committee.

[42] Thomas, pp. 283-285.

[43] *Commission d'enquête,* I, p. 356; Garnier-Pagès, X, p. 114; and statement of Trélat before the assembly's Committee of Public Works, July 15 (*Archives nationales.* C 928. *Comité des travaux publics. Minutes des séances,* pp. 37-39).

[44] Thomas relates (p. 285) that Trélat, on May 26, after inspecting the Monceau administration *for the first time,* had congratulated him upon his work and warmly thanked him for his promised coöperation in the problem of dissolution.

[45] Boulage, *secrétaire général* of the Ministry of Public Works, was also present.

Thomas vouches.[46] The director arrived promptly at nine. The
minister was seated at his desk. Without rising, he motioned
Thomas to a chair. "Monsieur Thomas," he said, "we ask your
resignation."[47] On what grounds was he being dismissed?
Thomas asked. No reason could be given, Trélat replied.
Thomas declares that he offered to give, in his resignation, as
motives for his withdrawal, his unwillingness to assume responsibility for the acts of the commission which had just been given
control of the Workshops. He would thus save Trélat from
an embarrassing situation. He was thanked and quickly penned
his resignation.[48]

Thomas then offered to assist with the installation of his
successor, but was told that he was to leave at once for Bordeaux on a mission for the government.[49] He protested that
he had no fitness for the task assigned him, which he viewed as
a mere pretext for his exile from Paris. Trélat was unyielding;
he must go *at once*. Thomas asked twenty-four hours respite
in which to arrange his affairs; his request was peremptorily
refused. He asked permission to take leave of his mother; he
was again refused. The director's further objections were swept
aside. A *commissaire de police* was introduced, and Thomas
was quickly escorted to a waiting carriage, in which he found
himself accompanied by two police officers. The minister's
final instructions were that the officers should show every con-

[46] Published in *La France nouvelle* in a *supplément,* which follows the number
for June 9, 1848, and in the numbers for June 18, 20, 23; reproduced by Thomas
(pp. 286 ff.); also separately published under Dumas' name: *Révélations sur
l'arrestation d'Émile Thomas . . . suivi de pièces justificatives* (Paris, 1848).

[47] Trélat's initial statements that Thomas had resigned and accepted the " mission " *voluntarily* yielded subsequently to a frank admission that the act had
been arbitrary (*Moniteur,* June 15, 1848).

[48] Dumas' account is of course very much to the credit of Thomas. Its outlines, however, have not been contradicted.

[49] Nominally he was to study the question of the prolongation of the *Canal des
Landes* from La Teste de Buch to Bayonne. Trélat also suggested that Paris was
not a safe place for Thomas at the moment (Thomas, pp. 289-290). In answering Taschereau's interpellation in the assembly, May 29, Trélat made it appear
that Thomas had constantly complained of the dangers he was running in Paris
(*Moniteur,* May 30).

sideration to the prisoner. " By the Chartres Road," Trélat called. And the carriage rolled off into the night.

The minister's purpose was clear: Thomas was to be made the victim of a veritable *lettre de cachet*.[50] The prisoner established amicable relations with his guards and was permitted to write his mother from Versailles and Chartres. But the minister's little comedy took an unexpected turn when both the prisoner and his guards were arrested outside Bordeaux. When they protested, they were shown a telegraphic order from the minister. They were later released from the *gendarmerie* at Bordeaux by an embarrassed official, who had just received a second telegraphic order with instructions to view the first as *non avenu*. Thomas was then asked to present himself to the *commissaire* of the Department of the Gironde [51] and, after refusing the " mission " upon which the minister had despatched him, was forced to cool his heels in Bordeaux until the by-elections in Paris were over.[52]

[50] Dumas comments:
    " En effet, changez la date: nous sommes au seizième siècle.
    " Changez les noms des individus et le lieu ou la scène se passe: nous sommes à Venise " (Thomas, p. 293).
  [51] The Provisional Government had replaced the prefects of the departments with interim officers, the *commissaires*.
  [52] It appears certain that, in counselling the removal of Thomas, Garnier-Pagès acted without consulting his colleagues of the Executive Commission. The latter learned of his dismissal only the next day when the *commissaire* of the Gironde telegraphed Recurt, minister of the interior, asking explanations of the order to arrest Thomas on his arrival. Recurt at once informed the Executive Commission, which immediately sent the second telegram. The latter, however, through a misunderstanding, was delivered to the *gendarmerie* only after Thomas' arrival. If the Executive Commission, however, was opposed to the removal of Thomas and his detention in Bordeaux, it took no steps to permit him to leave Bordeaux at once and indeed allowed him to be held there until after the elections. It must, therefore, bear the responsibility for the arbitrary act of one of its members. With respect to his candidacy, Thomas claims (pp. 326-327) that the government actually suppressed the votes he received in the sixth arrondissement, where the complete returns showed not one vote for him, although he had evidence that there should have been a considerable number. The fact that Thomas received fewer than 8,130 votes (that was the number received by the last candidate named among those not elected — *Moniteur*, June 10), despite the very considerable agitation in his behalf, lends weight to his assertion. On the whole

The evidence justifies us in concluding that the government had adequate reason to dismiss Thomas, if only because he threatened seriously to impede the execution of its program. But his arbitrary and illegal removal from Paris was a sad commentary on the weakness and inconsequence of the government's policy. There is no adequate reason to believe that Thomas planned to oppose the government's dissolution program with force. Some flurry would doubtless have been occasioned by his dismissal, no matter how temperately it had been accomplished, but his mysterious disappearance and the rumors to which it gave rise caused a violent repercussion in the Workshops, and the beginning of serious disorders in the streets which continued right down to the June Days. Again, if the government sought to remove Thomas to prevent his election to the assembly, the danger was surely inadequate to justify the arbitrary measures employed. The government should have foreseen that Thomas' influence as a deputy would probably be slight in view of the attitude toward the Workshops prevailing among the great majority of the assembly.[53]

In any event the government paid dearly for its intemperate action. When the character of Thomas' removal became generally known, a chorus of disapproval and censure of the government's weakness arose from newspapers of every *nuance*. Even those most critical of the Thomas administration insisted that his removal should have been accomplished in the light of day and not in the manner of the Italian princes of the Renais-

---

question of the responsibility of Garnier-Pagès, et al., see Thomas, p. 321; Dumas, in *La France nouvelle*, June 23, 1848; Garnier-Pagès, X, p. 114; *Commission d'enquête*, I, p. 356.

[53] Upon his return to Paris, Thomas complained formally to both government and assembly, asking an investigation of his whole administration and registering a whole series of protests against the arbitrary action from which he had suffered. Had his humiliating experience come at a time less filled with matter of greater moment, he might well have secured justice. As it was, the June Days intervened, and the authorization for judicial proceedings against the former minister of public works was finally defeated by a small margin in the assembly (Thomas, pp. 307-308, 311-318; for the attacks on Thomas, apropos his extravagance, etc., which the government permitted to appear in the *Moniteur*, see the number for June 4; cf. *Journal des travaux publics*, June 1).

sance.[54] Indeed the government, whose reputation had already sorely suffered, saw its prestige once again seriously compromised.

The great majority of the members of the National Workshops were still loyal to the cause of order on May 15. And in the ten days following, despite the concerted attacks on the institution by newspapers of the right and the menacing declaration of Trélat before the assembly, there was little indication of serious disaffection.[55] It was precisely the unfortunate disappearance of the popular Thomas that precipitated the first serious conflict between government and workers.[56]

Boulage, *chef du cabinet* to the minister of public works, had been present at the famous interview between Thomas and Trélat. Having reassured the director and promised to deliver a letter to his mother,[57] he arrived at Thomas' Monceau home at eleven-thirty o'clock the same evening. Bombarded with questions, Boulage declared that the director had been sent away to protect him against dangers threatening him in Paris, and that in any case Trélat would come on the morrow and give full explanations. When Trélat arrived at Monceau the

[54] See, e.g., the *Univers*, May 30; *France nouvelle*, May 31; *Peuple constituant*, May 30; *République*, May 30, June 2; *Presse*, May 30.

[55] This does not mean that there was *no criticism* of Thomas by the workers. When it was learned that a proposal was contemplated requiring members of the Workshops to accept work at wages fixed by employers, a warm protest was sent to the director by a large group of the delegates (some time between May 23 and 27). The same letter protested against the sending of workers to the provinces until the Constitution should have been completed. The letter terminated with a significant warning: "Nous ne sommes les instruments de personne; notre droit de citoyen nous garantit notre pleine et entière indépendance" (*Père Duchêne*, May 28-30). Earlier the same newspaper, which was of course a workers' journal, had published an article accusing Thomas of living in luxury in his château at Monceau (*ibid.*, May 7).

[56] There is ample evidence of Thomas' popularity right up to the time of his removal. See, e.g., letter to the *Liberté*, signed by the Workshops' delegates, May 22 (published May 28); petition of workers to the government, asking the return of Thomas "que nous regardions comme notre père" (*République*, May 29); and the letter of Flachat and Polonceau (Thomas, pp. 302-303).

[57] It said simply: "Chère mère, Je suis forcé de partir pour Bordeaux; ma sécurité personnelle n'est pas en danger: j'espère revenir bientôt. Émile Thomas" (Thomas, p. 292).

following morning, he was faced by an impatient group of between 200 and 300 persons — members of the administration, workers, friends of Thomas. Questions flew; the minister replied that the director had been sent to study *embrigadement* [58] in the Landes. The discussion soon became heated, and one of the assistant directors charged that Thomas had been *forced* to leave Paris. Thereupon the assistant directors resigned as a group. Meanwhile the workers had learned of Thomas' disappearance. Excitement ran high, and the police heard workers threaten that " they had arms . . . and would overthrow the government if it suppressed the National Workshops." [59] The agitation continued in the afternoon, and the attempt to post a proclamation from Trélat to the workers met with determined resistance, fostered by Thomas' assistants. The agent of the Executive Commission, charged with posting the proclamation, reported that a dangerous movement was being organized among the workers by members of the Workshops' administration. [60]

Trélat had been warned in advance of the excited state of feeling prevailing in the Workshops and of the danger he would run in attempting to present explanations before the club of the National Workshops' delegates. The minister's courage was quite equal to the occasion, however, and he was promised the protection of the assistant directors and Boucard, *chef du cabinet*. He had agreed to come on the afternoon of the same day, May 27. That afternoon the minister's exordium made

[58] It is not without interest to note that, whereas Trélat had proposed to Thomas a technical engineering project, the study of canal development, for which he was unfitted, the minister now described Thomas' mission as one dealing with *embrigadement;* i.e., the extension of the National Workshops' system.

[59] Report of the Prefect of Police to the Executive Commission, May 27 (*Commission d'enquête*, II, pp. 186-187).

[60] See the interesting, but prejudiced, reports of Falaiseau de Beauplan to the Executive Commission, written at two a.m. and three a.m., May 28 (*Archives nationales*. BB[30], no. 313, *liasse* 2). Dumas declares that, when Boulage and Trélat arrived in the morning, the workers wanted to hold the former as a hostage; that a revolt was about to break out and that only Madame Thomas succeeded in dominating the situation (*France nouvelle*, June 23, 1848). Thomas omits these details in his apologia.

a happy impression: his references to the shattering of the monarchy on the barricades of February were received by universal " bravos." Soon, however, impatient demands for news of Thomas interrupted his discourse.[61] · Trélat's replies were evasive. The crowd became more and more unruly and pressed close about the tribune. The prompt action of the assistant directors and a group of student officers from the *École centrale* permitted Trélat to escape by a hidden door at the rear of the riding school and safely to regain his carriage.[62]

When news of Trélat's misadventure reached the Executive Commission, the story had become distorted: apparently it was stated that the minister had been forcibly detained at Monceau and that the officers of the Thomas administration were implicated.[63] The Executive Commission promptly ordered the issuance of warrants of arrest for Pierre Thomas, Jaime, and others. And the minister of war was ordered to despatch to Monceau three regiments of the line, ten battalions of the *Garde mobile*, and 2,000 members of the National Guard.[64] At the same time Boulage was ordered to install Léon Lalanne, member of both Trélat's earlier committee of experts and of the newly created National Workshops' Commission, as direc-

---

[61] The account in the *Commune de Paris* (May 30) gives the substance of a speech by Pierre Thomas in which he referred to the government's orders of May 24 to Émile Thomas. This information doubtless made a bad impression on the workers.

[62] In addition to the account in the *Commune de Paris,* see the account of Boucard (Thomas, pp. 305-306), that of Delessard (p. 25), that in the *Presse* (May 28), and the letter of Chappon, of the *École centrale,* in the *Journal des Débats* (May 29) ; see also the Report No. 2 of Falaiseau de Beauplan (*Archives nationales.* BB³⁰, no. 313, *liasse* 2) and Lalanne: " Lettres sur les Ateliers nationaux. IV," *National,* July 23, 1848.

[63] Trélat later declared before the assembly's Committee of Public Works that he had been held prisoner by the delegates for three hours (*Arch. nat.* C 928. *Comité des travaux publics. Minutes des séances,* pp. 37-39), but the concordant evidence of other witnesses would indicate that this statement was an unwarranted exaggeration. In the same statement Trélat declared that Thomas' resignation was given voluntarily. See also *Commission d'enquête,* I, p. 355.

[64] Subsequent orders reduced the figures to two battalions of the line and two battalions of the *Garde mobile,* and the order to the National Guard was countermanded (*ibid.,* II, p. 44).

tor of the National Workshops. The new director arrived in the evening at Monceau at the head of a numerous detachment of troops and took over the administration with an impressive display of force.[65] That night troops bivouacked in the park at Monceau, patrols made their rounds in the neighborhood, and numerous groups of workers in earnest discussion gave rise to rumors of a *coup de main* for the morrow.[66]

Alarming reports accompanied continued agitation among the workers on the following day. Placards summoned the members of the Workshops to meet at their regular pay stations to sign a petition asking government and assembly for explanations of the " affaire Thomas." Rumors spread like wildfire, and fears of a possible insurrection were general in Paris.[67] The following morning, May 29, a rumor that the workers, supported by parts of the Eighth and Twelfth legions of the National Guard, were planning a demonstration against the assembly, was the basis for the general *rappel,* beaten at five o'clock, summoning all of the National Guard regiments to arms.[68] Meetings of workers were general during the day, but order was maintained. The delegates of the Workshops, meeting at Monceau in the afternoon, accepted the petition to the assembly, and decided that the new director should appear before them to give categorical explanations relative to the dis-

[65] Thomas, p. 307; Lalanne: " Lettres sur les Ateliers nationaux. IV," *National,* July 23, 1848; Delessard, p. 26.

[66] Reports of Falaiseau de Beauplan (*Arch. nat.* BB[30], no. 313, *liasse* 2).

[67] Report of the Prefect of Police (*Commission d'enquête,* II, pp. 187-188). It was reported that the workers would demand the maintenance of the Workshops and would secure their end by force if necessary. Even the judicious *Journal des Débats* (May 29) spoke of the "l'inquiétude qui s'est répandue dans Paris lorsqu'on a appris qu'une armée de plus de cent milles ouvriers désoeuvrés menacait de se mettre en insurrection ouverte. . . ." For the workers' petition, see *Commission d'enquête,* II, p. 297. When a deputation of a dozen Workshops' delegates came to protest to the government, " la commission exécutive leur parle avec une énergie qui les offusque et devant laquelle ils s'inclinent et se soumettent néanmoins " (Lalanne: " Lettres sur les Ateliers nationaux. IV," *National,* July 23, 1848).

[68] *Commission d'enquête,* II, p. 190; *National,* May 30; *Journal des Débats,* May 30.

appearance of Thomas. This Lalanne refused to do.[69] The evening witnessed continued agitation and minor collisions between workers and the National Guard. The latter appeared to act with less than its usual enthusiasm, discouraged, it was said, by the government's lack of energy; and it was rumored that the workers hoped to win support by causing disaffection within its ranks.[70]

Although active agitation among the workers had subsided temporarily on May 30,[71] the latter were given new cause for alarm when the Labor Committee's plan for the dissolution of the Workshops was accepted by the assembly on that day. The origins of that plan and its repercussions will be considered subsequently. Its adoption in the midst of the consternation caused by the mysterious disappearance of Thomas seemed peculiarly untimely. Moreover, on the same day, the government's earlier dissolution plan, as presented to Thomas, May 24, was published for the first time.[72] It is not strange that the workers had the impression that a general assault on the Workshops was preparing.

* * * * *

The agitation caused by the abduction of Thomas witnessed the end of the antagonism between the Luxembourg and the National Workshops and the recomposition of the essential unity of the working class, sundered by the activities of the Provisional Government. In place of their earlier " loyalty " to the cause of order, the members of the Workshops now abruptly turned to coöperation with their brother workers of the Luxembourg.

When the deputies had assembled in early May, the solution of the unemployment problem was of most immediate importance. The question could be attacked: (1) through the

[69] Commission d'enquête, I, pp. 174, 192; Vraie République, May 31; Liberté, May 31.

[70] Commission d'enquête, II, pp. 192-193.

[71] Ibid., pp. 194-195. See, however, the rumor of a plot to burn the buildings at Monceau (Journal des Débats, May 31).

[72] Journal des Débats, May 30; published also in Commune de Paris (May 31), which reached a large group on the left.

"organization of labor," that is, by a socialist experiment; (2) by the indefinite continuance of the Workshops, awaiting the eventual revival of business; (3) through the repudiation of the " guarantee of work " and the return of workers to their employers, subject to the conditions which had earlier prevailed.[73] It was soon apparent that the great majority of the assembly preferred the third alternative and would accept the second only on condition that a radical transformation be made in the Workshops. In the face of the hostility of the assembly and later of the government also, the members of the Workshops inevitably turned more and more to the first solution, which seemed to offer the only means of escaping the return of preëxisting conditions. Into this changing psychology the propaganda of the Luxembourg penetrated with increasing readiness. Apparently the arrest of Thomas served merely to accelerate greatly a movement already well formed.

Although Louis Blanc had resigned as president of the Luxembourg Commission and the latter had ceased to exist after the demonstration of May 15, the delegates had preserved an organization and continued their propaganda activities.[74] Marie accuses them of having exerted wide influence on the workers; employers were subjected to the pressure of the strike, violence was resorted to, businesses were ruined.[75] The police reported that the Luxembourg delegates were an important element in the disturbances at the end of May and the beginning of June, and accused them of forcing workers, by intimidation, to leave their employers and enroll in the National Workshops.[76] These are statements impossible of verification on the basis of the present state of our evidence. We have, however, certain precise indications of the coöperation of the Luxembourg and the National Workshops.

On May 28 a meeting took place at which there were present

---

[73] The analysis is Renard's (*République de 1848*, p. 63).

[74] See above, p. 19; *Commission d'enquête*, II, pp. 169, 226-227. The activity of the Luxembourg group can be gauged by the frequency of the meetings noted in the *Vraie République*, May 26 and ff.

[75] Cherest, pp. 219 ff.; cf. *Commission d'enquête*, I, p. 246.

[76] *Ibid.*, II, pp. 169, 226-227.

a "large number" of presidents of democratic clubs and delegates of the Luxembourg and of the National Workshops. At this meeting an invitation was issued for a meeting on the following evening for the purpose of drawing up a slate of candidates to the assembly for the Department of the Seine in the by-elections of June 4. The latter meeting included the presidents of the democratic clubs, and the delegates of the workers' *corporations* (i.e., those formerly represented in the Luxembourg parliament), of the *Gardes mobile et républicaine,* and of the National Workshops.[77] The list of candidates, upon which agreement was reached in the "most complete spirit of fraternity"[78] and which each group was to support wholeheartedly, included: Cabet, Caussidière, Pierre Leroux, Proudhon, Kersausie, Thoré, Lagrange, Raspail, Adam, Malarmet, and Savary (the last three being workers).[79] The appearance of such names as those of Cabet, Proudhon, and Leroux on a list sponsored by delegates of the Workshops suggests the change which had recently been wrought in the mentality of their members.[80]

Whereas the workers had gone down to stunning defeat in the April elections, their coöperation in the by-elections of June 4 bore fruit: this time, of the eleven successful candidates in the Department of the Seine, four were choices appearing on the workers' union list — Leroux, Proudhon, Lagrange, and Caussidière.[81] But it must be admitted that, despite the coöp-

[77] *Vraie République,* May 29.
[78] *Vraie République,* June 4.
[79] *Ibid.,* June 2.
[80] For continuing attempts at official influence, see the *Vraie République* (June 4) where it is claimed that, when the lists were distributed in the National Workshops, those at the top were the lists agreed upon at the meeting of the various democratic groups but that the other lists contained other names.
[81] Some notion, though by no means a precise one, of the progress of democratic opinion between elections is given by the comparative strength of four of the candidates of the left (*Peuple constituant,* June 14):

	April 23	June 4
Pierre Leroux	40,284	91,375
Lagrange	25,570	78,682
Raspail	52,093	71,977
Cabet	20,616	68,360

erative effort of these democratic groups, the workers revealed a great lack of regimentation. They were told by leading organs of the left that the majority had abstained from voting in the April elections and were warned of the dangers of inertia.[82] And yet, of the total number of those eligible to vote in the Department of the Seine (414,317), only 248,372 exercised the privilege.[83] In short, in spite of the heightened agitation among the workers and their suspicions of the good faith of the assembly, the total vote in the Department of the Seine declined from about 300,000 (April 23)[84] to 248,372 (June 4). Such apathy on the part of the workers as a whole is little short of astounding. It becomes increasingly clear that the agitation of these weeks was the work of a militant minority and that a large part of the working class was indifferent to the appeals of its leaders.[85]

The coöperation of the Luxembourg and the National Workshops continued after the elections — and without interruption right down to the June Days. The two groups met again on June 10[86] and on June 13;[87] and on the latter date there appeared a joint proclamation to the "Workers" warning them against the machinations of the reaction, Bourbon, Orleanist, or Napoleonic: ". . . rien maintenant n'est possible en France que la République démocratique et sociale. . . . Pas plus d'empereur que de roi!" At the foot of the proclamation appeared the names of the officers of the two groups.[88]

---

[82] See, e.g., *Commune de Paris*, May 31; *Représentant du peuple*, June 2.

[83] *Vraie République*, June 9.

[84] *Représentant du peuple*, April 30, 1848.

[85] See, e.g., comments of *Peuple constituant* (June 12) on the apathy of the workers in the matter of the ballot. The same situation had apparently prevailed in the case of the election of the officers of the National Guard (see *Commune de Paris*, April 8).

[86] *Vraie République*, June 9 (contains announcement of the meeting).

[87] *Commission d'enquête*, II, p. 207.

[88] *Réforme*, June 12, 13; republished in Blanc: *Révolution de 1848*, II, pp. 136-137. The warmth of the feeling existing between the two groups is attested in two letters, one from Bacon, president of the Workshops' delegates, to the delegates of the Luxembourg, June 4, and another from one Auguste Sibert, of the National Workshops, to the Luxembourg delegates, June 9 (*Archives nationales.* C 942, *liasse* III).

II

Following the events of May 15 the question of dissolving the Workshops drew the almost daily attention of the assembly. The general tenor of the discussion was one of decided moderation, however. The assembly seemed reassured by Trélat's remarks of May 17 and willing to coöperate with the government.[89] Moreover, it was known that the assembly's Labor Committee was discussing a solution of the whole question. Nevertheless, this tone of moderation was destined to change abruptly when the ferment within the Workshops, caused by Thomas' dismissal, convinced many deputies of the need for decisive action. Meanwhile this change of heart was foreshadowed by the proposal of Léon Faucher, May 24, envisaging the dissolution of the Workshops.[90] The discussion was set for May 27. On that day, when the storm within the Workshops gave added weight to the deputy's defence of his scheme, Faucher made a frontal attack upon the institution. The Workshops, he said, sheltered an unorganized mob, accessible to political agitation and the influence of conspirators.[91] They should be dissolved forthwith. It may be imagined with what disquietude the violence of the deputy's remarks was received by the workers! [92]

The predominant importance of the National Workshops' question inevitably gave to the assembly's Labor Committee a position of special significance and power. Its membership embraced a wide variety of interests. Among the workers were Agricol Perdiguier, Astouin, Peupin, Dobremel, Martinetz, Julien, and Corbon, the latter chosen president. The socialists

---

[89] The assembly promptly granted a 3,000,000-franc appropriation asked by Trélat, May 22 (*Moniteur*, May 23, 25). The same bill carried 3,800,000 francs for public works outside Paris, whose importance Trélat stressed as a means of employing members of the Paris Workshops.

[90] *Moniteur*, May 25. For other proposals respecting the dissolution of the Workshops, see *ibid.*, May 20, 21.

[91] *Ibid.*, May 28. " Encore quelques mois de ce régime, et nos ouvriers, que le travail doit faire vivre, que le travail ennoblit, descendraient au rang de prolétaires, en attendant qui'ils devinssent les prétoriens de la République."

[92] See, e.g., the *Vraie République*, May 30.

included Considerant, who attempted to reassure his colleagues by declaring that his ideas were inapplicable at the moment; Louis Blanc, who later opted for another committee; Leblond; Pascal Duprat; and Girard. Among the supporters of " free coöperation " were Wolowski; the Protestant minister, Coquerel; Alcan; Boussingault; Fourneyron; and Parrieu *fils*. Agricultural interests were represented by Falloux, Vogué, Thourret, and Dezeimeris. But the dominant figure in this essentially conservative committee was the Vicomte de Falloux, who was destined to assume a rôle of the first importance in the succeeding weeks.[93]

Falloux, whose pretensions to a noble ancestry of some antiquity are belied by the prosaic fact that his grandfather, an honest cattle merchant, had been ennobled by Louis XVIII only in 1823, had been raised in the pious atmosphere of a Catholic and royalist household. This training in loyalty to the church, so capably begun by his mother, was continued at the hand of a far more able woman, the distinguished Madame Swetchine, who had been converted to Roman Catholicism by Joseph de Maître. Falloux's formal studies in Paris were completed by travel abroad, where he made numerous contacts in aristocratic circles and visited, among others, the Comte de Chambord. Cold, reserved, possessed of a very superior intelligence and a complete command of himself under all circumstances, Falloux was *par excellence* an " homme du salon."

In 1846, Falloux was elected to the Orleanist Chamber, where during the succeeding two years he sat among the tiny group of legitimists. He understood at once the opportunities which the February Revolution offered the Catholic party. Indeed he embraced the Republic with such effusion and pursued an electoral campaign so openly democratic and so ostensibly anti-clerical that he was obliged privately to reassure certain of his Catholic friends.[94] Elected to the Constituent

[93] On the organization and the composition of the Labor Committee, see the introduction to the *Proc.-verb. du Com. du travail*.

[94] E. Veuillot: *Le Comte de Falloux et ses mémoires* (Paris, 1888), pp. 18 ff.

Assembly, he inscribed himself on the roll of the Labor Committee, for whose discussions he declared himself especially
fitted by reason of his long interest in charitable works, the
exact character of which remains somewhat obscure.[95] As
member of the Labor Committee he devoted himself unreserv-
edly to the question of the dissolution of the National Workshops. A reporter successively of two different committees
dealing with this question, he rapidly emerged from obscurity
and assumed a place of prominence among older and more
experienced colleagues. Falloux's character explains so much in
his policy that it seems worth while to quote the shrewd judgment of Tocqueville, who knew the man, had worked with him,
and admired him.

> In the course of my political career, I don't know that I have ever
> encountered a more extraordinary type. He possessed at once the two
> characteristics most necessary for the conduct of parties: an ardent con-
> viction which drove him constantly toward his end, from which he was
> deflected neither by disappointments nor by dangers; and a mind both
> supple and firm, which devoted to the execution of a single plan an
> extraordinary multiplicity and variety of means. He was sincere in the
> sense that, as he put it, he considered only his cause and not his personal
> interest, but he remained at the same time very cunning, and [he pos-
> sessed] an uncommon and very effective kind of cunning, for he succeeded
> in believing for the moment the *mélange* of truth and falsehood which he
> was about to serve to others. . . . [96]

The influence of Falloux was so considerable in the whole
question of the dissolution of the National Workshops, that the
problem may profitably be examined from the point of view of
the policy which he sponsored.

Immediately following the June Days, when the Workshops
were the object of almost universal odium, Falloux publicly
voiced his disappointment that the assembly's special committee (the second of which he had been reporter) had received
so little credit for the dissolution, which had finally been
effected by an *arrêté* of General Cavaignac, without the inter-

[95] *Ibid.*, pp. 11-12.
[96] Tocqueville: *Souvenirs,* pp. 336-337.

vention of the assembly.[97] Falloux appeared well satisfied with
his activity and disappointed that it had received so little prominence. During the year following, however, the attacks of the
left succeeded in transferring a measure of the odium for the
June Days to those who had urged the dissolution of the National Workshops, and to Falloux in particular. Finally, when
the question came before the assembly by accident on May 24,
1849, Falloux, who had quite apparently undergone a change
of heart, disclaimed all personal responsibility for the decisions
reached.

> . . . when you isolate me in the question of the National Workshops
> [Falloux told his colleagues], you seem to forget that I was never anything
> but the reporter of committees of the Assembly, and that all the proposals
> that I made had been sanctioned by it. . . . Not for a moment did I have
> my own way, not once did I use my own initiative. . . .[98]

Is it true that Falloux never once acted upon his own initiative? Is it true that he was merely the mouthpiece of committees of the assembly? One must recur to his record in the
period following the invasion of the assembly, May 15.

The Labor Committee met for the first time on May 17. On
that day or shortly thereafter, a subcommittee of three was
appointed to study the question of the Workshops in detail.
It included Falloux, Beslay, who played a relatively moderate
rôle in the Commune of 1871, and the Fourierist, Considerant.[99]
It is perfectly obvious that the subcommittee was dominated
by Falloux. In subsequent statements, some of them made
long years after the June Days, Falloux insisted upon the conciliatory character of the policy of the Labor Committee, of
its subcommittee, and particularly of himself. The subcommittee's aim was to make a careful study of the whole problem
before any decisive step should be taken and then to avoid all
measures which might be considered in any sense provocative.
Accordingly Duclerc, minister of finance, was consulted as to

---

[97] *Moniteur*, July 6; for the *arrêté* of Cavaignac, see *ibid.*, July 4.
[98] *Moniteur*, May 25, 1849.
[99] Falloux: *Mémoires*, I, p. 328.

the availability of funds for the necessary public works. Two weeks were passed in conferences at the ministry of public works, particularly with the newly appointed National Workshops' Commission. The individual workshops were inspected. Finally, assured that funds and work projects were ready, the subcommittee made its report, asking the appointment of a somewhat larger group for the preparation of the decree. This was done and the enlarged subcommittee prepared the decree, which was voted by the assembly.[100] Throughout, Falloux's description gives the impression of complete unanimity within the Labor Committee on the whole question and of the greatest deliberation and calm on the part of the subcommittee. The contrast between Falloux's apologiæ and the impression made by a day-by-day reading of the stenographic minutes of the Labor Committee is striking.

In the period of eight days after its appointment the subcommittee investigated the problem of the Workshops. Duclerc and certain other ministers were consulted, Monceau was visited and Thomas was questioned.[101] But it is of course obvious that Falloux did not spend two weeks in conference at the ministry of public works, particularly with the National Workshops' Commission, for his report was made to the Labor Committee on May 25, and the latter commission was appointed only on that day. Elsewhere Falloux admits that up to the time of the adoption of the draft decree by the committee, he had only once consulted the commission, and then for about an hour.[102] Moreover, his report of May 25 indicates clearly that Falloux had been content with a hasty reconnaissance which had apparently served merely to confirm him in his opinion that energetic measures were necessary.

On May 25, he told his colleagues of the Labor Committee that those who faced the Workshops' problem could be divided into three groups: " Those who do not wish to have them dissolved, those who do not dare, and . . . those who dare and

---

[100] Falloux: *Mémoires*, I, pp. 328-329; *Moniteur*, May 25, 1849.

[101] *Arch. nat.* C 928. *Min. sténog. du com. du travail*, May 25.

[102] *Ibid.*, May 29.

wish but cannot because they encounter obstacles and lack energy adequate to the execution of such a plan." In which of these categories did the Committee wish to range itself? The situation had become too complex for the subcommittee to offer a solution and it asked the advice of the committee. But in any case Falloux wished to make one point clear: those who did not *dare* to dissolve the Workshops were suffering from an illusion. They were constantly being told that they were faced by an army of 115,000 men and that if the Workshops were suppressed, this army would revolt. This was not true, said Falloux. What with false enrollments, the Workshops numbered only 80,000 men, a large proportion of them well-intended and ready to return to work in their own trades. But even supposing resistance, continued Falloux,

have you not the National Guard, honest workers, all the manufacturers who ask only the use of a certain energy. Take what measures you prefer, we guarantee that we will not find serious resistance; and in case we do encounter it, let us not be afraid to use force, force without the shedding of blood, but that moral force which belongs to the law.[103]

Falloux's statement is of capital importance. It reveals that he favored energetic action from the beginning, that he believed (or feigned to believe) that serious resistance would not develop, and that in case it did develop he was convinced that it could and should be met with force of arms. For one does not put down "serious resistance" with "moral force," and Falloux's mention of the National Guard is significant. It is indeed likely that Falloux already believed that serious resistance would develop. Émile Thomas had told him just that,[104] and the remarks of his colleagues during the succeeding days indicate clearly that the fear of a rising was constantly in their minds. For the present Falloux was content to leave the proposal of specific measures to his colleagues. Coquerel and Rondeau favored immediate and radical action. But the consensus of opinion was that the situation was dangerous and that

[103] *Arch. nat.* C 928. *Min. sténog. du com. du travail,* May 25.
[104] *Ibid.*

further investigation should precede specific action. Accordingly it was decided that the ministers of public works, the interior, and commerce, and the prefect of police should be summoned to give evidence.[105]

On the following day, May 26, the draft of the decree prepared by the subcommittee for submission to the assembly was read to the Labor Committee. In the discussion of Falloux's report the majority clearly favored rapid action but was anxious above all to avoid any measure provocative of revolt. Trélat was introduced at this point. The minister urged that the committee coöperate with his newly appointed National Workshops' Commission in finding a solution for the problem. The latter commission had that very morning recognized the necessity of taking an accurate census of the workers as a basis for the execution of any program. The minister declared the census to be the work of only forty-eight hours. When Trélat was asked by Falloux if he was opposed to the subcommittee's report, the minister's reply was ambiguous. He opposed nothing in the report, Trélat declared; indeed its proposals had been adopted by the government three days earlier;[106] but, he added, " since then we have perceived serious obstacles to the application of these views." Later, after further ambiguities, Trélat concluded on a contradictory note: " Ce décret me paraît excellent, les mesures sont excellentes. Je n'ai aucune objection à leur faire." The minister's statements appear to have made a very poor impression indeed.[107]

What is of capital interest in Trélat's admission is that the government was already in retreat from its advanced position of May 24. The " serious obstacles " encountered doubtless refer to the opposition of Thomas. The appointment of the National Workshops' Commission, May 25, committed the government to a policy of further study of the problem. On the other hand, it will be remembered that Thomas was removed

---

[105] *Arch. nat.* C 928. *Min. sténog. du com. du travail,* May 25.

[106] Trélat doubtless referred to the government's decisions of May 23, which Thomas was instructed to put into force, May 24.

[107] *Arch. nat.* C 928. *Min. sténog. du com. du travail,* May 26.

on May 26, the evening of the same day on which the meeting above took place. This final display of resolution on the part of the government was probably not unconnected with the fact that Trélat clearly perceived that the temper of the Labor Committee would permit no further dilatory tactics in the solution of the problem. But the violent reaction to Thomas' abduction was too much for the government, which once more lapsed into a policy of vacillation.

On the following day, May 27, Marie appeared before the committee. Like Trélat, he urged the necessity of a census as the basis of any program, but, whereas the minister had declared that the census could be taken in two days, Marie admitted that " about a week " would be necessary. Its results should be awaited, he declared, before the proposal of any law. The member of the Executive Committee also emphasized the difficulty of sending workmen from Paris to distant points; previous attempts to get workers to accept places in Lyon, for instance, had failed.

Coquerel answered Marie by an unequivocal declaration for immediate dissolution; the government " is as embarrassed as we are by the National Workshops, . . . it is waiting for us to give it the courage to dissolve them." Marie replied, warmly defending the Workshops as an imperious necessity. "Would you rather have agitation in the public square . . . one rising after another? . . . Is it possible to dissolve the National Workshops, and to announce that the *ateliers* which existed yesterday no longer exist today, and that the 115,000 men there occupied are to be scattered about Paris, penniless and unaided? " The definitive solution of the problem must rest upon the revival of private industry. "With the aid of the assembly, the Executive Commission hopes to restore a condition of confidence in which credit and industry can revive. And that cannot be done in a day! " Marie concluded.

Falloux answered Marie in scathing terms.

We are asked for time! [he said] But time is not *for* us, it is *against* us. Every day lost spells discredit for the Republic, for the National Assembly, for all the public authorities . . . [time] multiplies all our difficulties, and in a week we shall have . . . more than 140,000 workers on strike.

It is evident . . . that there exists in . . . the different ministries a kind of systematic opposition to the solution of the question of the National Workshops; . . . they are making this question an *epouvantail* to force us to pass this or that . . . measure, and they say to the National Assembly: you do not want to accept such and such a measure, how then do you wish the National Workshops to be dissolved?

The question of the National Workshops is a political question. . . . It is not necessary to discharge men without providing them with means of support, but the government is sufficiently strong to rely upon its armed resources. This question of the transformation of the National Workshops must be confronted frankly and supported by the authority of the National Assembly.

Marie vigorously denied Falloux's assertion that the government was preserving the Workshops in order to exert influence on the assembly. He was simply urging a further study of the facts, he said. In the end his remarks seem greatly to have mollified certain members of the committee, and it was agreed that the National Workshops' Commission should be consulted before final action was taken. Falloux appeared little impressed with the desirability of further delay, but consented to be a member of a committee to consult with Trélat's group of experts.[108]

On May 29, Falloux reported the results of his conference with the National Workshops' Commission.[109] This was proceeding in a deliberate and unimpressive fashion with the census and other problems, but Falloux declared that it was doing nothing which would assure an early solution. Meanwhile enrollments had not been stopped, and the commission admitted that the membership included some 8,000 to 10,000 liberated criminals. The commission had recognized that the Labor Committee could not accept these " faits monstrueux," and had declared that the decree which the latter proposed (subject to minor alterations) would be a source of great strength to it in dealing with the Workshops problem. The

[108] *Arch. nat.* C 928. *Min. sténog. du com. du travail*, May 27.

[109] He was apparently a committee of one.

Labor Committee then proceeded to the final discussion of the draft decree as proposed by the subcommittee. The most important change effected by the committee was the elimination of the article dealing with optional military enlistments, which General Duvivier and others believed might seem to the workers to contain a threat of constraint. But the discussion of the return of workers to their homes in the provinces revealed either an unwarranted optimism as to the ease with which the departments could provide work for those returning, or more probably a willingness to pass the responsibility to the local authorities so long as Paris might be rid of the plague of unemployed. The bland *insouciance* with which the committee brushed aside this thorny question reflected the extent to which an immediate solution had become an *idée fixe* with its members.[110] Whereas the violent reaction of the workers to Thomas' dismissal induced increasing caution on the part of the government, that same reaction influenced the Labor Committee to demand swift action in the suppression of the source of the danger. Falloux in particular urged that questions of detail be left for subsequent solution, that the events of " today and tomorrow " might well be of a character to make the adoption

---

[110] See, e.g., the comment of Demesmay: " Dans tous les départements de la France il y a de grands travaux publics qui sont en cour d'exécution et renvoyer les ouvriers à ces travaux, ce n'est pas une difficulté." But he gives no specific examples of such " grands travaux publics " and does not explain why workers continued to come to Paris from the provinces seeking work (*Arch. nat.* C 928. *Min. sténog. du com. du travail,* May 29). The conservative *Journal des travaux publics* subsequently (June 8) expressed its fears of the unfortunate results of this measure and urged that adequate work projects be found before the workers were sent home. The *Commune de Paris* (June 1) pointed out that this policy would revolutionize the provinces, a fact which the politicians failed to see. The ease with which certain elements believed the problem could be solved is nothing short of astounding; the *Organisation du travail* (June 6) published a *communiqué* declaring that the census of June 7 was expected to reduce the numbers enrolled from 115,000 to 90,000; that a third of the 90,000 would be returned to their homes in the provinces where local administrations would procure them work; that public works already provided would care for 25,000; that private industry would " easily " occupy 20,000 to 25,000 more as soon as differences between workers and employers had been arranged; and that there would then remain only a small fraction to be cared for!

of the decree urgent. Falloux was empowered to present the decree at once.[111]

The provisions of the decree were sufficiently moderate, but the tenor of Falloux's report was much less so. Although he insisted that the committee's purpose was not to throw men out of work but to provide other means of employing them, Falloux's speech bristled with ill-concealed animosity toward the Workshops. It was obviously his purpose to be rid, at the earliest moment possible, of this "grève permanente et organisée," this "foyer actif de fermentation menaçante."[112] The discussion of the measure on the following day, May 30, although punctuated by two sharp attacks on the workers by industrialist deputies, was decidedly moderate in tone. The principal preoccupation of the deputies was quite obviously to find a measure which promised to put an end to the army of the unemployed in Paris, perennial threat to the existence of the assembly itself.

The proposal was quickly adopted, in almost precisely the form in which it had been reported out of the Labor Committee, except for the addition of Article 5:

(1) Piece-work was to be substituted as rapidly as possible for work by the day, and could be undertaken either by individual workers or by workers' coöperatives.[113]

(2) Special appropriations were to be provided for the ministries of public works, commerce, and the interior in order to accelerate, "par voie d'avances et de primes," the revival of departmental and communal works and of private industry.

(3) Workers with less than three months' domicile in the Department of the Seine and who had no other means of livelihood there, were to receive, for themselves and their families, a transportation allowance and an indemnity.

(4) The present law was to be applicable in departmental towns and communes upon the request of the municipal councils.

(5) The provisions of Article 3 were not to apply to workers who came

---

[111] *Arch. nat.* C 928. *Min. sténog. du com. du travail*, May 29.

[112] *Moniteur*, May 30.

[113] "Art. 1ᵉʳ. Le travail à la tâche sera substitué, sous le plus bref délai possible, dans les ateliers nationaux, au travail à la journée. Il sera livré directement, aux prix des devis, sans rabais et sans intermédiaire d'entrepreneurs, soit à des ouvriers associés, soit à des ouvriers isolés, suivant la nature des travaux."

regularly each year to Paris and who could show a residence there of six months during the preceding year.[114]

The passage of the law and the long discussion which preceded it had given the workers an ample view of the temper of the assembly. It remained to be seen with what despatch the government would execute the law.

*   *   *   *   *

The acts of the government in the period immediately following the rising of May 15 clearly witnessed its determination to seek an early and radical solution of the Workshops' problem. But, concurrently with the stubborn opposition of Thomas to the brusque instructions of May 24, the government underwent a change of heart, apparently alarmed by the prospects of too precipitate action. Thenceforth, until the middle of June, the government attempted, first, to bridle the precipitation of the Labor Committee and then, after May 30, to mitigate the assembly's dissolution decree through inaction. Both policies failed. The Workshops' policy of the government during the entire period between May 15 and the June Days was indeed characterized alternately by haste and inertia. No one policy was ever adopted and followed consistently. The result was that the government rapidly lost prestige, and the control of the Workshops' question soon passed effectively into the hands of the assembly. The execution of the projected census nicely illustrates the way in which the government attacked the whole dissolution problem.

The necessity for a census had been evident to the government from the beginning. It was obvious that such measures

[114] *Moniteur*, June 4. The tenor of the law is most evident in the wording of the preamble: " Considérant que le travail des ateliers nationaux est devenu improductif; que son maintien dans les conditions actuelles serait en contradiction avec une bonne administration de la fortune publique, avec le retour de l'ordre et la reprise des opérations industrielles ou commerciales; qu'il constituerait une aumône déguisée; que le plus grand nombre des travailleurs inscrits aux ateliers nationaux réclament eux-mêmes le moyen de gagner plus librement leur existence, et refusent de prélever plus longtemps sur la fortune publique des deniers que n'appartiennent qu'aux orphelins, aux infirmes et aux vieillards, . . ."

as the dismissal of workers without Paris domicile required a census to determine who these workers were. Trélat's first step, on assuming office, was to instruct Thomas to proceed at once with an enumeration.[115] Thomas insisted upon the difficulties of forcing the workers to give information prejudicial to themselves, and pointed out that the alphabetical list at Monceau would furnish all other details. Moreover, the task was a difficult one and would require a week, he said.[116] In any event the enumeration was undertaken, but the results were disappointingly inadequate.[117] It was for this reason that the government insisted that a new census be made and asked that the Labor Committee await its results before laying a dissolution project before the assembly. This the committee refused to do. Its members obviously distrusted the sincerity of the government's interest in early dissolution, and of course it is possible to interpret the whole census program as a mere manœuvre on the part of the government to forestall early action.

In place of the refractory Thomas, the government had now placed in charge of the Workshops a "hand-picked" commission and, subject to it, an obedient instrument in the person of Léon Lalanne. Lalanne had had a not undistinguished record as a government engineer. A graduate of the *École polytechnique* in 1831, he had served as an engineer of the *ponts-et-chaussées* and was the author of a number of inventions which received the very favorable attention of the Academy of Sciences. He had also taken an active part in the construction of the Paris-Sceaux Railroad in 1846.[118] It will be recalled

[115] *Moniteur*, May 30 (statement of Trélat to the assembly).

[116] Thomas, pp. 263-264. Cf. Trélat's statement (*Moniteur*, May 30) and Lalanne: "Lettres sur les Ateliers nationaux. IV," *National*, July 23, 1848.

[117] Trélat's statement to the Labor Committee (*Arch. nat.* C 928. *Min. sténog. du com. du travail*, May 26; see similar statement of Marie, *ibid.*, May 27). Thomas declares that the "recensement presque terminé était mis, le 22 mai, à la disposition de la Commission"; and that the statistical table of the workers by trade was handed on later to Falloux and Thiers (Thomas, p. 329). For the table in question, see Thomas, pp. 376-378.

[118] *Dictionnaire des parlementaires français*, III, p. 547. Subsequently (between 1852 and 1861) he was engineer for railroad construction projects in Wallachia, western Switzerland, and northern Spain. In 1862 he reëntered the French

that he had been made a member, first, of Trélat's extra-
parliamentary committee and, later, of the National Workshops' Commission. It was quite natural that his appointment as director of the Workshops should bring with it a
general, though by no means complete, substitution in the
administration of students of the *École polytechnique* (where
the government engineers received the first stage of their training) for those of the *École centrale*.[119] Trélat made numerous
other changes in the Workshops' system, one of the most important of which was the suppression of the central club. He
substituted therefor an innocuous committee of fourteen delegates, one for each arrondissement and two for the suburbs.
The latter group remained consistently responsive to official influence until the June Days. It should be noted that the suppression of the central club did not prevent the delegates from
maintaining their organization intact. Their influence upon the
workers continued, and played an important rôle, particularly
in connection with the coöperative efforts of the Workshops
with the former delegates of the Luxembourg.[120]

Immediately following its appointment, the National Workshops' Commission undertook the execution of the required
census,[121] which was duly announced for June 7.[122] At five
o'clock on the morning of the seventh the Workshops' brigadiers met to receive census return blanks from their lieuten-

service to become, in 1876, director of the *École des ponts-et-chaussées*. He was
made *membre libre* of the *Académie des sciences* in 1879 and elected senator in
1883.

[119] *Peuple constituant*, June 9; *Liberté*, June 19.

[120] The club was dissolved June 2 by suppressing the pay of the delegates, but
the latter continued their activities and formed " une sorte de contrôle indé-
pendant de l'administration " (*Commission d'enquête*, II, p. 143; Lalanne: " Lettres sur les Ateliers nationaux. VI," *National*, August 16, 1848).

[121] Lalanne pays high tribute to the commission, the *procès-verbaux* of whose
meetings have unfortunately been lost. On its plans for industrial rehabilitation
and the solution of the workers' problems, so far as we know them, see Lalanne:
loc. cit.; Proudhon: *Confessions*, pp. 123-124; and C. Robin: *Histoire de la
Révolution française de 1848* (Paris, 1849-1850, 2 vols.), II, p. 321.

[122] *Moniteur*, June 2. On the preparations for the census, see further Lalanne:
" Lettres sur les Ateliers nationaux. IV, V," *National*, July 23, August 6, 1848;
Journal des Débats, May 29; *Arch. de la Seine. Mairies* O²ᵇ, nos. 4600-4605.

ants. Between seven o'clock and noon the census blanks were duly filled out under the direction of the brigadiers and then returned to the lieutenants, to be rechecked and handed on to the chiefs of service. The administration of the Workshops, however, soon discovered that this census could be considered only preliminary and that dependable results must be based upon two further operations. First, the identity and presence of each worker must be rechecked by visits of trusted *contrôleurs* at the workers' domiciles. Second, the information given in the census returns must be verified, particularly with reference to the length of the worker's sojourn in Paris (to be checked by examining his passport, consulting his landlord, and so on). A census commission was then to be selected from the census takers to make recommendations for dismissal or maintenance of each worker, the latter to be passed upon by the central administration of the Workshops.[123]

The minute details and complicated character of the census have been developed at length because they have a very real bearing on the subsequent course of events. The primary issue between the government and the assembly had now become that of the *speed* with which the Workshops should be dissolved, and the government insisted that the census must precede the execution of any program which might be adopted.

The results of the census were painted in a rosy hue by Mary, vice president of the National Workshops' Commission, in a report to the Labor Committee, June 10. In place of 119,000 workers "enrolled" on the books of the administration, the returns showed but 103,500 legitimate members of the Workshops.[124] Mary then went on to develop at length the complicated operations by which the administration proposed further to verify the figures. Although he spoke also of the other plans of the government for the execution of the assembly's law of May 30, it was evident that the process, as measured by the time which further census operations must involve, would neces-

[123] *Arch. de la Seine. Mairies* O²ᵇ, no. 4605; see also nos. 4603 and 4604.
[124] It was expected, however, that the number would be increased to 106,000-107,000 by the addition of a sick list, etc.

sarily be a slow one.[125]   In actual fact the census at the homes of the workers was accomplished only on the eve of the insurrection (June 20), and the work of checking the lists, under the direction of the mayors, was probably far from complete at that time.[126]

III

The government's activities in the early days of June apparently encouraged Falloux in the belief that the assembly's decree would be executed with despatch.   On June 3 he told the Labor Committee that the decree had been rightly comprehended by the workers, that preparations were being made for the census, and that sources of employment were being found by the minister of public works.[127]   On June 5 a letter from " a member of the National Workshops' Commission " informed the Labor Committee that " les plus heureux résultats " could be reported for those Workshops in which the piece-work basis, provided by the decree, was already in operation.[128]   Elaborate measures were taken to provide travelling expenses and an indemnity of five francs for those workers who were to be returned to their homes in the provinces.[129]   In the case of public works then being organized in the departments as an outlet for the unemployed,[130] units of forty to fifty workers were to be

[125] For Mary's report on the census of June 7, see *Proc.-verb. du com. du travail*, pp. 36-38; *Arch. nat.* C 928. *Min. sténog. du com. du travail*, June 10.

[126] It is very difficult to see how the operations could have been completed by June 25, had the insurrection not taken place, as Lalanne claims (" Lettres sur les Ateliers nationaux. V," *National*, August 6, 1848). The task of compiling results for the census of June 20 was relatively simple, but that of verifying the workers' statements on their sojourn in Paris was necessarily extremely long and complicated.   Lalanne declared that the census of June 20 made a reduction of about 6,000 and that the verification by the mayors would have led to another reduction of about the same number (Lalanne, *loc. cit.*).

[127] *Proc.-verb. du com. du travail*, pp. 27-28.

[128] *Proc.-verb. du com. du travail*, pp. 28-29.

[129] *Commission d'enquête*, II, pp. 171-173.

[130] The earlier difficulties of Thomas with the government engineers will be recalled.   Apparently the latter, who had been quite unable to find projects for the Thomas administration, officered by students of the *École centrale*, at once discovered a whole series of projects when Lalanne became director (Renard: *République de 1848*, p. 72).

formed under the orders of government engineers and sent out from Paris, Mary explained to the Labor Committee on June 10.[131] He also noted that measures had been taken to prevent all further immigration from the departments; the minister of the interior had the previous day advised the prefects to announce by official poster that no more workers could be received in Paris.[132] The government likewise proposed appropriations for provincial public works totalling 11,340,000 francs, which were promptly granted by the assembly.[133] And preliminary measures were taken for the early sending of workers to these projects in the departments.[134]

Despite the apparent activity of the government in certain directions, however, it was obvious to the proponents of immediate dissolution that these steps were not leading to the rapid execution of the assembly's law of May 30. It may be urged that the law could not well have been executed more rapidly, especially the section providing loans for the revival of private industry. Be that as it may, Falloux finally became convinced that the government had no serious intention of proceeding to a rapid dissolution of the Workshops. The discussions of the question by the Labor Committee prior to the adoption of the decree of May 30 had apparently convinced Falloux that the majority of the committee did not share his eagerness for a brusque solution of the problem. In any event he now proceeded to a series of manœuvres whose object was clearly to circumvent the too pacific Labor Committee and to take the question effectively out of its hands in the interest of immediate action.[135]

On June 14, with the president and the majority of its members absent, Falloux reported to the Labor Committee that the

[131] *Proc.-verb. du com. du travail*, p. 37.

[132] *Arch. nat.* C 928. *Min. sténog. du com. du travail*, June 10.

[133] *Moniteur*, June 11.

[134] *Arch. nat.* F[14], no. 9317, correspondence with the prefects of the Maine-et-Loire and the Indre-et-Loire.

[135] See, e.g., *Univers*, June 15. The importance of this step eluded certain of the left newspapers; the new committee is not mentioned at all by the *République* and the *Peuple constituant* for June 15.

assembly's decree of May 30 was in no sense being executed
and that the government seemed to wish to escape the control
of the assembly by not asking appropriations. Instead the
government was employing funds for the Workshops whose use
had been authorized by no vote of the assembly. He mildly
asked the committee if he should interpellate the minister of
public works on this subject during a meeting of the assembly.
Another member, Dezeimeris, at once demanded that the interpellation should take place that same day, and to this the members present unanimously agreed.[136]

Falloux grasped eagerly at the opportunity presented by the
"mandate" of the Labor Committee, but he went considerably
further than a mere interpellation of the minister. Apparently
he gave Trélat a strong hint that it was high time that the
government regularized its financial policy by asking an appropriation. When Trélat acceded and presented a *projet* calling
for an appropriation, Falloux made a frontal attack on the
government, denouncing its attempts to avoid the control of the
assembly by indirection. He opposed sending the *projet* to the
Labor Committee, because "the question is too serious for
three members . . . to accept henceforth the responsibility."
Instead he asked the appointment of a special committee of the
assembly, chosen in the *bureaux* and unrelated to the Labor
Committee. This special committee was to investigate the various questions relating to the appropriation asked and indeed
all questions relating to the Workshops. Trélat defended himself weakly and raised no objection to Falloux's motion, which
was promptly adopted.[137]

The swift and subtle series of moves by which Falloux manœuvred the question of the National Workshops out of the
hands of the Labor Committee and had it placed in those of a
special committee, was characteristic of his methods. It is true
that the trick was somewhat too patent and that Corbon obliged
Falloux to admit to the assembly that his act had been sanc-
tioned by only a small number of the Labor Committee. Fal-

---

[136] *Proc.-verb. du com. du travail*, p. 42.
[137] *Moniteur*, June 15.

loux quickly retired behind the half-truth that he had spoken
only in the name of the subcommittee of three.[138] But the
victory was none the less Falloux's. The question was taken
from the Labor Committee, which contained elements of opposition to Falloux's policy and given to a special committee
which, chosen in the *bureaux,* represented a cross-section of
sentiment in the assembly. Falloux well knew that the majority
of the assembly was alarmed by the presence of the army of
idle workers in Paris and hence that the majority of each
bureau (the *bureaux* were chosen by lot) would reflect this
sentiment. As a result the new committee would be sympathetic
with the brusque action which he favored. Falloux's anticipa-
tions were well founded. The special committee included such
deputies as Goudchaux, who had in a speech of the previous
day demanded the immediate dissolution of the Workshops;
and Charles Dupin, who had recently acquired an unfortunate
reputation among the workers by his speech on " Les ouvriers
qui ne sont pas de bon Paris." Moreover, the committee contained no members of the Labor Committee, save Falloux and
Dezeimeris (whose support of Falloux on June 14 suggests
coöperation), and no member of the subcommittee on the National Workshops, except Falloux.[139] From the mere stand-
point of expert knowledge, Falloux held a commanding position.

In his *Mémoires* Falloux insists upon the unanimity of opinion existing within the special committee. He figures merely
as the official mouthpiece of the committee. "... there was
unanimity in the committee of fifteen members as there had
been in the subcommittee of three, demanding dissolution 'à
peu près immédiate,'" Falloux declares. "M. Dupont de Bussac, belonging to the most advanced left element, separated
himself from us no more than had M. Beslay and M. Considerant."[140] This statement is curious, to call it by no other

[138] *Moniteur,* June 15.

[139] For the personnel, see Falloux: *Mémoires,* I, pp. 330-331; certain more
moderate elements also came into the committee, e.g., Dupont de Bussac (see
Organisation du travail, June 18).

[140] Falloux: *op. cit.,* I, p. 333.

name, for further on Falloux admits that Dupont de Bussac actually resigned in protest against the brusque policy of the committee.[141] Again Falloux states that but for him a dissolution measure would have been adopted in twenty-four hours; that he insisted that a program of amelioration of workers' conditions (inspired by the Comte de Melun) should proceed concurrently with plans for dissolution.[142] That Falloux supported such measures at this time seems in the highest degree unlikely. The program he describes could only have been executed slowly, whereas his activity, notably on June 23, clearly reveals Falloux as a proponent of a speedy solution. Moreover, the proposals would have been welcomed by the Labor Committee, to which he did not submit them in the course of nearly a month.

The special committee held five meetings in the course of three days,[143] and on June 19, Falloux was empowered to present a report to the assembly,[144] whose character will be considered presently.

The renewed hostility to the Workshops of Falloux and his colleagues is to be attributed not alone to the failure of the government to act with greater despatch. It reflected also the incessant agitation among the workers since the disappearance of Thomas. The increasing danger from the idle army of workers alarmed the deputies, as the too deliberate policy of the government exasperated them. A consistent reading of the Paris press during the first three weeks of June conveys a strong impression of almost uninterrupted disorder. The secret reports of the police confirm and extend this impression.[145] The streets were the scene of perennial agitation among the workers. Strong weapons had been forged for the ubiquitous revolutionary agitator in the denunciations of the workers from the tribune of the assembly. If the deputies had

[141] *Ibid.*, I, pp. 337-338.
[142] *Ibid.*, I, pp. 331-332.
[143] *La Presse*, June 18, 19; Falloux: *Mémoires*, I, p. 333.
[144] *Ibid.*, I, p. 333.
[145] *Commission d'enquête*, II, pp. 196 ff.

stigmatized them as idlers and wasters of the public moneys, the government seemed no less hostile. The generally popular Thomas had, they believed, been the object of a brutal and unwarranted dismissal. And his successor had suppressed the club of the Workshops' delegates, symbol of justice for the workers' cause.

As the days passed, the street gatherings grew more disorderly. To the discussion of the Workshops, the organization of labor, the proposed trial of Louis Blanc, was now added an ominous note. Passersby would hear groups singing, to the air of the "lampions": "Nous l'aurons, nous l'aurons!" and the reply sometimes "La République démocratique et sociale," sometimes "Poléon . . . Poléon!" For the popularity of the Prince, fostered by propaganda addressed to the proletariat, made rapid progress in the early days of June. His victory in the by-elections to the assembly, June 4, only served to enhance his prestige, and street parliaments were already naming Louis Napoleon as new head of the Republic. Workers from La Villette sent a petition to the assembly asking that he be proclaimed consul.[146] It was believed that the Bonapartists were making strenuous efforts to win adherents in the National Workshops,[147] and Thomas himself was suspected, probably not without reason, of being a Bonapartist sympathizer.[148]

The continued agitation among the workers alarmed both government and assembly, which replied with a Draconian law forbidding street meetings of armed men (*attroupements*), and even gatherings of those unarmed "qui pourrait troubler la tranquillité publique." Such meetings could be disbanded by force, and prison sentences extending as high as ten years were to be imposed on offenders. An *attroupement* was declared to be "armed" when several of its members were seen to be carry-

[146] *Commission d'enquête*, II, pp. 198 ff.; *Journal des Débats*, June 17; Lebey, I, pp. 300 ff.

[147] Blanc: *Révolution de 1848*, II, pp. 136-137; Lamartine: *Révolution de 1848*, II, pp. 345-346.

[148] Lebey, I, pp. 300-301, 305-306, and sources there cited; Stern, II, pp. 314-315.

ing arms or when even *one individual* bore arms, provided he were not at once expelled by the others. Even those indirectly connected with the incitement of such gatherings — printers and distributers of posters — came within the purview of the law's severe provisions.[149]

The law at once drew unmeasured denunciation from the left press. The workers had fought behind the barricades to win a right which was now brusquely and unjustly withdrawn. Although the measure was declared to exceed "toute la fureur des lois de septembre," the workers were warned against overt acts which would play into the hands of the "reaction."[150] Indeed, in the vituperative attacks of the press one senses already the presence of extreme tension presaging the irruption of two weeks hence. These very attacks of the left press, continued now without interruption, were unquestionably an element of the very first importance in further arousing, and especially in crystallizing, the exacerbated spirit of the proletariat. It is unfortunate that the influence of the press cannot be measured with greater precision.

With the passage of the drastic law on *attroupements*, street meetings did not cease. On the contrary, they increased and became more menacing, despite very numerous arrests.[151] Meanwhile a further widening of the breach between the workers and the party of order was occasioned by the projected "Banquet de 25 centimes." The modest price was intended to make possible the attendance of all the workers of Paris at a monster "banquet," in the planning of which the delegates of the National Workshops had taken a prominent part.[152] The

---

[149] *Moniteur*, June 8 and 9; Duvergier: *Collection complète des lois*, Vol. 48, p. 325, note. The law was proposed by Recurt, June 5, discussed and adopted, June 7. The law on *attroupements* of April 10, 1831 (*ibid.*, Vol. 31, pp. 296-299) was much less severe than that of June, 1848!

[150] On the reactions of the press, see, e.g., *Commune de Paris*, June 7; *Vraie République*, June 7; *Liberté*, June 7; *La République*, June 8; *Peuple constituant*, June 9; see also *Commission d'enquête*, II, p. 201, and *Père Duchêne*, June 13-15.

[151] *Commission d'enquête*, II, pp. 201 ff. No fewer than 750 arrests were made on June 11 (*ibid.*, II, p. 204; cf. *Organisation du travail*, June 12).

[152] *Père Duchêne*, June 3, and days following; *Commission d'enquête*, II, pp. 197, 286.

prospect of such a gathering alarmed the bourgeoisie and gave rise to rumors of every description. The newspapers of the left protested that there could be no thought of civil war when the wives and children of workers were invited; and they scouted the rumor that the prisoners of Vincennes (including Barbès and Albert) were to be delivered.[153] Although official attempts to influence the members of the Workshops to absent themselves from the banquet failed, the workers' delegates themselves finally decided to postpone the *fête* until July 14,[154] the decision apparently reflecting the extreme hostility of official Paris to the whole proceedings.

*　　　　*　　　　*　　　　*

Viewed long after the events — always a relatively facile procedure — the situation had become, by the middle of June, a well-nigh hopeless impasse. The assembly was becoming hourly more alarmed by disorders in the street;[155] drastic measures and denunciations of the workers followed swiftly one upon another. In turn, the attacks of the assembly and the conservative press alarmed the workers and drove them more and more into the arms of revolutionary agitators. The whole formed a vicious circle, from which, given the psychology of the parties concerned, there seemed to be no issue save through the arbitrament of force. It remains to indicate briefly the actions and reactions of government and assembly, on the one hand, and of the workers, on the other, in the days immediately preceding the insurrection. These events served merely to exaggerate the tension already existing between the two groups.

If the attitude of the assembly with reference to the National Workshops was not already sufficiently clear to the workers, it was rendered more explicit by the attack on the institution,

[153] *Vraie République*, June 8.

[154] *Père Duchêne*, June 13-15; *Vraie République*, June 12; *Commission d'enquête*, II, p. 291.

[155] For vivid impressions of the fears of the conservatives, see Tocqueville: *Souvenirs*, pp. 200 ff.; Faucher, I, 219 (and cf. 205-207); and the report of a conversation of Nassau Senior with Beaumont, Molé, Tocqueville, and Cousin, May 25 (E. d'Eichthal: *Alexis de Tocqueville* [Paris, 1897. See bibliography for full title], p. 227).

June 15, by Michel Goudchaux, erstwhile member of the republican opposition under the July Monarchy. The speaker bluntly declared that "the National Workshops must disappear . . . in their entirety; [they] must go, in the provinces as well as in Paris; it is not a question of their diminution . . . they must disappear!" Goudchaux turned his attack from the institution to the workers themselves. "Les ateliers nationaux ont produit jusqu'à présent une chose dont nous n'avons pas d'exemple, je le dis, c'est-à-dire des ouvriers qui cessent d'être honnêtes!"[156] Goudchaux's unmeasured language drew a despairing rejoinder from the Workshops, widely placarded in Paris on June 18:

> Why do the National Workshops so greatly excite your disapproval, Citizen Goudchaux? It is not their reform that you ask, it is their complete suppression. But what is to be done with the *hundred and ten thousand* workers who rely on their modest daily wage as the means of existence for themselves and their families? Shall they be surrendered to the evil counsels of hunger, to the incitements of despair?[157]

The workers once again saw their rights threatened when the minister of justice, Bethmont, was interpellated, June 16, on the subject of the press laws. Bethmont declared that the July Monarchy's law on *cautionnement* for newspapers (requiring an initial "guarantee deposit" of 100,000 francs) was still on the statute books and that, although it had been unenforced since the February Revolution, the government had no intention that it should remain so. To be sure the government intended shortly to bring in a law which would *somewhat* reduce the requirements.[158] But it was understood at once that the en-

---

[156] *Moniteur,* June 16.

[157] *Commission d'enquête,* II, pp. 293-294. The savage attacks on the workers are more easily understood when it is realized that it was quite generally believed that a struggle in the streets between the forces of "order" and those of "anarchy" was inevitable. Goudchaux subsequently declared that he foresaw the insurrection, but that he considered it inevitable; that if it had come later, there would have been 10,000 dead, and that if it had come in March or April, it would have been a mere skirmish! (*ibid.,* I, p. 289).

[158] *Moniteur,* June 17. The law on *cautionnement* was among the famous "September Laws"; for its details, see Duvergier: *Collection complète des lois,* Vol. 35, pp. 265-268.

forcement of the *cautionnement* would result in the immediate suppression of the great majority of the left newspapers, whose necessarily modest subscription rates made impossible the raising of any considerable deposit sum.[159] Criticism from the left press, even bitter attacks on the law, greeted the minister's pronouncement,[160] and the typesetters of Paris sent a petition to the assembly, protesting against this assault on the "press of the poor" and arguing cogently that such a law would add their numbers to those already in the National Workshops.[161]

Three days after the unfortunate remarks of Bethmont touching the press laws, Falloux came to the tribune to present a report in behalf of the assembly's special committee on the National Workshops, adopted at his suggestion on June 14. The execution of the assembly's law had not yet been seriously undertaken, declared the report. Moreover, the expenditures of the administration had at times anticipated the appropriations of the assembly. In order to regularize this situation and to provide for the drawing up of a definitive solution for the Workshops' problem, the committee's bill proposed three measures:

(1) The appropriation of 3,000,000 francs, sought by the minister of public works, should be granted.
(2) Further appropriations should not exceed 1,000,000 francs at a time.
(3) The powers of the special committee should be continued until the assembly should decide otherwise.[162]

These measures were anything but reassuring to the workers. For, if they were adopted, the future of the Workshops would

[159] Five days later the Executive Commission was considering a very much milder law; the *procès-verbal* for the session of June 21 speaks of a "'loi nouvelle sur la presse qui repousserait le principe du cautionnement et exigerait la signature des articles'" (Seignobos: "Les procès-verbaux du Gouvernement provisoire et de la Commission du pouvoir exécutif," *Revue d'histoire moderne et contemporaine*, VII, p. 596).

[160] *Représentant du peuple*, June 18; *Peuple constituant*, June 18; *Père Duchêne*, June 20-22.

[161] *Représentant du peuple*, June 21.

[162] *Moniteur*, June 20.

be in the hands of a group known to be hostile to the institution and favorable to the thesis of immediate dissolution. Further evidence of the temper of the assembly was given the workers on the same day in a series of violent measures, happily not adopted, proposed by another deputy, Turck; among them were the following: within five days all workers not resident in Paris for one year were to be given passports and travelling expenses to return to their communes; all those having adequate outside means of support (*l'aisance*) were to be prosecuted as thieves; Paris workers with trades were to return at once to private industry, the latter to be given credit assistance; strikes were to be forbidden henceforth and punished as "rébellion à la loi." [163]

On the following day, June 20, the protracted session of the assembly was devoted in almost its entirety to the discussion of the National Workshops, apropos the measures proposed by the special committee. The debate was at times tempestuous, and the general sense of the speeches was hostile to the workers. Victor Hugo, in his first appearance in the tribune, deplored the corrupting influence of the Workshops on honest workers. His speech, which was characterized by more warmth than clarity, warned the socialists against excesses and conjured up the twin spectres of "la guerre civile et la guerre servile." Léon Faucher pictured an army of from 50,000 to 60,000 unemployed waiting to be enrolled in the Workshops and having equal rights to aid with those already members. Since work could not be found to employ this mass of idle workers, it were better to destroy the Workshops and to give the workers outright charity. La Rochejacquelein declared that substantial credit assistance to building contractors in Paris would make possible the employment of 50,000 workers of the building trades, now members of the Workshops. Caussidière rose to warn his colleagues of the dangers of unconsidered haste. The National Workshops, he declared, "font le club du désespoir tous les

soirs sur le boulevard." The workers ask for bread, or in
despair they will throw themselves on the bayonets that await
them. Caussidière's bizarre language, contrasting strangely
with the traditions of the tribune as well as with the sound
common sense of much that he said, easily won the oratorical
honors of the day, notably when he declared in picturesque
phrase "qu'il faut aujourd'hui jeter toutes les divisions dans
un sac."

In the end the report was adopted, and the hostile special
committee of the assembly was empowered to draw up a definitive plan for the dissolution of the Workshops. It is significant
that this stormy session, the most considerable yet devoted to
the question of the Workshops, was reported in the *Moniteur*
of June 21. That same day the preparations were made for
the demonstrations of June 22, which led directly to the insurrection.[164] But the grievances of the workers were destined
to be reinforced by an attack from still another quarter. For
the government, which had recently shown its hostility to the
social revolution in Marie's proposal for a law on *attroupements*, now joined actively in the assault on the Workshops.

The workers' reaction to the assembly's law of May 30 had
been sufficiently violent during the two weeks following its
passage. That the opposition was not more violent doubtless reflected the fact that, due to the inertia of the government,
the law's provisions remained virtually unexecuted. The workers were threatened with an "exil en province," it is true, but
as the days passed and no contingents left for the departments,
the proletariat doubtless became conscious that the government
itself had no desire for precipitate execution of the law. But
the Executive Commission soon changed its tone, and seemed
eager to give at least the appearance of substantial coöperation
with the assembly. Suddenly, in place of the *future possibility*
of an exile to the provinces, the workers were faced with the

---

[164] Seignobos (*Révolution de 1848*, p. 99) points out that the assembly had
not dissolved the Workshops but that it had now effectively taken from the
government the means of continuing them.

immediate reality of peremptory orders from the government.[165]

Before the assembly, June 19, Trélat read an impressive list of projects to which workers were to be sent, either immediately or within a few days. On the basis principally of the appropriations granted earlier in June,[166] there were already employed on such projects some 2,000 workers, the minister declared. By the end of the week another 5,000 would be sent. And eventually the projects actually being developed would employ 17,000 workers.[167] Actually Trélat was far too optimistic in his estimates: the total number of departures for June 22 was fifty-six, that for June 23, thirty-six,[168] and that for June 24, perhaps 400.[169] It is obvious that the government had accomplished but little in the direction of the execution of this aspect of the assembly's law. But the very fact that the government appeared to have begun seriously the deportation of workers to provincial projects caused a violent reaction[170] and was the principal ostensible cause of the demonstration of June 22, precursor of the insurrection. The feeling that the government now meant to execute the assembly's will was further empha-

[165] Apparently the government began by trying to induce the workers to volunteer for work in the provinces (on an " enlistment " basis, the *Représentant du peuple,* June 20, declares). Apparently when this scheme did not give the desired results, peremptory orders were issued, requiring the workers to leave (see the instructions of Lalanne, *République,* June 23, and elsewhere).

[166] See above, p. 121.

[167] *Moniteur,* June 20. It is difficult to reconcile Trélat's statement that 2,000 workers were already employed with the fact that the machinery for the issuance of the essential *feuilles de route* was set in operation only June 20 (Lalanne: " Lettres sur les Ateliers nationaux. IV," *National,* July 23, 1848). Moreover, Lalanne stated before the Labor Committee, June 21, that only 300 workers had thus far been sent to projects in the provinces, but promised that the end of the week would see this figure increased by 1,000 (*Proc.-verb. du com. du travail,* p. 52).

[168] *Commission d'enquête,* I, p. 303.

[169] *Ibid.,* I, p. 228. The fact that the total amount paid to workers returning to the provinces as *secours de route* was only 925 francs (see below, p. 167) indicates that the total number " deported " from Paris was altogether inconsiderable.

[170] *Ibid.,* I, pp. 302-303, II, pp. 168, 212-214; Stern, II, p. 364; *Journal des Débats,* June 23.

sized by the census at the homes of the workers, June 20,[171] for it was known that the census would reveal those who had no right to remain longer members of the Paris Workshops.

Finally, on June 16, the Executive Commission had adopted once again a plan for obligatory enlistments in the army.[172] The plan previously adopted had remained a dead letter. It required that workers, aged eighteen to twenty-five, should be offered an enlistment of two years in the army; if they refused, they were to be dismissed from the Workshops.[173] The Executive Commission's decree meant that thousands of workers were to be faced peremptorily with the alternative of an army enlistment — with the inevitable hardships, low pay, separation from their families — or the dismal prospects of pro-

---

[171] See above, p. 119, also *Commission d'enquête*, I, p. 41. Thomas (pp. 343-344) lists a further group of provocative measures, which he alleges Lalanne took on June 21: the *bureau de secours* was suppressed, the prices of the products of the shoemaking and tailoring establishments (established by Thomas and including members of the Workshops in those trades) were increased fifty per cent., the medical dispensary was suppressed, and orders were given for the immediate cessation of work in the Workshops. The latter measure particularly seems highly unlikely. Thomas rushed to see Falloux and prophesied a revolt, but the latter declared his fears exaggerated.

[172] The decision on enforced military enlistments has almost invariably been a subject of confusion by writers on the period. Renard, for example, declares that an *arrêté* of the government, of June 21, provided that workers aged 18 to 25, were to enroll in the army and that the others were to hold themselves in readiness to leave for works in the provinces (*République de 1848*, pp. 75-76). Seignobos follows Renard (*Révolution de 1848*, pp. 99-100). There was no such *arrêté* of June 21. Two separate announcements by the government have been confused. June 19, Trélat announced to the assembly the early sending of large numbers of workers to the provinces; this measure was in execution of the assembly's decree of May 30. The *Moniteur* of June 22 contained the notice on the decision regarding military enlistments, worded in such a way that it seemed to refer to an earlier decree, actually adopted June 16 but never published.

[173] Garnier-Pagès, X, p. 423. Garnier-Pagès quotes the *procès-verbal*: " ' 16 juin. La Commission du Pouvoir exécutif décide que, dans le délai de cinq jours, les ouvriers des Ateliers nationaux, âgés de 18 à 25 ans, devront contracter un engagement de deux ans dans l'armée; et, s'ils refusent, ils seront exclus des Ateliers.' " It will be noted that the decree of June 16 was to apply to *all* workers between the ages specified, whereas the earlier decision of the government had applied only to bachelors.

tracted unemployment. " La famine ou l'esclavage," comments Proudhon.[174] The adoption of this harsh measure at the time when a mass attack was being made upon the Workshops by the assembly could scarcely be viewed by the workers as other than an outright provocation, a counsel of despair to those who needed no further incitement to revolt.

Why then did the government readopt this highly obnoxious measure? In the face of the silence of the members of the Executive Commission, it is difficult to explain. The wavering character of its policy during this whole period prepares one to expect anything. This particular decision may well have reflected the government's serious alarm and the feeling that only vigorous measures would save the situation. And yet the government waited six days after adopting the measure before it was announced. It seems more likely that the continued attacks on the weakness of the government's policy, both in the press and in the assembly, had finally convinced its members that a show of resolution was essential if the government were to save itself in the approaching storm.[175] In short, it was forced to align itself with the assembly's policy of speedy dissolution in spite of its own better judgment — or shall we say, in spite of its fears?

The *Moniteur* of June 22 contained a notice, inconspicuously placed on the first page, that " The Executive Commission has given orders that enrollments [in the army] shall begin tomorrow in the National Workshops." There followed a casual reference to the " recent decision " requiring enlistment, and a further irritating statement that the execution of the measure had been deferred in order " to leave to all the young workers the time to make the choice with the necessary deliberation"! Actually the measure had never before received official publication.[176] The decision had been reached only on June 16.

---

[174] Proudhon: *Confessions*, p. 126. *République* (June 22): ".. on les place dans la triste alternative ou de devenir soldats ou de mourir de faim."

[175] On the rapid loss of prestige of the government, and especially of Trélat, see *Journal des Débats*, June 21; *Peuple constituant*, June 20, 21; *République*, June 21; *Lampion*, June 23.

[176] It appears nowhere in the *Moniteur* prior to June 22. The casual publica-

It was officially communicated to Lalanne only on June 20.[177] It became known to the workers when they were already in a state of acute agitation, and was a subject of violent protest during the demonstrations of June 22, which led directly to the insurrection of the following day.

tion of a similar decision of the government (*Journal des Débats,* May 30, and elsewhere) in no sense justifies the reference in the notice of June 22: "On se rappelle qu'une décision récente a prescrit que les ouvriers, etc."

[177] Lalanne: "Lettres sur les Ateliers nationaux. VI," *National,* August 16, 1848.

CHAPTER VI

THE JUNE DAYS

I. The Insurrection Precipitated by Agitation in the National Workshops.
II. Extent of Participation by the Workshops. III. The Final Dissolution.

FROM 1848 to the present time the traditional view of the June insurrection has insisted that the National Workshops were the cause, if not the army, of the insurrection. To what extent is this true? It is with this problem that the present chapter is concerned. It is essential first to notice in some detail the events directly leading to the insurrection, and the connection therewith of the Workshops, so far as we know it. The present account makes no attempt to deal in detail with the June Days themselves, the history of which has yet to be written.[1]

I

The immediate origins of the insurrection are to be found in a meeting held in the Faubourg Saint Marceau on June 21. It was attended by a group of leaders from the National Workshops and very possibly by delegates of the Luxembourg and representatives of the revolutionary clubs. It seems most probable that the purpose of the meeting was to arrange a protest for the morrow against the dissolution plans of the government and that the question of an eventual resort to the barricades was deferred until the answer of the government should be received.[2] Rendezvous was appointed at the Place du Panthéon at eight o'clock the following morning.[3]

[1] The insurrection awaits an adequate, full-length monograph. The most satisfactory account is that by Charles Schmidt (*Les journées de juin 1848* [Paris, 1926]), but it is brief and lacks the critical apparatus.

[2] If this were not the case, it is difficult to understand why a formal protest to the government was made at all. Valuable time would have been gained by the erection of the barricades on the twenty-second.

[3] The accounts are not concordant. Cf. Garnier-Pagès, XI, p. 60; *Commission*

That this group constituted in the beginning a sort of general staff for the badly regimented forces of the insurrection is evidenced by the rôle of one Louis Pujol, a lieutenant in the National Workshops, who had been the moving spirit in the secret meeting of June 21. Revolutionary fanatic and member of Blanqui's club, Pujol had appeared prominently in the invasion of the assembly on May 15.[4] At the age of twenty-six he had already had a turbulent career: dismissed from a seminary as a youth, he had enlisted in the African *chasseurs*, and after numerous adventures, the Revolution of February had found him in prison, from which he won release by virtue of an ode in praise of Lamartine. The eloquence and extravagance of his language had secured him dominion over the workers,[5] and for the short space of a day and a half he was to appear as leader of the insurrection.[6]

Early on the morning following the secret meeting of June 21, several hundred members of the National Workshops made their way from the Place de la Bastille toward the Panthéon. But the workers, in a state of heightened agitation, were led, not to the Panthéon, but to the Petit Luxembourg, seat of the

d'enquête, I, p. 183 (deposition of Chenu, always subject to suspicion); cf. Stern, II, p. 364.

[4] *Commission d'enquête,* I, p. 319.

[5] For his incendiary language Stern (II, pp. 365-366) refers us to a pamphlet published in 1848, *Prophétie des jours sanglants,* in which, referring to those who govern the Republic, Pujol declares: " ' Ils espèrent réserver les jours d'agonie pour le peuple et garder pour eux les fêtes et l'ivresse de l'or.' "

[6] Garnier-Pagès, XI, pp. 60, 71-72; Schmidt, p. 35. On the colorful incidents in Pujol's subsequent career, see H. Monin: " Notice sur Louis Pujol," *Révolution de 1848,* I (1904-1905), pp. 132-135. He was wounded during the June Days, then arrested. Later, when he was about to be deported to Cayenne, his sister secured an amnesty for him. Soon, however, he was obliged to flee to Spain by reason of his suspected affiliation with a secret society. There he fought on the side of the insurgents in the revolution and was made, with his friend, Captain Delmas, " national historiographer." He soon fled to England with a mistress who left her husband but took with her two small children. After various adventures in London, he abandoned his mistress, secured a modest tutorship, and married an English woman. He then went on to America and founded a girls' boarding school in New York. During the Civil War he rapidly rose to the rank of colonel in the northern army. Finally in 1866, while transporting arms to Juarez's party in Mexico, he perished in a shipwreck.

Executive Commission, where they protested noisily against the deportation of workers from Paris and enforced enlistments in the army. Marie was the only member of the government who had as yet arrived at his office. Vassal, *commissaire de police* charged with the protection of the palace, urged Marie to admit the workers within the court, trap them by shutting the gates, and then arrest the whole group. This summary procedure did not appeal to Marie as either expedient or legal. He agreed instead to receive five delegates. Pujol and four workers were accordingly admitted.[7]

Marie, who immediately recognized Pujol as one of the mob which had invaded the assembly on May 15, denied him the right to speak. Pujol was insistent. Marie turned to the others: "Have you need of Pujol's permission? Are you his slaves?" The workers broke their silence, and a bitter denunciation of the government's policy followed: they had been tricked by lying promises and now were to be forced to leave Paris to work in unhealthful conditions — to die of fever and want. To this policy their answer was peremptory: they would *not* leave Paris, they would *forcibly* resist such "inhuman laws." Marie angrily replied that the assembly's decision would be enforced at all costs. The delegates retired in a rage.[8] They were at once bombarded by the impatient questions of the waiting workers, to whom the outcome of the conference was evident in the angry faces of the delegates. Presently the crowd moved on to the Place Saint Sulpice, where Pujol harangued them, standing on the brim of the fountain. The speaker distorted Marie's language: it was made to appear that he had characterized *all* of the workers as "slaves." Pujol was answered by a tempest of shouts: "À bas Marie! À bas la Commission exécutive! À bas l'Assemblée!" A battalion of the regular army was rushed up to clear the square. With rendezvous

[7] Garnier-Pagès, XI, pp. 71-73; Cherest, p. 250; Stern, II, p. 365; *Commission d'enquête*, I, p. 319.

[8] Garnier-Pagès, XI, pp. 73-74; Cherest, pp. 251-254; Stern, II, pp. 366-368; *Commission d'enquête*, I, pp. 229, 319-320, II, pp. 179-181.

appointed in the Place du Panthéon at 6 o'clock in the evening, the crowd broke up to seek reinforcements in the National Workshops and elsewhere.[9]

Thus far the demonstration of the workers, effectively controlled by the " general staff " of the June 21 meeting, was directed against the policy of the government toward the National Workshops. Its original purpose was to protest against the decision on enforced enlistments and the departures of workers for the provinces, in short, against the imminent, though not yet decreed, dissolution of the Workshops. Only when the government proved adamant in its determination to execute these measures did Pujol's group determine to resort to the barricades. The decision of this militant group was destined to draw only a minority of the members of the Workshops into the movement. But the widely ramified elements of discontent, long secretly preparing for an eventual rising, seized the occasion and hurled themselves into the insurrection.[10]

The police reports furnish a concise but vivid picture of the uninterrupted demonstrations which followed. Shortly before eleven o'clock, a group of between 250 and 300 workers, with a National Workshops' banner at its head, was observed moving in the direction of the Place du Palais National. Soon thereafter another column of 500, also with a Workshops' flag, was reported marching along the Rue de la Tixanderie, the workers loudly acclaiming their determination to die rather

[9] Garnier-Pagès, XI, pp. 75-78; Cherest, pp. 252-253; *Commission d'enquête,* I, p. 271; *Journal des Débats,* June 23.

[10] Marrast and Carlier, " directeur de la police au cabinet du Ministère de l'Intérieur," subsequently declared that the insurrection had been set for July 14 (the day of the popular " Banquet à 25 centimes ") and that the " factieux " were impelled to strike earlier by the opportunity offered in the revolt within the Workshops (*Commission d'enquête,* I, pp. 247, 323). On the extensive preparations of the insurgents, see the opinions of General Lamoricière (*ibid.,* I, p. 307) and Colonel Allard (*ibid.,* I, pp. 220-221). But cf. Proudhon's view that the arrangement of the streets suggested a natural strategic plan for the erection of the barricades and that the habit of resorting to barricades had by now everywhere produced *barricadeurs* (*ibid.,* I, p. 337).

than to leave for the Sologne.[11]   Similar and even more violent sentiments were expressed by groups gathered near the Hôtel de Ville at noon. Shortly before one o'clock some 200 members of the Workshops were seen marching along the Rue Saint Victor, shouting the hour of the rendezvous: " Ce soir, à six heures, au Panthéon! " At two o'clock a crowd which had assembled in the Place du Panthéon set out for the Luxembourg, shouting: " À bas Lamartine! vive Napoléon! " Everywhere the hour of the rendezvous was made known, everywhere the Workshops were the subject of agitated discussion.

As the afternoon progressed the workers grew more numerous in the Place du Panthéon; by seven o'clock a milling crowd of from 4,000 to 5,000 had gathered. Suddenly two huge columns began to move off, one in the direction of the Faubourg Saint Marceau, the other down the Rue Saint Jacques. The latter procession, numbering some 3,000 workers and carrying a dozen National Workshops' flags, followed a circuitous route to the Place de la Bastille to shouts of " Du travail! du pain! nous ne partirons pas! " What was apparently the same procession, but now increased to between 8,000 and 10,000 and carrying a great number of flags, passed the Hôtel de Ville at nine o'clock. The latter was now heavily guarded by troops, and a crowd estimated at 100,000 was densely packed in the square and in the streets adjoining.[12]

The column soon proceeded again along the Rue Saint Jacques. Shouts of " Vive Barbès, ou du plomb! " rang out. The shops closed as the procession drew near. Presently it was again in the Place du Panthéon. There Pujol, surrounded by torches and flags of the National Workshops, harangued the crowd. " The people have been deceived! you have done nothing more than change tyrants, and the tyrants of today are more odious than those who have been driven out. . . . You must take vengeance! and to avenge yourselves, you have an

---

[11] " Ils ajoutent qu'ils prendront les armes contre l'Assemblée Nationale, et qu'ils seront secondés par la garde mobile" (*Commission d'enquête*, II, p. 212).

[12] Garnier-Pagès, XI, p. 91.

invincible weapon in the barricades."[13]   The workers were
summoned to gather at six o'clock the following morning. The
unyielding tactics of the government were to be answered by
force.

　　　*　　　　*　　　　*　　　　*　　　　*

While the demonstrations in the streets continued uninterruptedly, the Executive Commission was feverishly seeking
measures for the effective control of the now alarming course
of events. Attempts to arrest Pujol, his companions of the
morning conference at the Luxembourg, and a group of fifty-
six delegates of the Workshops, were fruitless. Lacking the
addresses of the workers in question, the government appealed
to Lalanne. The director declared himself unable to furnish
even such elementary information in the face of the chaotic
state of the records of the Workshops' administration![14]   It is
in the highest degree unlikely that such an action would have
checked perceptibly the course of the insurrection.[15]   And
indeed by the morning of the 23rd the government had adopted
a contrary policy: instead of attempting to arrest the insurrection in its inception, it had decided that it should be allowed
to crystallize in such a way that effective mass military action
could be taken against it. This was the work of Cavaignac,
minister of war, supported by Lamartine. The plan was attacked by Ledru-Rollin and the other members of the Executive Commission, whose consent was only won at six o'clock on
the morning of June 23.[16]   Whatever wisdom there may have

[13] Garnier-Pagès, XI, pp. 95-96.

[14] " L'armée de 103,500 hommes à laquelle je commande, n'a pas d'autre contrôle que les bulletins de recensement; et ces bulletins sont encore entre les mains
des vingt-cinq maires de Paris et des principales communes de la banlieue. Tant
qu'on ne m'aura pas rendu ces bulletins, je resterai dans l'impuissance de pren-
dre aucune mesure radicale, sans être arrêté dans l'exécution" (letter of Lalanne,
June 22, 1848, Commission d'enquête, II, p. 180). On the whole incident of the
attempted arrests and the dilatory tactics of the government, see ibid., I, 332,
361-362, II, pp. 44-45, 179-181; Cherest, pp. 253-255; and cf. Garnier-Pagès,
XI, p. 82.

[15] Cherest, pp. 257-258.

[16] P. Quentin-Bauchart: Lamartine, homme politique; la politique intérieure
(Paris, 1903), p. 363; le Général Ibos: Le Général Cavaignac. Un dictateur
républicain (Paris, 1930), pp. 162-163.

been in this course from a military point of view, it unquestionably permitted the insurrection to magnify itself considerably, and allowed other large elements of discontent to incorporate themselves with the protesting groups from the National Workshops.

*   *   *   *

At the same hour when the government's decision was taken, several thousand workers gathered in the Place du Panthéon. Pujol harangued the manifestants, who, with flags unfurled, then took their way toward the Place de la Bastille. There, with the crowd on its knees about the *Colonne de juillet,* Pujol invoked the heroes of the Bastille. "Liberty or death!" demanded the speaker. "Liberty or death!" the mob responded.[17] The procession then marched on, brigadiers of the National Workshops at its head. At the end of the Rue Saint Denis it halted. A whistle sounded. The crowd stopped an omnibus, dragged the driver from his seat, forced the passengers to the ground, and overturned the vehicle, shouting "To the barricades!" Armed men rushed together from every direction. The insurrection had begun.[18]

On the first barricade, which rapidly assumed large proportions, appeared a flag bearing the words, "Ateliers nationaux, 4ᵉ arrondissement, 5ᵉ section."[19] Other barricades followed in quick succession, and by noon all of the east of Paris was organized for war. Henceforth the movement became infinitely more complex, and the elements from the National Workshops, which had taken a leading rôle up to this point, were virtually lost sight of in the chaos of the fighting.

*   *   *   *

With the excited agitation of the workers hourly thrusting the Republic nearer the verge of civil war, the assembly's special committee on the Workshops continued the preparation of a definitive solution of the problem. Falloux's activities on June 23 throw clear light both on his determination to have a speedy

[17] Schmidt, pp. 38-39.

[18] *Journal des Débats,* June 24; *Réforme,* June 24; Schmidt, p. 39.

[19] *Ibid.,* p. 40; *Organisation du travail,* June 24.

solution of the question and on the dominant position which he
occupied in the committee. The committee met at ten o'clock
on the morning of the 23rd. A draft decree, providing for the
dissolution of the Workshops within three days, followed by
the payment of a transition dole at the homes of the workers,
was ready for presentation to the assembly. The decree was
scheduled to have been presented only on June 24. The insurrection had already begun. When it seemed to certain members
of the committee that the presentation would now be untimely,
even provocative (as it subsequently seemed also to the assembly), Falloux insisted not only that the report be presented but
that it be presented that very day, June 23. From the length
and warmth of Falloux's speech to his colleagues it is obvious
to what extent he felt obliged to influence them to follow the
course he had set for himself. He even threatened them with
resignation.[20] Despite all his efforts, two of his fourteen colleagues voted against his proposal, and one of these resigned.[21]

Falloux's naïve explanation, or more properly his two explanations of the episode, are revealing of his policy. Before the
assembly on May 24, 1849, in defending his actions on June 23,
he declared:

. . . I said to my colleagues: The civil war has begun; the responsibility is neither yours, nor that of anyone in this assembly. There is something of which I must think, however, my honor, and this is how I conceive
it: if the misguided workers who attack us are defeated tomorrow, I will
never consent to sponsor a measure which they regard as disastrous to
them. . . . I will not allow them to think that I awaited their defeat to
proclaim here what you have for a long time believed desirable and necessary. I am the reporter of the Committee on the National Workshops
today, this very morning, or I will never be; for, after the battle, I declare
to you that I will resign. . . .[22]

Curiously enough this account of Falloux's speech is probably accurate. In any event none of the members of the special
committee who were present in the assembly on May 24, 1849,

[20] *Moniteur,* May 25, 1849.
[21] Falloux: *Mémoires,* I, pp. 337-338. De Montreuil and Dupont de Bussac
voted *contra;* the latter resigned in protest.
[22] *Moniteur,* May 25, 1849.

contested it. But one is permitted to believe that Falloux was thinking on June 23, not of justice for the workers, but of the triumph of the forces of order. This he admits in his *Mémoires,* written thirty years later. There he does not so much as allude to the cause of the workers:

> Paris had at that time only two defensive forces, the National Guard, almost unanimously of the same sentiment as the assembly, and the *Garde mobile.* The *Garde mobile* had been organized in February. Some of its battalions had obeyed the call of duty on May 15, but on the latter date this young militia, composed for the most part of Parisians, had been given only a brief test and its attitude remained very doubtful. The army of the party of order needed, therefore, to feel that it was energetically supported by the assembly, . . . and, when our committee met on the morning of June 23, it had but one question to discuss: should it await the outcome of the struggle already begun before announcing its decision, or ought it give at once to the National Guard and the *Garde mobile* pledge of its resolute coöperation and proof of its determination to face all dangers in common? [23]

The latter decision was taken. The forces of order were to present a united front in the face of the " forces of anarchy." But when Falloux came to the tribune that same afternoon, he was faced by resistance, even to the reading of his report. That morning Falloux had given his colleagues of the committee to understand that he wished to avoid everything that might irritate the workers. But the language of his report, which he had drafted himself *after* the conclusion of the morning meeting of the committee,[24] was not particularly reassuring for the workers. The abuses in the Workshops, said Falloux, " have paralyzed industry, alarmed the provinces, disturbed confidence, and as a result have struck at the very sources of the public wealth." He asked the " dispersion radicale de ce foyer actif, concentré, d'agitation stérile." But this time Falloux had gone too far. Many of his colleagues in the assembly obviously feared the provocative effect which the decree might have on the workers, and the discussion was postponed to the Greek calends.[25]

[23] Falloux: *Mémoires,* I, p. 337.
[24] *Ibid.,* I, p. 338.
[25] *Moniteur,* June 24.

II

From its very nature, the problem of the extent of the participation of the members of the National Workshops in the June insurrection can never be satisfactorily solved. On July 3 Cavaignac, who had no desire to minimize the achievement of the army in suppressing the insurrection, declared to the assembly that the *highest* estimate he had been given of the total number of the insurgents was 50,000.[26] Since the number enrolled in the Workshops was between 105,000 and 106,000, continued the president of the council,[27] and since a large number of the insurgents were unquestionably not members of that organization, it was mathematically obvious that only a minority from the Workshops could have been present behind the barricades.[28] The highest estimate of this latter number is that of Quentin-Bauchart, the very hostile *rapporteur* of the assembly's well-known Committee of Investigation on the June Days, who refers to the " 25,000 or 30,000 workers of the National Workshops who formed the heaviest battalions in the insurrection." [29] Lalanne, interested in presenting a favorable record for the organization which it was his function to control, estimates the total number of participants at from 5,000 to 6,000.[30] The truth lies somewhere between these two

[26] Léon Faucher, a naturally prejudiced witness, gives (I, p. 225) the number as 60,000. The prefect of police, Trouvé-Chauvel, estimated the total number of insurgents as between 40,000 and 50,000 (*Commission d'enquête*, I, p. 358). The number of arrests was estimated at 25,000 (Renard: *République de 1848*, p. 82) ; half of this number was released without examination after a few days, for lack of space (Stern, II, p. 479). No comment is needed on the difficulty of making any satisfactory estimate of the total number involved.

[27] Cavaignac was made " chef du pouvoir exécutif " on the morning of June 24, after which the Executive Commission resigned. After the insurrection he relinquished his powers as interim dictator and was given in turn the executive power as " président du conseil des ministres."

[28] *Moniteur,* July 4, 1848.

[29] Quentin-Bauchart: *Études et souvenirs,* I, p. 203.

[30] *Commission d'enquête,* I, pp. 303-304. This figure was based on the verbal reports of the *chefs d'arrondissements,* and Lalanne admits that it was at best only " une appréciation conjecturale." The director seems also to have been in-

obviously prejudiced estimates, probably nearer Lalanne's
figure.[31] In any event, even if 20,000 members from the Workshops participated, that would mean only a minority of one in
six, since there were actually about 120,000 men still receiving
pay, June 22,[32] and not 106,000 as Cavaignac stated later.

What are the reasons for this seemingly anomalous situation?
When the institution was being attacked from all sides and
when its dissolution seemed imminent, why did not a much
larger proportion of the workers take up arms in support of
their "rights"?

The government's decision to continue the pay within the
Workshops during the insurrection was apparently a factor of
primary importance in securing the neutrality of the great
majority of the workers. This policy did not of course affect
those who answered the call to arms and fought with the
National Guard from the outset.[33] It affected that large group
(probably a majority) who refused to answer the National
Guard *rappel*, who refused to take arms against their brother
workers; but who, their daily wage assured, were apparently
unwilling to invite the risks to themselves and their families

fluenced, in arriving at this figure, by the fact that a twentieth of the workers
failed to appear for their pay, June 23. Marie gives the same figure as Lalanne
(*ibid.*, I, p. 320).

[31] A *bordereau* of the Ministry of Finance, listing sums paid to each of the
arrondissements during the period June 27 - July 4, throws some light on the
question of the number of participants from the Workshops (*Arch. nat.* C 920
A, *Dossier* 256). If it is assumed that pay was made for each of the seven days
noted (Sunday, July 2, excluded), the total of 1,004,987 francs has then to be
divided, first by seven, and then by 1.33, the average daily wage in francs of
the workers. From this number of approximately 108,000 must be deducted a
number representing the budget for the officers and members of the administration, etc. This figure cannot be fixed exactly, but it would still leave the
number of workers well above 100,000. If it can be assumed that the participants in the insurrection did not present themselves for their pay (which it
seems unlikely they would do), then we have an indication that the total
participation was fewer than 20,000 (deducting 100,000-105,000, as the number
being paid June 27 - July 4, from the total enrollment of 120,000).

[32] Lalanne: "Lettres sur les Ateliers nationaux. I," *National*, July 14, 1848.

[33] Cf., e.g., Delessard, p. 28.

involved in openly joining the insurgents — at least not until
the success of the movement seemed assured.[34]

Faced with a situation which demanded immediate action,
Lalanne decided on his own responsibility, June 23, to continue
the pay.[35] This measure was subsequently approved by General Cavaignac, Trélat, and Sénard, president of the assembly.[36] The pay was continued at the regular stations, and the
officers of the Workshops were instructed simultaneously to
use every influence to induce their workers not to join the insurgents.[37] Both Cavaignac and Lalanne subsequently defended this policy as having induced an overwhelming majority of the workers to abstain from participation in the insurrection.[38] And it seems only natural that the immediate
cessation of their means of livelihood would have exasperated
thousands of workers and would have driven them into the
arms of the insurgents.[39] On the other hand, the policy was

[34] *Commission d'enquête*, I, p. 325; see also *ibid.*, I, p. 367; A. Pagès-Duport:
*Journées de juin. Récit complet des événements des 23, 24, 25, 26 et des jours
suivants* (Paris, 1848), p. 102; and *Démocratie pacifique*, July 1, 1848. Bouniols
(p. 243) refers to a meeting of 2,500 members of the National Workshops in the
Salle Barthélemy on the night of June 22-23. This group calmly voted a list of
demands and a "démarche pacifique" to be made to the minister of public
works. From the latter they receievd a vaguely encouraging reply at 6 o'clock
the morning of June 23. Bouniols gives no source, but the meeting very probably
took place; it witnesses the existence of both militant and more pacific elements
within the Workshops, and explains to a degree the small participation of the
workers.

[35] Lalanne: "Lettres sur les Ateliers nationaux. VII," *National*, August 26,
1848.

[36] *Commission d'enquête*, I, p. 303; *Moniteur*, July 4, 1848.

[37] Lalanne: "Lettres sur les Ateliers nationaux. VII," *National*, August 26,
1848. Lalanne had sufficient funds to make the usual pay on June 23; about a
twentieth of the workers did not appear. But the ministry of finance refused
to honor a requisition for an additional 200,000 francs, with the result that the
director was obliged to empty his reserve and then had only 80,000 francs for
the pay of June 24. June 25 was Sunday, which was not a day of work, and
on June 26 no pay was made for the first time. On that day Lalanne was advised by Cavaignac that henceforth the function of paying the workers was to
be transferred to the *mairies*. The director immediately resigned.

[38] Lalanne: *loc. cit.*; *Moniteur*, July 4, 1848.

[39] Lalanne (*loc. cit.*) declares that in many places workers awaited their pay
patiently, whereas at other stations, where funds were not available, the insurrection made many recruits.

subjected to harsh criticism by those who believed that the pay had actually nourished the insurrection.[40]   When General Lamoricière discovered that Lalanne had issued *laisser-passer* to officers of the Workshops bearing the pay money, he fulminated: " If this man is not brought to me and shot, I will answer for nothing." [41]   In so far as the pay was made in the territory of the enemy and to members of the Workshops receiving the inactivity dole, nothing could prevent workers from leaving the fray long enough to receive their pay.   And there is scattering evidence that the pay actually did aid the insurrection in numerous cases.[42]   If, however, the continuance of the pay was a substantial factor in inducing 80,000 or 100,000 men to abstain from the insurrection, it was money well spent from the point of view of the government.

The influence of the government's policy becomes clearer when the general character of the movement is considered. If members of the Workshops were immobilized by the continuance of their pay, the large numbers of unemployed, to whom admission to the Workshops had been refused in recent weeks, were probably in many instances driven to revolt by hunger.[43] Lalanne estimated that there were approximately 20,000 unemployed cabinetmakers alone in the Faubourg Saint Antoine at the time of the insurrection,[44] and Léon Faucher declared to the assembly, June 20, that the number of unemployed in

[40] *Commission d'enquête,* I, p. 42; but see the further qualification on p. 43.

[41] *Ibid.,* I, p. 304.

[42] *Ibid.,* I, pp. 234, 275, 300, 306-307, 333-334; Delessard: *Souvenirs,* pp. 29-30. Lalanne himself expressed fears on this score, and in transferring the system of pay to the *mairies* (June 26), urged that only workers showing a certificate of service in the National Guard should receive their wages (letter of June 26 to the mayor of the eleventh arrondissement, *Arch. de la Seine. Mairies* O²ᵇ, no. 4613).

[43] Cf. conversation of Tocqueville with Nassau Senior, May 17, 1853 (D'Eichthal, p. 328). General Duvivier, mortally wounded during the insurrection, warned those in power on his death bed: " ' Ces pauvres ouvriers ont besoin d'être contenues, mais il faut faire quelque chose pour eux; il faut leur donner du travail, il faut que la main de la Patrie s'ouvre ' " (quoted by Schmidt, p. 127).

[44] *Commission d'enquête,* I, p. 302.

Paris, outside the Workshops, was between 50,000 and 60,000.[45] By forbidding further enrollments in the Workshops, government and assembly had taken from these men the only possible immediate source of livelihood.[46] It is not difficult to believe that it was from this group that the heaviest contingents for the insurrection were recruited.

But these men were not influenced merely, or even primarily, by hunger. They had been disillusioned by the failure of government and assembly to keep faith with promises made in February — promises which were, it is true, unwillingly given, vague, impracticable in large measure. And the persistent attacks on the workers in June convinced these workers that the return of the economic conditions of the July Monarchy was being hastened by the forces of the " reaction," that there was little hope of achieving the economic improvement for which they had fought in February. Hence, goaded by hunger, preferring sudden death to the torture of want,[47] these men resolved to risk all in the hope of realizing those vague aims of social regeneration which, struggling to become explicit since the beginning of the revolution, they believed would assure the future felicity of the worker.

That this was so, that the June Days were a crusade for an ideal, despite all the barbarities committed (and these were not restricted to the *barricadeurs*), is attested by the very *naïveté* of the insurgents' aims. The report of the Committee of Investigation on the June Days reproduces two posters of capital interest published by the insurrectionists. Here appear none of the excesses subsequently attributed to the insurgents by a frightened bourgeois press (indeed one of the posters insists that the Republic is a defence of property!). The workers ask merely what they have been asking since the February

---

[45] *Moniteur*, June 21.

[46] See especially the significant letter of Lalanne to the Executive Commission, June 13, stressing the serious character of the situation as a result of the cessation of enrollments (" Lettres sur les Ateliers nationaux. VI," *National*, August 16, 1848).

[47] See, e.g., *Commission d'enquête*, I, p. 326.

Days, the establishment of the " République démocratique et sociale." [48] Their " Republic" remained a vague utopia, far less defined for them even than for leaders like Louis Blanc, whose ideas at the end of June were still so nebulous that he deplored the coming of civil war at a time when nothing was "ready for the *immediate solution* of the problem of poverty! " [49] It was this enthusiasm for a symbol, this religious fervor for a vague principle that explains the heroic tenacity, the superb resistance of those who held the barricades. "It is this sort of revolutionary religion," said Tocqueville afterwards, "that our bayonets and our cannon will not destroy." [50]

The June Days were then the work of a militant minority among the proletariat, fired by utopian aspirations which the government and assembly would not, and in some measure could not, satisfy. These militant, though apparently little coördinated, elements had for some time been resolved to resort to force, as the extensive character of their preparations attests. They merely availed themselves of the opportunity offered by the decision of Pujol and his Workshops' followers to precipitate the conflict. [51]

III

The proportion of the Workshops' members actually participating in the insurrection may have been relatively small, but government, assembly, and the mass of public opinion were at once convinced that the Workshops had been the cause and, in large measure, the army of the revolt. [52] The newspapers of the right opened a violent attack upon the institution and

[48] For the posters, see *Commission d'enquête,* II, p. 290; cf. *ibid.,* II, p. 289; cf. Pagès-Duport, p. 97, and *Commission d'enquête,* I, p. 38.

[49] *Ibid.,* I, p. 115.

[50] Letter of Tocqueville, July 21, 1848 (parts of which are cited by Renard: *République de 1848,* pp. 85-86) ; cf. Stern, II, p. 370. On elements and causes, see also Renard: *op. cit.,* pp. 84 ff.; Proudhon (*Commission d'enquête,* I, p. 337); cf. *ibid.,* II, p. 129.

[51] Cf. *Commission d'enquête,* I, p. 366.

[52] See, e.g., Barrot, II, p. 285, who declares that the Workshops " formaient, sinon la totalité, au moins une grande partie de l'armée qui combattait en juin." Barrot was president of the Commission of Investigation on the June Days.

demanded the instant dissolution of this "armée de guerre civile." [53] No story was too exaggerated to lack hearers. Even the ordinarily sane *Journal des Débats* suggested that the extreme cruelties of the insurgents probably reflected the presence of 22,000 liberated criminals in the ranks of the Workshops. [54] Similar tales were widely credited. To be sure, the organs of the center and left urged moderation and a just appreciation of the workers' grievances. [55] But the "great fear" of the days of the barricades had blasted their influence. Madame Agoult, who was not given to overstatement, declared that the insurrection left society a "prey to a feeling of terror incomparable to anything since the invasion of Rome by the barbarians." [56] So great was the exodus from Paris for the provinces and foreign parts that the prefecture of police was obliged to take special measures to care for the "enormous crowds" seeking passports. [57]

The civil war at an end, the question of the Workshops again appeared on the assembly's official order of business for June 29. But its discussion was postponed at Cavaignac's request. The president of the council of ministers had determined to resolve the matter without the intervention of the assembly. On July 3 he came to the tribune merely to defend formally the policy embodied in the executive decree which definitely abolished the Workshops. He knew of course that he was preaching to the converted.

[53] *Constitutionnel*, June 30: "Que les ateliers nationaux soient immédiatement dissous, ainsi que le gouvernement en a donné aujourd'hui la promesse. Ces prétendus ateliers n'étaient qu'un camp ouvert pour la révolte; un piège dressé aux bons ouvriers sans travail, pour les embaucher au service de l'émeute; un foyer de conspiration; une école de barricades. Il faut donner par d'autres moyens efficaces du travail aux bras inoccupés, mais se hâter de licencier cette armée de guerre civile. . . ."

[54] *Journal des Débats*, June 29.

[55] *National*, July 3, 4; *Démocratie pacifique*, June 28, July 1; *Réforme*, July 4; *Peuple constituant*, July 4. The conservative Catholic *Univers* took the same point of view (July 3).

[56] Stern, II, pp. 472-473; see also pp. 478 ff., Renard: *République de 1848*, pp. 81-82 and *passim*, and the *Constitutionnel*, June 30.

[57] Robin, II, pp. 358-359.

The Workshops, originally organized for a laudable purpose, had been perverted, and had escaped from the control of the administration, declared Cavaignac. Attempts to dissolve the institution peacefully were fruitless. Indeed it was when the workers realized that these efforts were sincere that they hurled themselves into the civil war. It was true that only a minority from the Workshops had participated in the insurrection, admitted the president of the council. But if the *great majority* of the members of the Workshops did not fight behind the barricades, they were none the less " perhaps sympathetic " with the insurrection. The institution was a menace to the Republic. Already the function of paying the workers had been transferred from the Monceau administration to the *mairies*, and today, declared Cavaignac, " I can announce to the assembly that the National Workshops of Paris are completely dissolved, that they have ceased to exist." [58]

*   *   *   *   *

With the suppression of the Workshops the history of the institution itself naturally ends. Of its members, some were destined to be " transported " as insurgents, some continued to be given aid at the Paris *mairies*, some were sent to work projects in the provinces,[59] others still were returned to their homes in the departments. But the subsequent fate of these men is a story which, though of great human interest and not without some historic significance, forms more properly an aspect of the later social and economic history of the Second Republic.

[58] *Moniteur*, July 4.
[59] See, e.g., C. Schmidt: " Les ouvriers des Ateliers nationaux au chemin de fer d'Orléans," *Révolution de 1848*, XXIII (1926-1927), pp. 781-787.

CONCLUSION

IT is perfectly evident that the Provisional Government was faced at the outset with an unemployment problem demanding immediate remedy. Action was the more urgent by reason of the imperious demands of the still armed forces of the social revolution. It is difficult to see, therefore, how some such concession as the National Workshops, serving at once to care for the unemployed and to placate the social revolutionaries, could have been avoided. It is none the less true that the imminence of the dissolution of the Workshops precipitated the June insurrection. Could the latter have been avoided, had the government and assembly pursued other policies toward the National Workshops?

Before the assembly was convened the Workshops had become an agglomeration of more than 100,000 men. Under the exceptional business conditions prevailing it was not unnatural that unemployment should have reached these proportions. Moreover, the revolutionary government, but recently established, was far from functioning efficiently; it experienced real difficulties in preventing large numbers of unemployed from coming to Paris from the provinces. But the fact that the government proved completely ineffective in finding work projects to employ at least a good part of these men involves it in a heavy responsibility. Falloux later charged that the plans for the projects so readily found by the government engineers under the Lalanne administration had long since been elaborated. And the charge is, at least in some degree, justified.[1] In any event it was the province of Marie to oblige the engineers to yield their coöperation. His failure to do so resulted in the formation of an idle army of the proletariat of

[1] Certain of these projects (plans, estimates, etc.) can be examined in the *Archives nationales*. C 920 A. At least two of them had been prepared several months previous to the time they were voted.

menacing proportions and demoralized personnel. It is difficult
to believe that a vigorous policy would not have found serious
employment for a large proportion of these men in and near
Paris. It is true of course that Marie and the majority of his
colleagues viewed the Workshops merely as an unavoidable
concession to the radicals and as a temporary expedient at
best. But this did not prevent them from perceiving the danger to public order of this growing army of idle men. Whatever their view of the social question may have been, their
responsibility was clear: it was to provide serious employment
for the members of the Workshops pending the return of
normal conditions.

Having permitted this army to accumulate in Paris without
serious employment, the Executive Commission (it included
five members of the former Provisional Government) determined brusquely to dissolve it. This policy, which might well
have precipitated an insurrection at once, was not carried into
effect, and yielded for a period to a program of moderation. But
the government's policy — or lack of policy — had none the
less a direct influence on the insurrection in June. One of its
members, Garnier-Pagès, was directly responsible for the arbitrary removal of Thomas. The latter act, to which the other
members of the government gave their subsequent tacit assent, caused a very serious repercussion in the Workshops and
marked the beginning of the disaffection of the workers.
Moreover, in the end, the government abandoned its policy of
moderation and weakly joined the assembly's assault on the
Workshops, promulgating the unfortunate decision on enforced
military enlistments.

While the government vacillated, the assembly resolutely
took in hand the problem of the dissolution of the Workshops.
Falloux at least — and certain of his colleagues — were subject to none of the government's hesitations. Falloux was
from the beginning partisan of a rapid solution of the question. His statements before the Labor Committee bear witness
that he faced even the prospect of an insurrection with equan-
imity. When the government failed to take measures which

looked to the speedy execution of the assembly's decree of May 30, Falloux cleverly manœuvred the question out of the hands of the too pacific Labor Committee and had it placed in those of a special committee chosen in the *bureaux*. He dominated the special committee, especially by reason of his expert knowledge of the question. He continued to urge an early solution, and, even after the insurrection had begun, he insisted upon the immediate presentation of a bill envisaging dissolution within three days. This act even his colleagues in the assembly, favorable as they were to an early solution, regarded as provocative. It can be said with assurance that, in so far as the campaign for the dissolution of the Workshops was a cause of the insurrection, Falloux's responsibility for the decisions taken was a heavy one.

But even if the responsibilities of government and assembly could be nicely determined, there would remain a much larger question. When the decisions of government and assembly are examined more closely, it will be seen that they were the manifestations of far deeper causes. If the insurrection in June was inevitable, as many have believed both then and since, it was rendered so by the essential dichotomy of the Revolution, by the opposition of two fundamentally different theories of society and of government. Did the Revolution signify merely the adoption of universal suffrage, with the preservation intact of the existing economic system, in short, the formation of a regime in which the landed aristocracy and the bourgeoisie would continue to dominate the scene? Or did the Revolution and universal suffrage constitute merely a vestibule to the far wider and somewhat intangible perspectives of a society regenerated in the interests of the worker? These opposing ideas are brought into focus in the case of the establishment of the National Workshops. The forces of " order " saw in them a temporary expedient, the workers a gage to the social revolution. When, therefore, the former undertook the dissolution of the Workshops, the workers believed themselves the victims of a cruel deception. What the social revolutionaries could not accomplish by peaceful means

in the face of the hostility of the vast majority of their coun-
trymen, they determined to achieve by force. Hence the insurrection in June, which doomed not only the social revolution but the Republic itself.

APPENDIX

APPENDIX I

NUMBERS ENROLLED IN THE NATIONAL WORKSHOPS

Growth of the Workshops

March 15	14,000
March 31	28,350
April 15	64,870
April 30	99,400
May 15	113,010
May 31	116,110
June 15	117,310

WITH the exception of that for March 15, the figures are derived from a table given by Lalanne.[1] In the case of the enrollment, as of March 15, Thomas' figure of 14,000[2] seems to be nearer the truth than Lalanne's of 5,100, especially since the latter subsequently accepted the number given by Thomas.[3] The workers of the *banlieue* were admitted to the Workshops, between May 1 and May 12. On the latter date the enrollments were in theory stopped.[4] Lalanne stated that the number receiving pay, as of June 7, was actually higher than his figures indicated — between 119,000 and 120,000.[5]

The census of June 7 gave a total number legitimately enrolled of 103,184.[6] It was to this figure that those on the payroll of the Workshops should have been reduced.[7] The *contrôle simultané* of June 20 at the *mairies* revealed a further reduction of 6,000, and it was estimated that the further verification of workers' statements by the mayors (*contrôle*

---

[1] Lalanne: "Lettres sur les Ateliers nationaux. I," *National*, July 14, 1848. These figures were selected (apparently as being the most reliable) for the report of the Committee of the *Cour des comptes* on the accounts of the Workshops' administration (*Commission d'enquête*, II, p. 156).

[2] Thomas, p. 89.

[3] Lalanne: *Rectification historique*, p. 3.

[4] *Arch. nat.* C 920 A, *Dossier* 256.

[5] Lalanne: "Lettres sur les Ateliers nationaux. I," *National*, July 14, 1848.

[6] Lalanne: "Lettres sur les Ateliers nationaux. V," in *National*, August 6, 1848. But Mary, vice president of the National Workshops' Commission, in a report to the assembly's Labor Committee, June 10, declared that it was expected that the total would be increased to 106,000 or 107,000 by the addition of a sick list, etc. (see above, p. 119).

[7] For the reasons why the reduction was not made promptly see below, p. 166.

moral) would lead to another reduction of about 6,000, making a total number enrolled of 91,000 or 92,000.[8]

Thomas' own fragmentary figures on the growth of the Workshops are erratic and unreliable. He speaks of a total of 25,000 for March 16,[9] and of a total of 14,000 for March 17![10] He gives 30,000 as the total on March 21.[11] Elsewhere Thomas gives a total of 66,000 for April 16[12] and of 120,000 for May 26.[13] Both these latter figures approximate those given by Lalanne.

*   *   *   *   *

The phenomenal growth of the Workshops has been the subject of repeated comment by the present writer. No figures are available to show just what elements composed the Workshops; i.e., to what extent the membership was native Parisian or composed of workers from the provinces and from abroad; how many liberated criminals the institution included; etc. An embarrassing influx of the provincial unemployed was one of the most serious problems facing the administration from the first.[14] There is evidence of a substantial immigration of foreign workers, notably from Belgium, to take advantage of the employment offered by the Paris Workshops.[15] Stories that the Workshops were peopled with liberated criminals were of course current.[16] Carlier, of the minister of the interior's police, estimated that half of all the *libérés* in France, about 12,500, were in Paris.[17]

---

[8] Lalanne: "Lettres sur les Ateliers nationaux. V," in *National,* August 6, 1848.

[9] Thomas, p. 197.

[10] *Ibid.,* pp. 97-98.

[11] *Ibid.,* p. 146.

[12] *Ibid.,* p. 197.

[13] *Commission d'enquête,* I, p. 351.

[14] Address of Recurt to a deputation of workers from Ivry (*Moniteur,* March 24, 1848). *Commission d'enquête,* II, p. 171; Garnier-Pagès, IX, p. 80; Thomas, pp. 207-208; Cherest, p. 191.

[15] Caussidière warned foreign workers that they could not enter the Workshops and would be expelled from France (*Moniteur,* March 20, 1848). Cf. *Commission d'enquête,* I, p. 246; II, p. 170; and Garnier-Pagès, II, p. 26.

[16] See, e.g., *Journal des Débats,* June 29, 1848.

[17] *Commission d'enquête,* I, p. 246; cf. *ibid.,* II, p. 173.

APPENDIX II

THE FINANCES OF THE NATIONAL WORKSHOPS, WITH SPECIAL REFERENCE TO THE SYSTEM OF ACCOUNTING

ON the subject of the finances and the system, or systems, of accounting of the National Workshops, two reports of fundamental importance exist. One, the report of a committee of three appointed by the minister of public works, June 1, 1848,[1] to examine the accounts of the Thomas administration, may be consulted in the *Archives nationales*.[2] The other, the report of a committee of three members of the *Cour des comptes*, appointed July 8, 1848, by the Committee of Investigation on the June Days, exists as part of the report of the latter committee.[3] Whereas the first deals only with the Thomas regime, the latter surveys the whole period of the existence of the Workshops. The latter report, however, was prepared with considerable haste — the Report of the Committee of Investigation on the June Days appeared August 3, 1848 [4] — while the former was accomplished with greater care.[5]

In accordance with the order of June 27 from the Committee of Investi-

---

[1] *Moniteur*, June 2, 1848. The *Commission spéciale pour la liquidation du compte des ateliers nationaux pendant la gestion d'Émile Thomas* included Eveillé, government engineer; Roy, *inspecteur des finances*, who had organized the system of accounting used by the Workshops' administration; and Gonssolin, one of the former assistant directors of the Workshops under Thomas. Etienne, of the *Cour des comptes*, was subsequently added to the committee (*Commission d'enquête*, II, pp. 168-169).

[2] *Archives nationales*. C 920 A. *Dossier* 256. Hereafter cited as *Archives nationales. Rapport de la Commission pour la liquidation du compte d'Émile Thomas*. The report was submitted to the minister of public works some time after the first of October. It bears no date.

[3] *Commission d'enquête*, II, pp. 141 ff. The *Rapport fait au nom de la Commission chargée d'examiner le projet de loi relatif au règlement des comptes de 1848, par M. Théodore Ducos, représentant du peuple. Séance du 25 juin, 1851* (Paris, 1851, 191 pp.) adds nothing of importance. It can be consulted in the *Moniteur*, June 26, 1851, and elsewhere.

[4] *Moniteur*, August 4, 1848.

[5] See above, p. 108 ff. The committee investigating Thomas' regime subjected some 500,000 documents to verification (*Archives nationales. Rapport de la Commission pour la liquidation du compte d'Émile Thomas*).

gation on the June Days, the official papers of the National Workshops administration had been seized and put under seal. These papers were turned over to the Committee of the *Cour des comptes*. They concerned, as indicated above, only the period posterior to the dismissal of Émile Thomas as director.[6] The papers for the Thomas regime had already been placed at the disposal of the committee of three investigating the accounts of the Thomas regime. The latter committee furnished the former with information on the Thomas administration so that the one report might present a picture of the entire period.[7]

Faced with the chaotic conditions existing when he became director and the multiple demands of his new and strange position, Thomas at first neglected the organization of an adequate system of accounting.[8] Indeed such a system was virtually nonexistent in the first days of the Thomas administration. Receipts and expenditures were simply entered in a notebook, and the funds for the wages of the workers were distributed at Monceau against receipts from the thirty-two chiefs of service who received the pay money. The latter then divided their allotments among the captains, who did the same with their lieutenants. In turn the lieutenants distributed to each brigadier sufficient funds for the pay of fifty-five men, the brigadiers repartitioning the money among the squad leaders, the latter finally paying the men. Since account blanks were collected from all squad leaders daily, the complexity of the accounting system is evident. The temptations for petty graft in such an organization need no emphasis. And it was on the basis of this primitive system that some 1,400,000 francs were expended in the course of less than a month.[9]

Finally Thomas, who admits that he had had no experience of public finance, became alarmed at the heavy responsibility with which he was burdened by reason of the absence of an adequate accounting system. He laid the situation before Garnier-Pagès, and Roy, *inspecteur des finances*, was promptly delegated to organize a system of accounting and to exercise general surveillance over its functioning. Roy at once instituted the system employed generally in the public administrations.[10]

---

[6] *Commission d'enquête*, II, p. 141.

[7] *Commission d'enquête*, II, p. 141. The report complains, however, that the documents were inadequate for the attainment of satisfactory results, especially since great speed was necessary (*ibid.*, II, pp. 145-146).

[8] *Archives nationales. Rapport de la Commission pour la liquidation du compte d'Émile Thomas.*

[9] *Commission d'enquête*, II, pp. 143-144; *Archives nationales. Rapport de la Commission pour la liquidation du compte d'Émile Thomas.* This sum apparently includes the expenditures prior to the appointment of Thomas as well as those following, and until about March 25, 1848.

[10] *Ibid.*; *Commission d'enquête*, II, p. 144, cf. II, pp. 174-175; Thomas: *Ateliers nationaux*, pp. 137-139. Thomas praises Roy's work warmly. On Thomas' earlier financial difficulties, see also *ibid.*, pp. 76-77.

Roy's system functioned very satisfactorily as far as balancing the books of the central administration was concerned,[11] but the more fundamental weaknesses in the system of making the pay remained. These Roy aimed to remedy by changes embodied in a regulation of April 10, prepared in accord with Thomas. Henceforth the pay was to be made directly by the brigadiers, instead of by the squad leaders, in the presence of an *agent de paie*. The points at which the pay was to be made were to be announced in advance, so that the *chefs* could be present, if they desired. Upon receiving his wage each man was to present his *livret*, which was to be initialled by the brigadier.[12] The regulation offered certain very obvious advantages, but it met with such serious opposition from the workers that it was suspended until it could be approved by the workers' delegates. This was finally done on May 11.[13]

Meanwhile further sweeping reforms had been effected in the system of making the pay and of accounting. As of May 1, the funds were to be distributed daily from a newly established central *caisse*, not to the thirty-two chiefs of service but to the fourteen *chefs d'arrondissements*, thus reducing the number of those directly responsible to the central administration. For each *chef d'arrondissement* a *sous-caissier* was appointed, who was to keep the accounts for the *arrondissement*, to exercise surveillance over the accounts of the chiefs of service, and to make a report to the central administration every five days of expenses, accompanied by the necessary supporting documents. The chiefs of service were to function in the same way in respect to the accounts of their subordinates. The daily funds were to be distributed among the hierarchy, passing successively through the hands of the *chefs d'arrondissements, sous-caissiers*, chiefs of service, captains, lieutenants, and brigadiers. The pay was to be made everywhere simultaneously.[14]

Although this system left much to be desired, it was superior to that which it replaced, provided only it had been executed. Whether the system was vitiated through the fault of the administration or whether the situa-

[11] *Commission d'enquête*, II, p. 144; cf. *Archives nationales, loc. cit*. The system of accounting used for the pay of the members of the central administration was of Roy's devising (*Archives nationales, loc. cit.*), although Thomas does not mention the fact.

[12] *Archives nationales. Rapport de la Commission pour la liquidation du compte d'Émile Thomas.* It was further provided that each man's name was to occupy every day the same place on the *feuille de paie* (to promote efficiency in checking), that there were to be two roll calls a day, that fines should be instituted for irregularities in the reports of brigadiers, and that the latter should be obliged to deposit a guarantee sum of fifteen francs.

[13] *Ibid.* Cf. the brief and inadequate account in the *Commission d'enquête*, II, p. 144.

[14] *Ibid.*, II, pp. 144-145; cf. *Archives nationales. Rapport de la Commission pour la liquidation du compte d'Émile Thomas.*

tion was beyond all remedy, the regulations were not carried out and the disorder only increased.[15]

It was at this point that Thomas was brusquely removed from office. Unfortunately the accounts of his regime were further compromised by the "imprudent zeal" of his friends. For, instead of insisting that his papers be put at once under seal, it appears that his subordinates seized and destroyed a certain number of documents which they found in his office. For that reason it was impossible for Thomas to account for various sums which he had received on his own responsibility.[16]

Both reports present a clear record for Thomas, the central administration, and the higher ranks of the administrative hierarchy generally. Such irregularities as were found were the results of imprudence, inexperience, or faulty organization, and in no sense reflected dishonest intent. Thomas was cleared of charges that he had wasted the state's moneys in the purchase of horses and carriages,[17] a charge frequently found associated with accusations of extravagance in the maintenance of Thomas' Monceau household. The director had unfortunately failed in the beginning to have a regular allowance made him for household expenses. This was done April 1; he was given sixty francs a day, six francs each for the ten persons eating at his table. In connection with the expenses of furnishing his Monceau headquarters, the report of the committee found nothing exorbitant.[18] The committee concluded that, although Thomas may have lived somewhat too well at the expense of the state in the beginning, he left office perhaps poorer than when he had assumed it.[19]

For the higher ranks of the administration, the reports bear much the same testimony as in the case of Thomas. The accounts of the central *caisse* at Monceau and those of the *sous-caissiers* revealed no trace of embezzlement.[20] The same was substantially true of the accounts of the chiefs of service,[21] although three of the latter had serious unexplained shortages.[22] In general the statement may be made also of the captains and lieutenants; in short, the funds intended for the workers' pay actually reached the brigadiers intact.[23]

---

[15] *Ibid.; Commission d'enquête*, II, p. 145. The former report notes that the new regulation remained essentially a dead letter.

[16] *Archives nationales, loc. cit.*

[17] *Archives nationales. Rapport de la Commission pour la liquidation du compte d'Émile Thomas.* In view of the extensive need of carriages by the administration, Thomas bought horses and carriages on his own responsibility. They were later sold, if not with profit, at least without loss.

[18] *Ibid.*

[19] *Ibid.*

[20] *Commission d'enquête*, II, p. 146.

[21] *Ibid.*, II, p. 146.

[22] *Archives nationales. Rapport de la Commission pour la liquidation du compte d'Émile Thomas.*

[23] *Commission d'enquête*, II, p. 148; cf. *Archives nationales, loc. cit.*

More serious criticisms were levelled at certain of the administrative branches. Serious irregularities appeared in the administration of the *bureau de secours*.[24] The Workshops' delegates prepared the lists of needy workers. Five inspectors and sixty subordinates verified the lists. The delegates then received the requisitions for bread, etc., and distributed them. But the inspectorate was adequate to the verification of only about one-tenth of the lists daily presented. And there was no check to determine whether the requisitions reached the proper persons. The diverting of public moneys under these conditions can well be imagined. The committee was told that, of the total expense of this service, one-quarter (80,000 francs) disappeared as the result of fraud.[25]

A system of accounting for the thousands of tools used by the Workshops was virtually nonexistent. The tools had been lent by the military engineers and had heedlessly been allowed to pass from hand to hand. The result was that 24,000 francs was owing in the end to the engineers.[26] Abuses were reported also in the case of the bureau for medical aid; no suspicion was cast upon the disinterestedness of the doctors at the head of the organization, but it was pointed out that there was no means of determining whether or not a worker was receiving pay both from the dispensary and from his brigadier.[27]

If the officers of the grade of lieutenant and higher were generally cleared of the suspicion of embezzlement, it was precisely with the brigadiers that the flagrant abuses appeared, and they extended to the squad leaders and to the workers themselves. The abuses were of many kinds, and very often the proof of fraud was incontestable. The account blanks (signed daily by the workers) contained signatures obviously counterfeited, or of workers whose absence could be demonstrated.[28] Sometimes a considerable number of signatures appeared in the same hand; sometimes the signature of one individual changed from day to day. Again certain brigades, for a period of a month, would show not a single absence, setting up a serious presumption of fraud. Other irregularities included the omission of signatures where the pay had been made, supplementary pay without justification, etc.[29] Superficially it would seem that simultaneity in making the pay and the elaborate precautions against fraud would have been more

[24] See above, p. 19.

[25] *Commission d'enquête*, II, pp. 150-151.

[26] *Archives nationales. Rapport de la Commission pour la liquidation du compte d'Émile Thomas.*

[27] *Ibid.*, certain minor irregularities were also reported: e.g., the purchase of furniture was left to the *chefs d'arrondissements*, with the result that some offices were furnished in mahogany.

[28] But cf. *Archives nationales, loc. cit.* The latter report declares that the signing of one person for another was rather rare.

[29] *Commission d'enquête*, II, pp. 146-147; on this whole question, see also *Archives nationales. Rapport de la Commission pour la liquidation du compte d'Émile Thomas.*

effective. Actually the captains and lieutenants failed to exercise the necessary surveillance; " the inspectors did not inspect "; and the *agents de paie*, rebuffed by the central club, were badly received and became accomplices of the growing disorder or were helpless to prevent it. The result was that a large number of workers received double or triple pay in different *arrondissements*.[30]

The *livret* was another source of irregularities. Very often the *livrets* of discharged workers were kept by the brigadiers, who then continued to use them, either drawing the workers' pay themselves, or lending the *livrets* to others on a share basis. The abuses were multiplied from the time when a worker who had lost his *livret* was permitted to have a second for the nominal charge of fifty centimes.[31]

The election of brigadiers by the members of the respective brigades was another source of weakness in the system. Owing their position to the workers, the brigadiers lacked adequate authority and were often forced to be silent spectators of, if not actual accomplices in, the numerous abuses committed. Only too frequently, however, it was the brigadiers themselves who gave to their men an example of fraud or insubordination.[32] Complaint of this class of subordinate officers was general.[33]

As a result of the irregularities enumerated,[34] the Committee of the *Cour des comptes* was of the opinion that perhaps more than 1,000,000 francs disappeared in this way.[35] But the report gives no adequate supporting evidence for this estimate, and Thomas himself believed that the figure should be much lower.[36] That part of this sum was diverted to a secret treasury for the eventual support of the insurrection, the committee doubted. The character and condition of the men concerned seemed to preclude the possibility; moreover, the tendency of the workers to waste their pay was notorious.[37]

The judgments on the administration of Lalanne are solely those of the Committee of the *Cour des comptes*. Despite the fact that Lalanne had announced a reduction of 14,000 in the numbers legitimately enrolled in the Workshops as a result of the census of June 7, the total sum paid out daily by the *caisse* at Monceau to the *chefs d'arrondissements* remained

[30] *Commission d'enquête*, II, p. 147.

[31] *Ibid.*, II, p. 147.

[32] *Commission d'enquête*, II, pp. 147-148.

[33] See, e.g., *ibid.*, I, p. 302; Lalanne: " Lettres sur les Ateliers nationaux. III," *National*, July 19, 1848; *Gazette des tribunaux*, March 13, 1849; *France nouvelle, supplément* to June 9, 1848.

[34] Some idea of their extent is given by the reductions in the numbers legitimately enrolled, made possible through the census operations (see above, pp. 133-134, and *Commission d'enquête*, II, p. 148).

[35] *Ibid.*, II, pp. 148, 155.

[36] *Ibid.*, II, p. 155.

[37] *Ibid.*, II, pp. 148, 152.

ths same.[38] The explanation given to the committee of this apparently anomalous situation was the following: The necessary verification of the census at the *mairies* had encountered unexpected obstacles and was completed only June 20. Meanwhile the administration was powerless to eliminate those fraudulently receiving pay, being unprovided with the necessary lists upon which to proceed. When the latter were finally ready, the *chefs d'arrondissements* were ordered to act upon them, but the insurrection was at hand and the order remained unexecuted. In the view of the committee, the failure to rectify the brigade lists at once and thus to save the treasury considerable sums exposed the administration of the Workshops to serious criticism.[39]

In summary it may be said that, in the question of the finances of the Workshops, both Thomas and Lalanne personally emerged with a perfectly clean record. Thomas' mistakes were a result of his inexperience or reflected the difficulties he faced.[40] Lalanne inherited a situation over the difficulties of which neither the strength nor the courage of the director could be expected to triumph, in the opinion of the Committee of the *Cour des comptes*.[41]

COST TO THE STATE OF THE NATIONAL WORKSHOPS
(In francs)

Thomas Administration (through May 28, 1848)	7,068,025.89
Lalanne Administration	4,298,925.07
Payments by Paris *mairies* (June 27 - July 4, 1848)	994,987.00
Payments by Thevenet, *liquidateur* (subsequent to July 4, 1848)	220,000.00
Ateliers de Belleville	31,420.50
Secours de route, paid to workers returning to their homes in the provinces	925.20
Repayment by *mairies* of " guarantee sums " (brigadiers, *et al.*)	36,367.00
Printing bill — *Imprimerie nationale*	16,306.75
Salaries, etc., of members of Liquidation Commission	8,694.95
	12,675,652.36
Expenses remaining to be paid (as of December 31, 1848)	85,000.00
	12,760,652.36
To which is usually added the payments made in the National Workshops (Women)	1,732,598.00
Grand Total	14,493,250.36

[38] *Commission d'enquête,* II, p. 149; but cf. the figures cited by Thomas (p. 390) which show considerable variation from day to day.

[39] *Commission d'enquête,* II, pp. 149-150.

[40] *Archives nationales. Rapport de la Commission pour la liquidation du compte d'Émile Thomas;* Cherest, p. 205; and cf. references in this appendix to Thomas: *Ateliers nationaux.*

[41] *Commission d'enquête,* II, pp. 152-153.

The Grand Total and the individual items were made up from scattering sources; no complete itemized account exists, to the writer's knowledge.[42] The most satisfactory single analysis is contained in the Report by Lacrosse, minister of public works, to Deputy Etienne, of the assembly's Finance Committee, December 31, 1848.[43] Lacrosse arrives at a total of 14,488,235.57 francs (14,488,000 francs in round numbers). Since the appropriations previously made totalled 12,000,000 francs,[44] and since the assembly subsequently (February 10, 1849) granted a further appropriation of 2,488,000 francs for the definitive liquidation of the Workshops,[45] the total given by Lacrosse seems unquestionably to be the correct one. The composite itemized figures above give a total of only something more than 5,000 francs higher than Lacrosse's total.

The total for Thomas' regime (7,068,025.89 francs) is taken from a report of December 20, 1848, which accompanied a letter of January 9, 1849, from Roy, secretary of the Commission on the Liquidation of the Workshops, to the minister of public works.[46] The figures for the Lalanne regime were derived from a study of the same report, which gives also the figures for the payments by Thevenet. The payments made by the Paris *mairies* can be found, in itemized form (by day and by *arrondissement*) in a *bordereau* attached to a Report of the Ministry of Finance, February 2, 1849.[47]

The items "Ateliers de Belleville," "Secours de route," "Repayment by *mairies* of 'guarantee sums,'" "Printing bill," and "Salaries, etc., of members of the Liquidation Commission" appear in a letter of Lacrosse, minister of public works, to Deputy Etienne, of the assembly's Finance Committee, January 26, 1849.[48] The estimate of 85,000 francs remaining to be paid is to be found in a report by Lacrosse, accompanying a letter to Etienne, December 31, 1848.[49] An itemization of this latter sum can be found in a letter of Lacrosse to Etienne, January 30, 1849.[50]

The final figure on the expenses of the National Workshops (Women) of 1,732,598 francs was given in a report by Roy, published in the *Moni-*

---

[42] The assembly's law of February 10, 1849, appropriating 2,488,000.00 for the liquidation of the Workshops, required that a final account be rendered within three months (*Moniteur*, February 11, 1849). But no such report had been made, declared the Ducos Report of June 25, 1851 (*Moniteur*, June 26, 1851).

[43] *Archives nationales.* C 920 A, *Dossier* 256.

[44] *Ibid.,* and cf. "Note A," attached to the Report of the Ministry of Finance, February 2, 1849 (*Archives nationales, loc. cit.*).

[45] *Moniteur*, February 11, 1849.

[46] *Archives nationales.* C 920 A, *Dossier* 256. Cf. that given in the Report of the *Commission d'enquête*, II, p. 156.

[47] *Archives nationales, loc. cit.*

[48] *Ibid.*

[49] *Ibid.*

[50] *Archives nationales.* C 920 A, *Dossier* 256.

teur, January 17, 1849.[51] In the Workshops for Women shirts and other articles of wearing apparel were made for the army, National Guard, etc. The total income from the sale of these products was 1,403,080.97 francs, making the net cost to the state 329,517.03 francs. An average of 25,000 women was employed during the period of the existence of the Workshops, April 1-June 26, 1848.[52]

[51] The total actually given is 1,732,608 francs, the result of an error in subtraction.

[52] Report of Roy (*Moniteur,* January 17, 1848).

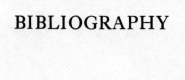

BIBLIOGRAPHY

BIBLIOGRAPHY

I. UNPUBLISHED MATERIALS

UNPUBLISHED materials consulted are to be found in the *Archives na-tionales* and in the *Archives de la Seine*.[1] Other collections (e.g., those of the *Conservatoire des arts et métiers, Bibliothèque de la ville de Paris, Bibliothèque du Sénat*) yield nothing. The collection formerly in the *Archives de la Chambre des députés* has now been transferred to the *Archives nationales*. Of primary importance in the latter collection are the *minutes sténographiques* of the Labor Committee of the National Assembly. The *minutes sténographiques*, along with the published but much briefer and less adequate *procès-verbaux*, permit us to present a full-length picture of the activities of this important committee, in so far as the National Workshops are concerned. The *minutes sténographiques* likewise give us a much clearer view of the character of the policy of Falloux, who spoke at length before the committee on several occasions during those meetings for which we possess the minutes.

The comparatively few papers in the *Archives de la Seine* are none the less of importance. They include instructions from the mayor of Paris to the mayors of the arrondissements on various occasions and help to reconstruct a picture of the cumbrous administrative system of the Work-shops. They also throw light on numerous other questions, such as the census of June 7.

Archives nationales

BB^{18}, 1473. *Liasse* 6882 includes reports on certain officers of the Workshops guilty of malversation.

BB^{30}, 313. *Liasse* 2 contains two reports of one Falaiseau de Beauplan on the repercussion in the Workshops to the dismissal of Thomas.

F^{14}, 9317. *Liasse* 1 contains interesting letters on the subject of send-ing workers to railroad projects in the provinces.

C 920 A. *Dossier* 256 includes the important report of the " Com-mission spéciale pour la liquidation du compte des Ateliers nationaux

---

[1] On the archival materials for the period, see Charles Schmidt: *Les sources de l'histoire de France depuis 1789 aux Archives nationales* (Paris, 1907) ; Pierre Caron: " Sources manuscrites parisiennes de l'histoire de la Révolution de 1848 et de la deuxième République," *Revue d'histoire moderne et contemporaine*, VI (1904-1905), pp. 85-119; and Pierre Caron: " Note sur les sources de l'histoire de la deuxième République aux Archives nationales," *Révolution de 1848*, I (1904-1905), pp. 57-60.

pendant la gestion d'Émile Thomas" and other papers of interest relative to the finances of the Workshops. *Dossiers* 254, 257, 258, etc., contain plans, estimates, etc., on the projects for which appropriations were voted by the assembly, June 10.

C 925. Includes the original of the *Procès-verbaux des déliberations du Comité du travail.* (See below, p. 176.)

C 928. *Liasse* 1 is made up of the " Minutes sténographiques provenant du Comité du travail de l'ancienne Assemblée constituante de 1848," for the meetings of May 24, 25, 26, 27, 29, 30, 31 and June 5, 6, 8, 10. The others, fortunately of secondary importance for this study, have been lost. *Liasse* 3 contains the *Comité des travaux publics. Minutes des séances.*

C 942. *Dossier* III includes letters on the healing of the breach between the delegates of the Luxembourg and those of the Workshops during the first half of June.

Containing some material of interest, but of secondary importance, are the following: BB^{30}, 312; BB^{30}, 314; BB^{30}, 315; BB^{30}, 320 A; C 915.

Archives de la Seine

Mairies. O^{2b}. The carton *Mairies* L-P 4332-4647 contains the papers on the Workshops, numbered consecutively 4574-4621.

II. PUBLISHED MATERIALS

The following list of published materials includes: (1) *Bibliographical Guides*; (2) *Collections of Official Documents*; (3) *Printed Works and Articles*; (4) *Newspapers.* Under *Bibliographical Guides* no attempt is made to provide anything like a complete list of bibliographies for the period; the writer has simply set down some of the finding lists which he found valuable in tracing the materials used. Under *Printed Works and Articles* the classification " Primary Sources " and " Secondary Works " has been eliminated: many of the works cited, written by the actors themselves, extend on both sides of the tenuous line which is supposed to separate the two groups. The works listed include two categories: (1) books to which reference is made in the footnotes; (2) other works which the writer has found to be of importance but to which he has had no occasion to refer in the notes. Obviously no attempt has been made to compile a general bibliography for the period in question; only works of immediate relevance have been included. The inclusion of general works readily available through the finding lists noted under Section 1 would have constituted a needless encumbrance of the bibliography.

1. *Bibliographical Guides*

Of first importance among the general finding lists for the whole period is the very comprehensive but complicated *Catalogue de l'histoire de*

France, published by the *Bibliothèque nationale.* Works published since 1867 can be traced in the following, roughly consecutive, lists:

Caron, Pierre. *Bibliographie des travaux publiés de 1866 à 1897 sur l'histoire de la France depuis 1789.* Paris, 1912. 831 pp.

Brière, G., et Caron, Pierre. *Repertoire méthodique de l'histoire moderne et contemporaine de la France.* Annual finding lists for the period 1898-1906. Published in the *Revue d'histoire moderne et contemporaine,* 1907-1914.

Caron, Pierre, et Stein, Henri. *Repertoire bibliographique de l'histoire de France.* Paris, 1923 - . Tome I (1923) for years 1920-1921, and later volumes.

Further bibliographical aids include:

Crémieux, Albert. *La Révolution de février.* (Full title below, p. 178.) Extensive bibliography includes a long list of memoirs for the period and a valuable section on the general histories, classified on the basis of the author's point of view toward the Revolution.

Pimienta, Robert. *La propagande bonapartiste.* (Full title below, p. 181). See especially his section on bibliography of the press.

Renard, Édouard. *Bibliographie relative à Louis Blanc.* Toulouse, 1922. 24 pp. Most complete existing bibliography on Louis Blanc. Useful for the study of the social question in general.

Renard, Georges. *La République de 1848. Notes et références, avec deux index alphabétiques. Complément de l'ouvrage publié par l'auteur sous le même titre.* Paris, 1906. 31 pp. References to nearly all the materials of importance for the period, with occasional critical commentaries. The emphasis is of course on social and economic questions.

Seignobos, Charles. *La Révolution de 1848. Le seconde Empire.* Paris, 1921. 426 pp. Contains summary bibliographical lists in the footnotes, with occasional valuable commentaries.

Stammhammer, Josef. *Bibliographie des Socialismus und Communismus.* Jena, 1893-1909. 3 vols.

Wassermann, Suzanne. *Les clubs de Barbès et de Blanqui.* (Full title below, p. 183.) Some useful comments on the memoirs, histories, and "left" newspapers of the period.

2. Collections of Official Documents

Assemblée nationale constituante. 1848-1849. *Compte rendu des séances de l'Assemblée nationale; exposés des motifs et projets des lois présentés par le Gouvernement; rapports de MM. les Représentants.* Paris, 1849. 10 vols. See convenient finding list: *Table analytique, par ordre alphabétique, de matières et de noms de personnes, du Compte rendu des séances de l'Assemblée nationale constituante (4 mai 1848 - 27 mai 1849) et des documents imprimés par son ordre.* Paris, 1850.

——. *Impressions. Projets de lois, propositions, rapports, etc.* Paris, 21 vols. Vol. XIII is the *Rapport de la Commission d'enquête sur l'insurrection qui a éclaté dans la journée du 23 juin et sur les événements du 15 mai.* Paris, 1848. 3 vols. in one. Alexandre Quentin-Bauchart, *rapporteur.* The *rapport* includes the extended depositions of political leaders of every *nuance*, and a variety of other documents. It is of capital importance for the history of the Workshops. It is badly organized, and preceded by a report of the committee which reflects the strongly bourgeois prejudices of its members toward the social revolution.

——. *Comité du travail. Procès-verbaux du Comité du travail a l'Assemblée constituante de 1848.* Paris, 1908. 328 pp. Forms No. 1 of the *Bibliothèque de la " Révolution de 1848."* The *procès-verbaux* of the Labor Committee are fundamental to a study of the question of the dissolution of the Workshops, although they become of distinctly secondary importance for those few meetings for which the *minutes sténographiques* exist. (See above, p. 174.) The introduction contains valuable material on the formation of the committee, its composition, etc.

Duvergier, J. B. *Collection complète des lois, décrets, ordonnances, règlemens, et avis du conseil d'état, etc.* [Title varies.] Paris, 1824 - . Includes laws, etc., from 1788 to the present, with valuable annotations.

3. Printed Works and Articles

Alton-Shée, Edmond, comte d'. *Mes mémoires (1826-1846).* Paris, 1869. 2 vols.
Souvenirs de 1847 et de 1848 pour faire suite à mes mémoires. (Œuvre posthume.) Paris, 1879. 329 pp.

[Anonymous.] *M. Émile Thomas.* Paris, n.d. 8 pp. Pamphlet published May 27, 1848, following removal of Thomas.

Apponyi, Rudolf, graf. *Vingt-cinq ans à Paris (1826-1852). Journal du comte Rodolphe Apponyi, attaché de l'ambassade d'Autriche à Paris, publié par Ernest Daudet.* Paris, 1913-1926. 4 vols. The reflections of the Hungarian nobleman, in so far as they apply to the radicals, need to be subjected to careful verification; he believes exaggerated stories at times, and is not always well informed. Otherwise the memoirs are valuable: his connections were wide, especially in Orleanist circles.

Aragon, Henry. *La vie politique de François Arago.* Toulouse, 1924. 225 pp. Substantially a group of documents loosely woven together by panegyrics of an admirer of Arago. A serious biography is needed.

Artz, Frederick B. *France under the Bourbon Restoration.* Cambridge [Massachusetts], 1931. 443 pp.

Audebrand, Philibert. *Souvenirs de la tribune des journalistes (1848-1852).* Paris, 1867.

Babaud-Laribière, F. S. L. *Histoire de l'Assemblée nationale constituante.* Paris, 1850. 2 vols.

Barante, A. G. P. B., Baron de. *Souvenirs du Baron de Barante de l'Académie française. 1782-1866.* Paris, 1890-1901. 8 vols.

Barrot, Odilon. *Mémoires posthumes de Odilon Barrot.* Paris, 1875-1876. 4 vols.

Blanc, Louis Jean Joseph. *Histoire de la Révolution de 1848.* Fifth edition, Paris, 1880. 2 vols. The eloquent pages of the socialist leader are at once a defence of the Provisional Government and an answer to Lord Normanby's attacks on the social revolution. Often inaccurate and occasionally thoroughly unreliable, Blanc's reminiscences need to be subjected to the critical control of other materials. This work is the combination of earlier works, notably *L'Appel aux honnêtes gens. Quelques pages d'histoire contemporaine.* Second edition, Paris, 1849. 168 pp. (the third edition, with some additions, appeared as *Pages d'histoire de la Révolution de février, 1848.* Paris, 1850. 359 pp.), and *1848. Historical Revelations: inscribed to Lord Normanby.* London, 1858. 517 pp.

——. *L'Organisation du travail.* First edition, Paris, n.d. 131 pp.

——. *La Révolution de février au Luxembourg.* Paris, 1849. 156 pp.

Blind, Karl. "The Paris National Workshops of 1848." *Nineteenth Century and After,* LX (1906), pp. 307-314. Answer by a German friend of Louis Blanc's to a reference by John Morley to the Workshops as the utter failure of a socialist experiment.

Bouniols, Gaston. *Histoire de la Révolution de 1848.* Second edition, Paris, 1918. 448 pp.

Bouton, Victor. *Profils révolutionnaires par un crayon rouge.* Paris, 1848-1849. 188 pp.

Cahen, Georges. "Louis Blanc et la Commission du Luxembourg (1848)." *Annales de l'École libre des sciences politiques,* XII (1897), pp. 187-225, 362-380, 459-481. Most satisfactory account of the organization and political activities of the Commission.

Calman, A. R. *Ledru-Rollin and the Second French Republic.* New York, 1922. 453 pp. Based on letters of Ledru in the *Bibliothèque de la ville de Paris.* A full length biography of Ledru remains to be written.

Castellane, E. V. E. B., le Maréchal, Comte de. *Journal du Maréchal de Castellane, 1804-1862.* Paris, 1895-1897. 5 vols.

Castille, Hippolyte. *Histoire de la seconde République française.* Paris, 1854-1856. 4 vols.

Caussidière, Marc. *Mémoires de Caussidière, ex-préfet de police et représentant du peuple.* Paris, 1849. 2 vols.

Chaboseau, A. "Les constituants de 1848." *La Révolution de 1848,* VII (1910-1911), pp. 287-305, 413-425; VIII (1911-1912), pp. 67-80. Valuable analysis of the professions, social status, previous legislative experience, etc., of the members of the National Assembly.

Changarnier, Théodule, le Général. *Campagnes en Afrique. 1830-1848. Mémoires du Général Changarnier.* Paris, etc., 1930. 328 pp.

Charléty, Sébastien. *La monarchie de juillet (1830-1848).* Paris, 1921. 407 pp.

Chenu, Adolphe. *Les Montagnards de 1848. Encore quatre nouveaux cha-pitres précédés d'une réponse à Caussidière et autres democssocs.* Paris, 1850. 144 pp.

Cherest, Aimé. *La vie et les oeuvres de A.-T. Marie, avocat, membre du Gouvernement provisoire, etc.* Paris, 1873. 385 pp. Of capital importance. The very favorable biography of the man to whom the organization of the National Workshops was entrusted includes long excerpts from the notes of Marie.

Circourt, Adolphe de. *Souvenirs d'une mission à Berlin en 1848, publiés pour la Société d'histoire contemporaine, par M. Georges Bourgin.* Paris, 1908. 446 pp. See especially the important introduction by Bourgin on the foreign policy of Lamartine, the Polish question, etc.

Clapham, J. H. *The Economic Development of France and Germany, 1815-1914.* Cambridge [England], 1921. 420 pp.
An Economic History of Modern Britain. Vol. I: *The Early Railway Age, 1820-1850.* Cambridge [England], 1926. 623 pp. Detailed account of the economic crisis in Great Britain in 1846-1847.

Crémieux, Adolphe I. M. *En 1848, discours et lettres de M. Ad. Crémieux.* Paris, 1883. 338 pp.

Crémieux, Albert. *La Révolution de février, étude critique sur les journées des 21, 22, 23, et 24 février 1848.* Paris, 1912. 535 pp. The standard monograph on the February Days, developing the thesis that the Revolution was no " surprise accidentelle " but an essentially proletarian movement.

Crémieux, Albert, et Génique, G. " La question électorale en mars 1848." *La Révolution de 1848,* III (1906-1907), pp. 206-212, 252-263.

Delessard, Er. *Souvenirs de 1848. L'École centrale aux Ateliers nationaux.* Paris, 1900. 30 pp. Reminiscences of one of Thomas' *aides.*

Delvau, Alfred. *Histoire de la Révolution de février.* Paris, 1850. 481 pp. Panegyric of Ledru-Rollin by his private secretary.

Deschanel, Émile. *Lamartine.* Fourth edition, Paris, 1893. 2 vols.

Dictionnaire des parlementaires français, comprenant tous les membres des assemblées françaises et tous les ministres français depuis le 1er mai 1789 jusqu'au 1er mai 1889 avec leurs noms, état civil, états de services, actes politiques, votes parlementaires, etc. Paris, 1891. 5 vols. Edited by Adolphe Robert, Edgar Bourloton, and Gaston Cougny.

Drevet, père. *Mystères de l'Hôtel-de-Ville. Révélations de Drevet père, président des Délégués du peuple. Faits et actes inédits du Gouvernement provisoire (février, 1848).* Paris, 1850. 93 pp. See especially for plan for the militarization of labor, similar to that later suggested by Émile Thomas.

Dreyfus, Ferdinand. *L'Assistance sous la seconde République (1848-1851).* Paris, 1907. 220 pp.

———. *Un philanthrope d'autrefois, La Rochefoucauld Liancourt (1747-1827).* Paris, 1903. 547 pp. See especially on *chantiers de charité,* 1788 ff.

Du Camp, Maxime. *Souvenirs de l'année 1848. La Révolution de février, le 15 mai, l'insurrection de juin.* Paris, 1876. 316 pp.

Dumas, Alexandre. *Révélations sur l'arrestation d'Émile Thomas suivi de pièces justificatives.* Paris, 1848. 54 pp. Reprint of his defence of Thomas in *La France nouvelle*, which see, below, p. 184.

Eichthal, Eugène d'. *Alexis de Tocqueville et la démocratie libérale suivie de fragments des entretiens de Tocqueville avec Nassau William Senior (1848-1858).* Paris, 1897. 354 pp.

Fagniez, Gustave. *L'économie sociale de la France sous Henri IV, 1589-1610.* Paris, 1897. 428 pp.

Falloux du Coudray, F. A. P., Vicomte de. *Discours de M. de Falloux, ministre de l'instruction publique, sur la situation du pays et sur les Ateliers nationaux, à la séance de l'Assemblée nationale du 24 mai 1849.* Paris, 1849. 34 pp. The reprint of his speech witnesses Falloux's anxiety to get his case before the public.

——. *Discours et mélanges politiques.* Paris, 1882. 2 vols.

——. *Mémoires d'un royaliste.* Paris, 1888. 2 vols. Of capital importance for the whole question of the dissolution of the Workshops, but thoroughly untrustworthy — needs invariably to be subjected to the verification of other witnesses.

——. "Les républicains et les monarchistes depuis la Révolution de février." *Revue des deux mondes*, IX (February 1, 1851), pp. 393-422.

Faucher, Léon. *Léon Faucher.* Third edition, Paris, 1888. 2 vols. Vol. I. *Biographie et correspondance*; Vol. II: *Vie parlementaire.* The biography in Volume I is by Madame Faucher, who published the work, first edition, 1867.

Fournière, Eugène. *Le règne de Louis-Philippe (1830-1848).* Paris, 1906? 583 pp. Vol. VIII of Jaurès, Jean: *Histoire socialiste (1789-1900).* Paris, 1900-1908. 13 vols.

Freycinet, Charles de. *Souvenirs. 1848-1878.* Paris, 1912. 403 pp.

Garnier-Pagès, Louis Antoine. *Histoire de la Révolution de 1848.* Paris, 1861-1872. 11 vols. Garnier-Pagès has written at once a general history of revolutionary Europe, and a detailed account of the Provisional Government and the Executive Commission, a defence of the Revolution by a moderate republican. Much of this part of the book is based on the reminiscences of the writer, whose pompous tendencies to overemphasize his own rôle are evident. In 1853 Garnier-Pagès was permitted to consult the Archives of the Ministry of Justice and those of the Chamber of Deputies. In the latter collection he used the *procès-verbaux* of the meetings of the Provisional Government and of the Executive Commission; to the fuller and much more important notes of Pagnerre he also had access. On the *procès-verbaux*, parts of which are published in the Report of the *Commission d'enquête sur l'insurrection . . . du 23 juin*, etc. (see above, p. 176), see the article by Seignobos (below, p. 182). The *procès-verbaux*, formerly in the *Archives de la Chambre des députés* and which should be in the *versement* of some years ago to the *Archives nationales*, the writer has not been able to find. (See *série* C 929 ff.)

Ibos, le Général. *Le Général Cavaignac. Un dictateur républicain*. Paris, 1930. 237 pp.

Juglar, Clément. *Des crises commerciales et de leur retour périodique en France, en Angleterre, et aux États-Unis*. Paris, 1889. 560 pp.

Keller, Émile. *Le Général de La Moricière, savie militaire, politique et religieuse*. Paris, 1874. 2 vols.

Lacombe, Charles. *Vie de Berryer (d'après des documents inédits)*. Paris, 1895. 3 vols.

La Gorce, Pierre de. *Histoire de la seconde République française*. Paris, 1887. 2 vols.

Lalanne, Léon. "Lettres sur les Ateliers nationaux." *Le National*, 1848: I — July 14; II — July 15; III — July 19; IV — July 23; V — August 6; VI — August 16; VII — August 26. The apologia of the second director of the Workshops is of capital importance. It is highly favorable to the policy of the Executive Commission and very critical of the Thomas régime.

——. *Rectification historique sur les Ateliers nationaux*. Paris, 1887. 9 pp. Extract from *Le Temps*, October 6, 1887. Answer to La Gorce's claim that abuses in the Workshops continued under the Lalanne regime. Of slight importance.

Lamartine, Alphonse de. *Histoire de la Révolution de 1848*. Brussels, 1849. 2 vols. The ornate literary apologia of the poet says too much or too little on every subject. Lamartine is made the central pivot about which the Revolution turns, while the National Workshops and kindred topics are almost wholly neglected.

——. *Lettre aux dix départements*. Paris, August 25, 1848. 36 pp.

——. *Trois mois au pouvoir*. Paris, 1848. 328 pp.

Lazard, Raymond. *Michel Goudchaux (1797-1862), son œuvre et sa vie politique*. Paris, 1907. 683 pp.

Lebey, André. *Louis-Napoléon Bonaparte et la Révolution de 1848*. Paris, 1907-1908. 2 vols.

Lecoq, Marcel. *L'Assistance par le travail*. Paris, 1906.

Levasseur, Émile. *Histoire des classes ouvrières et de l'industrie en France de 1789 à 1870*. Second edition, Paris, 1903-1904. 2 vols.

——. *La population française. Histoire de la population avant 1789 et démographie de la France comparée à celle des autres nations au XIX⁰ siècle, précédée d'une introduction sur la statistique*. Paris, 1889-1892. 3 vols.

Lévy-Schneider, L. "Les préliminaires du 15 mai 1848. La journée du 14, d'après un document inédit." *La Révolution de 1848*, VII (1910-1911), pp. 219-232.

Loustau, Pierre. *Louis Blanc à la Commission du Luxembourg*. Paris, 1908. 154 pp. Louis Blanc's "system" as developed before the Commission of the Luxembourg.

Marriott, J. A. R. *The French Revolution of 1848 in its Economic Aspect*.

Oxford, 1913. 2 vols. Volume I includes an " Introduction critical and historical " by the editor and a reprint of Louis Blanc's *Organisation du travail.* Volume II is a reprint of Émile Thomas' *Histoire des Ateliers nationaux,* followed by one page of superficial notes on obvious points. The editor's introduction is not a serious contribution to the subject. It is superficial, inaccurate, and succeeds in misunderstanding the question of the Workshops.

Marx, Karl. *La lutte des classes en France (1848-1850).* Translation by Léon Rémy. Published as one volume with *Le XVIII Brumaire de Louis Bonaparte.* Paris, 1900. 362 pp.

Melun, A. M. J., Vicomte de. *Mémoires du Vte. Armand de Melun.* Paris, 1891. 269 pp.

Ménard, Louis. *Prologue d'une révolution.* Paris, 1849. 270 pp.

Michel, Henri. *La loi Falloux, 4 janvier 1849 - 15 mars 1850.* Paris, 1906. 524 pp. Standard work on the Falloux law, with some interesting appreciations of other aspects of Falloux's career.

Monin, H. " Notice sur Louis Pujol." *La Révolution de 1848,* I (1904-1905), pp. 132-135.

Pagès-Duport, A. *Journées de juin. Récit complet des événements des 23, 24, 25, 26 et des jours suivants.* Paris, 1848. 125 pp.

Paris. Chamber of Commerce. *Statistique de l'industrie à Paris, résultant de l'enquête faite par la Chambre de commerce pour les années 1847-1848.* Paris, 1851. 1008 pp.

Pechan, Hermann. *Louis Blanc als Wegbereiter des modernen Sozialismus.* Jena, 1929. 136 pp.

Phipps, Constantine Henry, First Marquis of Normanby. *A Year of Revolution, from a Journal kept in Paris in 1848.* London, 1857. 2 vols.

Picattier, E. *Les Ateliers nationaux en 1848.* Saint-Etienne, 1899. 174 pp. Only existing monograph. Negligible.

Pierre, Victor. *Histoire de la seconde République française.* Paris, 1878. 2 vols. Vol. I is reprint of his *Histoire de la République de 1848.* Paris, 1873. 554 pp.

Pimienta, Robert. *La propagande bonapartiste en 1848.* Paris, 1911. 130 pp. Develops dichotomy of movement prior to June Days: simultaneous appeal of Bonapartism to forces of order and disorder.

Proudhon, Pierre Joseph. *Les confessions d'un révolutionnaire pour servir à l'histoire de la Révolution de février.* Third edition, Paris, 1851. 380 pp.

Quentin-Bauchart, A. *Études et souvenirs sur la deuxième République et le second Empire (1848-1870). Mémoires posthumes publiés par son fils.* Paris, 1901-1902. 2 vols. Vol. I (Première partie) has subtitle: *La République de 1848 depuis l'ouverture de l'Assemblée constituante jusqu'à la présidence décennale du Prince Louis-Napoléon.* Bonapartist from the outset, Quentin-Bauchart is a source of importance on the dissolution of the Workshops, and especially on the June Days (he was subsequently reporter of the Commission of Investigation on the June Days, see above, p. 175). Staunch supporter of the cause of order, his prejudices against the workers are evident.

Quentin-Bauchart, Pierre. *La crise sociale de 1848. Les origines de la Révolution de février.* Paris, 1920. 326 pp.

——. *Lamartine, homme politique; la politique intérieure.* Paris, 1903. 423 pp. Slight, especially on economic questions.

——. *Lamartine et la politique etrangère de la Révolution de février (24 février-24 juin 1848).* Paris, 1908. 458 pp. A definitive work on Lamartine's foreign policy remains to be written.

Regnault, Elias. *Histoire du Gouvernement provisoire.* Paris, 1850. 371 pp.

Renard, Édouard. *La vie et l'œuvre de Louis Blanc.* Toulouse, 1922. 192 pp. " Cet ouvrage n'est pas un ouvrage de critique mais une simple biographie." Convenient for leading facts in life of Blanc. A full-length portrait of Blanc and his times is needed.

Renard, Georges. "Mémoires relatifs à l'histoire de la deuxième République française (1848-1852)." *La Révolution de 1848,* IV (1907-1908), pp. 114-120. Reprinted from *Bulletin des bibliothèques populaires* (February, 1907), pp. 17-22.

——. *La République de 1848 (1848-1851).* Paris, 1906? 384 pp. Vol. IX of Jaurès: *Histoire socialiste.* Characterized by penetrating interpretation and original points of view, refreshing and even sparkling style. Of decided *tendance socialiste,* with the class struggle in 1848 overemphasized. Contains the most satisfactory account of the Workshops, despite its brevity.

——. *La Révolution de 1848 et les Révolutions du XIXᵉ siècle. 1830-1848-1870.* Paris, 1904-1905, and years following. Of fundamental importance for articles and reviews of works on the Revolution of 1848.

Robin, Charles. *Histoire de la Révolution française de 1848.* Paris, 1849-1850. 2 vols.

Saint-John, Percy B. *French Revolution of 1848. The Three Days of February, 1848.* Second edition, London, 1848. 383 pp.

Schmidt, Charles. *Les journées de juin 1848.* Paris, 1926. 127 pp.

——. " Les ouvriers des Ateliers nationaux au chemin de fer d'Orléans." *La Revolution de 1848,* XXIII (1926-1927), pp. 781-787.

Sée, Henri. *La vie économique sous la monarchie censitaire (1815-1848).* Paris, 1927. 191 pp.

Seignobos, Charles. " Les procès-verbaux du Gouvernement provisoire et de la Commission du pouvoir exécutif de 1848," *Revue d'histoire moderne et contemporaine,* VII (1905-1906), pp. 581-597.

——. *La Révolution de 1848. Le second Empire.* Paris, 1921. 426 pp.

Spuller, Eugène. *Histoire parlementaire de la seconde République suivie d'une petite histoire du second Empire.* Paris, 1891. 376 pp.

Stein, Lorenz von. *Geschichte der sozialen Bewegung in Frankreich von 1789 bis auf unsere Tage.* Leipzig, 1850. 3 vols.

Stern, Daniel (pseudonym of the Comtesse d'Agoult). *Histoire de la Révolution de 1848.* Second edition, Paris, 1862. 2 vols. Madame Agoult paints the Revolution on a broad canvas. Her wide associations and deep knowledge of the period have given us a work of the first importance. Aspects of the social revolution are developed in detail. Louis Blanc she treats with sympathy and understanding. The book cannot be neglected by any serious student of the period.

Tchernoff, J. *Le parti républicain sous la Monarchie de juillet. Formation et évolution de la doctrine républicaine.* Paris, 1901. 496 pp.

Thomas, Émile. *Histoire des Ateliers nationaux considérés sous le double point de vue politique et sociale; des causes de leur formation et de leur existence; et de l'influence qu'ils ont exercée sur les événements des quatres premiers mois de la République, suivi de pièces justificatives.* Paris 1848. 395 pp. The apologia of the organizer and first director of the National Workshops is the source of the first importance for their history. Thomas' self-righteous defence of his régime is frequently unconvincing, and there is no doubt that his policy was vitiated to a considerable extent in the end by his own excessive ambitions. But it is no less true that the Provisional Government viewed the Workshops as a *pis aller* and gave Thomas only half-hearted assistance in his difficult task. A careful study of the director's defence, in connection with the other available materials, has greatly strengthened the writer's view that, at least until the first of May, Thomas was about as successful as could be expected under the prevailing anarchic conditions. Thomas' dates are often inaccurate, and many of his statements, e.g., those attacking the policy of the Provisional Government, require the closest scrutiny and control through the other sources.

Tocqueville, Alexis de. *Souvenirs de Alexis de Tocqueville.* Paris, 1893. 431 pp.

Véron, Dr. L. *Mémoires d'un bourgeois de Paris.* Paris, 1853-1855. 6 vols.

Veuillot, Eugène. *Le comte de Falloux et ses mémoires.* Paris, 1888. 354 pp. Bitter attack on Falloux, in the light of his memoirs, and defence of Louis Veuillot.

Wassermann, Suzanne. *Les clubs de Barbès et de Blanqui en 1848.* Paris, 1913. 248 pp.

Weill, Georges. *Histoire du parti républicain en France (1814-1870).* New edition, Paris, 1928. 431 pp.

Whitehouse, H. Remsen. *The Life of Lamartine.* Boston and New York, 1918. 2 vols.

4. *Newspapers* [1]

L'Ami du peuple en 1848. An 1ᵉʳ de la République reconquise. February 27 - May 14, 1848. F. V. Raspail, editor. Appeared irregularly. Interesting for point of view of editor. Vitriolic attacks on Provisional Government.

L'Atelier, organe spéciale de la classe laborieuse, rédigé par des ouvriers exclusivement. September, 1840 - July 31, 1850. Appeared weekly

---

[1] All newspapers listed were published in Paris.

between February Revolution and June Days. Reflected system of Buchez, hence relatively conservative tendency.

La Commune de Paris, moniteur des clubs. March 9 - June 7, 1848. Edited by Sobrier and Cahaigne. "Socialist" in tendency; i.e., associated itself with all those "who sought to improve the lot of man." But denounced the communists and was unsympathetic with utopians in general, e.g., Louis Blanc.

Le Constitutionnel, journal du commerce, politique et littéraire. May 2, 1819 - December 31, 1855, and thereafter. Edited by Dr. Véron. Orleanist, Thiers *nuance*. Espoused the cause of Louis Bonaparte before the December election. Well informed and well written, if prejudiced, editorials on the National Workshops. After May 15 gave more attention to problem than other newspapers, the *Débats* possibly excepted.

La Démocratie pacifique, journal des intérêts des gouvernements et des peuples. August 1, 1843 - November 30, 1851. Fourierist organ, edited by Considerant. Consistent but mild defence of aims of social revolution.

La France nouvelle, journal politique et littéraire. May 20 - June 24, 1848. Legitimist. Alexandre Dumas, editor. Of interest primarily for articles by Dumas in defence of Émile Thomas. The latter appeared in a *Supplément,* following the number for June 9, and in the numbers for June 18, 20, and 23. Dumas' account, with minor changes, appears in Thomas' *Histoire des Ateliers nationaux,* pp. 286-308 and *passim.*

Gazette des tribunaux. Journal de jurisprudence et des débats judiciaires. Feuille d'annonces légales. The numbers for March 8, 1849 and ff. contain the account of the trial of Blanqui, *et al.,* for their participation in the events of May 15, 1848.

L'Illustration, journal universel. March 14, 1843 -   .

Journal démocratique et officiel des Ateliers nationaux. June 22-24, 1848. Only two numbers appeared, those for June 22-24 and June 24-27.

Journal des Débats, politique et littéraire. 1814-   . Conservative: supporter of Guizot prior to the Revolution and of "party of order" thereafter. Well informed and well reasoned editorials on the National Workshops, written from point of view of *haute bourgeoisie.*

Journal des travaux publics, de l'agriculture, des chemins de fer, des manufactures et des progrès de l'industrie. Bulletin officiel des adjudications administratives. January 9, 1848-   . Moderately conservative. Hostile to ideas of Louis Blanc, but favorable to reconciliation of labor and capital and to the organization of labor through the formation of coöperatives.

Le Lampion, eclaireur politique. May 28 - June 25, 1848, and few numbers following August 8, 1848. Legitimist organ of extreme reactionary tendency. Vicious attacks on National Workshops.

La Liberté, journal des idées et des faits. March 2, 1848 - June 16, 1850. Established as a legitimist organ, it supported the Provisional Government. Its support of the Executive Commission quickly crumbled after May 15. On June 12 it became suddenly and vigorously Bonapartist, causing some suspicions of its disinterestedness (see Pimienta: *Propagande bonapartiste*, p. 48, title above, p. 181).

Le Moniteur universel. January, 1811- . Beginning February 25, 1848, has title *Le Moniteur universel. Journal officiel de la République française.* Includes official acts of the government and National Assembly, stenographic reports of the sessions of the assembly, reprints from provincial newspapers, etc.

Le National, feuille politique et littéraire. January 3, 1830 - December 2, 1851. Organ of the moderate republicans. Consistent supporter of the Provisional Government (of which Marrast, its editor, was a member), but without abdicating its independence. Generally moderate in temper and sane in point of view. Was sometimes badly informed, as in the case of the *journée* of April 16, or failed to perceive the tendency of events, as in the case of the danger from the dissolution of the Workshops.

L'Organisation du travail, journal des ouvriers. June 3-23, 1848. H. Lacolonge, editor. Despite its socialist and "savagely revolutionary" character, the newspaper appears to have connived with the friends of Napoleon, and it had acknowledged Bonapartists among its editors (Robert Pimienta, p. 49 — see above, p. 181). Its founder, M. Clavel, was also a Bonapartist. It was one of that small group of newspapers which, while driving the workers on to insurrection, had at the same time relations, of a character unfortunately obscure, with the Bonapartists. It also had the sympathy of at least a part of the National Workshops (see number for June 6). Lacolonge, its editor, later directed the insurrection in the Faubourg Saint Antoine.

Le Père Duchêne. Gazette de la Révolution. An premier de la nouvelle République. April 10 - August 22-24, 1848; suspended from number of June 22-25 until number of August 13-15. Vigorous supporter of the workers' cause. Important particularly because of large circulation, which it was claimed was as high as 70,000 prior to June Days.

Le Peuple constituant, journal quotidien. February 27 - July 11, 1848. Edited by Lamennais, who declared he was "socialist" if socialism meant workers' coöperation, not if it meant the negation of property and the family. Lamennais was extremely patient with the Provisional Government and the assembly until about May 10; he then quickly passed into open opposition and declared that anarchy, if it came, would be the work not of the people but of monarchist conspirators.

La Presse. June 15, 1836 - December 31, 1855, and thereafter. Émile de Girardin, its editor and the founder in France of the cheap newspaper with a wide circulation, was a chameleon in politics. Having thrust the abdication into the hands of Louis-Philippe, Girardin quickly tired of the Provisional Government. In turn he attacked the Provisional Government, the Executive Commission, and Cavaignac, and then rallied to the support of Louis Napoleon.

La Réforme. July 29, 1843 - January 11, 1850. Organ of the left republicans, edited by Flocon. It was dominated by the ideas of Ledru-Rollin, but was sympathetic with social reform and included Louis Blanc among its subordinate editors.

Le Représentant du peuple, journal quotidien des producteurs. October 14, 1847 - August 21, 1848. Edited by Proudhon. Frequent editorials on his "system," and open attacks on the "reaction" prior to the June Days.

La République. February 28, 1848 - December 2, 1851. Editor, Eugène Bareste. Moderate "socialist." Treated government with great moderation until May 11, thenceforward increasingly critical, but fair.

L'Univers, religieux, philosophique, politique, scientifique, et littéraire. October 5, 1833- . Ultramontane Catholic organ of Louis Veuillot. Vigorously "anti-socialist" but with profound sympathy for workers. Its articles on labor problems were generally sound and well balanced.

La Vraie République. March 26 - August 21, 1848; suspended June 25 - August 8. Editor, Thoré, with collaboration of Barbès, G. Sand, Pierre Leroux, *et al.* Consistent and vitriolic attacks upon the government, the "reaction," the "royalists," *et al.*, following the convening of the assembly. Demands justice for the workers' cause without offering much in the way of a specific program of reform.

INDEX

INDEX

INDEX

(This index refers only to names, subjects, etc., discussed in the text.)

HARVARD HISTORICAL STUDIES
(Out of print titles are omitted.)

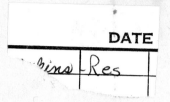